Paul the Allegorist

Paul the Allegorist

Galatians 4:21–31 and Its Implications for
Understanding Paul as an Interpreter of Scripture

ANDREW C. BURROW

Foreword by Todd D. Still

CASCADE *Books* • Eugene, Oregon

PAUL THE ALLEGORIST
Galatians 4:21–31 and Its Implications for Understanding Paul as an Interpreter of Scripture

Copyright © 2024 Andrew C. Burrow. All rights reserved. Except for brief quotations in critical publications or reviews, no part of this book may be reproduced in any manner without prior written permission from the publisher. Write: Permissions, Wipf and Stock Publishers, 199 W. 8th Ave., Suite 3, Eugene, OR 97401.

Cascade Books
An Imprint of Wipf and Stock Publishers
199 W. 8th Ave., Suite 3
Eugene, OR 97401

www.wipfandstock.com

PAPERBACK ISBN: 978-1-6667-8571-5
HARDCOVER ISBN: 978-1-6667-8572-2
EBOOK ISBN: 978-1-6667-8573-9

Cataloging-in-Publication data:

Names: Burrow, Andrew C., author

Title: Paul the allegorist : Galatians 4:21–31 and its implications for understanding Paul as an interpreter of scripture / Andrew C. Burrow.

Description: Eugene, OR: Cascade Books, 2024. | Includes bibliographical references and index.

Identifiers: ISBN 978-1-6667-8571-5 (paperback). | ISBN 978-1-6667-8572-2 (hardcover). | ISBN 978-1-6667-8573-9 (ebook).

Subjects: LCSH: Bible. Galatians IV.21–31—Criticism, interpretation, etc. | Paul, the Apostle, Saint—Theology. | Allegory. | Bible. Galatians—Criticism, interpretation, etc.

Classification: BS2685.52 B85 2024 (print). | BS2685.52 (epub).

09/10/24

Unless otherwise noted, Scripture quotations are from the New Revised Standard Version Bible, copyright © 1989 National Council of the Churches of Christ in the United States of America. Used by permission. All rights reserved worldwide.

Unless otherwise noted, translations of the Dead Sea Scrolls are from *The Dead Sea Scrolls*, edited by James H. Charlesworth (Tübingen: Mohr Siebeck, 1994–).

For my wife and daughter

Contents

Foreword by Todd D. Still | ix
Acknowledgments | xi
Abbreviations | xiii
Introduction | xxv

1   Paul's Interpretive Practice of Allegory in the Context
    of Galatians 4:21–31 | 1
    1. Introductory Comments | 1
    2. Six Interpretive Issues in Galatians 4:21–31 | 6
    3. Towards a More Precise Understanding of Paul's Interpretive
       Practice | 34

2   Evaluating the Criteria Used by Prior Scholarship When Examining
    Paul's Interpretive Practice of Allegory | 35
    1. The Criteria Used in Prior Scholarship for Selecting Comparative
       Examples | 36
    2. Examining the Criteria within the Ancient Interpretive Practice
       of Allegory | 41
    3. Results of the Examination | 68

3   Evaluating the Interpretive Schemata Used by Prior Scholarship to
    Examine Paul's Interpretive Practice of Allegory, and
    My Approach | 72
    1. Hellenistic, Alexandrian, and Palestinian Allegory | 73
    2. Typology | 75
    3. My Approach and Criteria | 80

4 Comparative Analysis 1: The Sectarian Texts of the Dead Sea Scrolls | 83
  1. The Authors of the Sectarian Texts as Suitable Comparative Examples | 84
  2. The Allegorical Practice of the Sectarian Texts | 93
  3. Galatians 4:22–25 and the Sectarian Texts | 99
  4. Contributions to Our Understanding of Paul's Interpretive Practice | 101

5 Comparative Analysis 2: The Works of Philo of Alexandria | 104
  1. Philo as a Suitable Comparative Example | 105
  2. The Allegorical Practice of Philo | 120
  3. Galatians 4:22–27 and *Legum Allegoriae* 1.63–76 | 123
  4. Contributions to Our Understanding of Paul's Interpretive Practice | 128

6 Comparative Analysis 3: The Epistle of Barnabas | 131
  1. Barnabas as a Suitable Comparative Example | 132
  2. The Allegorical Practice of Barnabas | 148
  3. Galatians 4:22–27 and Epistle of Barnabas 8, 10, 13 | 149
  4. Contributions to Our Understanding of Paul's Interpretive Practice | 154

7 Conclusion | 157
  1. A Short Review of Prior Criteria, Prior Interpretive Schemata, and My Approach | 157
  2. A More Precise Understanding of the Interpretive Practice behind Paul's Use of ἀλληγορούμενα | 158
  3. Its Significance for Other Interpretive Issues in Galatians 4:21–31 | 161
  4. Opportunities for Future Research | 164

Bibliography | 169
  Primary Sources | 169
  Secondary Sources | 173
Ancient Documents Index | 193

Foreword

WHEN TERTULLIAN POSED THE question "What has Jerusalem to do with Athens?" (*Praescr.* 7.9), he expected the faithful to say, "Little to nothing." Similarly, if a (goodly) majority of Pauline specialists were asked, "What has Paul to do with allegorical interpretation?" one could well anticipate hearing crickets if not a hearty "Nothing." Philo? To be sure. Origen? Without a doubt. Paul of Tarsus, the Jewish apostle to the gentiles? May it never be! What has the sober, circumspect Antiochene tradition to do with the interpretative flights of fancy that mark and mar the Alexandrian one? Paul foreshadows the Antiochene tradition and not the Alexandrian, does he not? Not a few of us were taught as much in our introductory New Testament courses back in the day.

In his provocatively titled volume *Paul the Allegorist*, Andrew C. Burrow skillfully and patiently probes the interpretative practice behind Paul's use of ἀλληγορούμενα in Gal 4:24. In so doing, Burrow is not only able to show how Paul engages in allegorical interpretation in Gal 4:21–31, but through a comprehensive, comparative analysis of this pertinent Pauline passage with Philo, the Dead Sea Scrolls, and the Epistle of Barnabas he is also able to establish convincingly that the interpretative practice of allegory was part of Paul's repertoire as a Jewish interpreter of Scripture in the Second Temple period. To be sure, it was not the only and certainly was not the primary interpretative tool in the leatherworker's toolkit, but neither was it missing altogether.

Over forty years ago now in a revision of an Emory University PhD dissertation, Richard B. Hays argued that if one were to truly understand Paul in general and Galatians in particular then one would need to acknowledge the centrality of "narrative" in Pauline thought.[1] Analogously, in *Paul the Allegorist* (which is a thorough revision of his doctoral thesis, which I was privileged to examine as an external reader), Andrew C. Burrow demonstrates that someone must be both knowledgeable and mindful of the ancient interpretative practice of allegory, which Paul himself employed, if they are to read well not only Galatians (4:21–31) but also the entirety of Paul's writings.

Todd D. Still
Baylor University, Truett Seminary
Waco, TX

---

1. See Hays, *Faith of Jesus Christ*.

Acknowledgments

THIS MONOGRAPH HAD ITS origin as a doctoral thesis, so I first must acknowledge the immeasurable impact of my doctoral supervisor, Chris Keith, and my co-supervisor, Mark S. Gignilliat. I am grateful to and thankful for them, and this project would not have been possible without their thoughtful and meaningful guidance. I also am grateful for my external reader, Todd D. Still, and my internal reader, James G. Crossley. The meaningful conversations with them during and after the viva helped me to determine my next steps for completing this monograph. Last, I would like to thank my former research assistants, Laura Bean and Maggie Hagelskamp. I would not have been able to complete this project as quickly or as efficiently without their help.

I also want to acknowledge others who provided feedback and support during the process of revision. Chief among these is David L. Eastman, for whom I cannot begin to express my thanks and my gratitude. His support remained unwavering, and his feedback was always what I needed to hear. I also would like to acknowledge Sean A. Adams, whose meaningful feedback helped me to restructure the project in the early stages of revision. Finally, I want to acknowledge those who have offered feedback or support in smaller but still important ways: John J. Collins, Brian Hinton, and Emma Hill.

During the life of this project, no one has been more important to me than my family. I am grateful for all who have supported me. Most importantly, I want to thank my wife and daughter. My wife has been a loving and encouraging companion, often telling me that she is my biggest fan. My daughter is the light of my world, who brings unimaginable joy.

Without their love and support, this project would not exist. They always have been and will remain my greatest source of strength and inspiration.

Abbreviations

HEBREW BIBLE/OLD TESTAMENT

Gen	Genesis
Exod	Exodus
Lev	Leviticus
Num	Numbers
Deut	Deuteronomy
2 Sam	2 Samuel
Ps	Psalms
Prov	Proverbs
Isa	Isaiah
Jer	Jeremiah
Ezek	Ezekiel
Dan	Daniel
Hos	Hosea

APOCRYPHA

1 Macc	1 Maccabees
2 Esd	2 Esdras

PSEUDEPIGRAPHA

2 Bar.	2 Baruch
2 Clem.	2 Clement

NEW TESTAMENT

Matt	Matthew
Luke	Luke
John	John
Rom	Romans
1–2 Cor	1–2 Corinthians
Gal	Galatians
Eph	Ephesians
Phil	Philippians
Col	Colossians
1 Thess	1 Thessalonians
1 Tim	1 Timothy
Phlm	Philemon
Jas	James

ANCIENT SOURCES

Ab urbe cond.	Livy, *Ab urbe condita*
Aen.	Vergil, *Aeneid*
An. pr.	Aristotle, *Analytica priora*
Ant.	Josephus, *Antiquitates judaicae*
Barn.	Epistle of Barnabas
Carm.	Horace, *Carmina*
Cels.	Origen, *Contra Celsum*

Comm. Gal.	Jerome, *Commentarius in epistolam ad Galatas libri III*
Comm. not.	Plutarch, *De communibus notitiis contra stoicos*
Cor.	Plutarch, *Caius Marcius Coriolanus*
Deipn.	Athenaeus, *Deipnosophistae*
De or.	Cicero, *De oratore*
Did.	Didache
Eloc.	Demetrius, *De elocutione*
Ep.	Horace, *Epistulae*
Geogr.	Strabo, *Geographica*
Hist.	Polybius, *Historiae*
Hom. Gal.	John Chrysostom, *Homiliae in epistulam ad Galatas commentarius*
In Galat.	Marius Victorinus, *In epistolam Pauli ad Galatas libri duo*
Inst.	Quintilian, *Institutio oratoria*
Is. Os.	Plutarch, *De Iside et Osiride*
Jejun.	Tertullian, *De jejunio adversus psychicos*
Let. Aris.	Letter of Aristeas
Lib. ed.	Plutarch, *De liberis educandis*
Marc.	Tertullian, *Adversus Marcionem*
Metam.	Ovid, *Metamorphoses*
Metaph.	Aristotle, *Metaphysica*
Mor.	Plutarch, *Moralia*
Od.	Homer, *Odyssea*
Praep. ev.	Eusebius, *Praeparatio evangelica*
Praescr.	Tertullian, *De praescriptione haereticorum*
Quaest. hom. Odd.	Porphyry, *Quaestionum homericarum ad Odysseam pertinentium reliquiae*
Rhet.	Aristotle, *Rhetorica*
Rhet. Her.	[Cicero,] *Rhetorica ad Herennium*

Strom.	Clement of Alexandria, *Stromateis*
Vit. poes. Hom.	Plutarch, *De vita et poesi Homeri*
Vit. Pyth.	Porphyry, *Vita Pythagorae*

DEAD SEA SCROLLS

1QpHab	Pesher Habakkuk
1QM	War Scroll
1QS	Rule of the Community
4QCat^a	Catena A
4QFlor	Florilegium
4QMMT	Miqṣat Maʿaśê ha-Torah
4QpIsa^a	Isaiah Pesher 4
4QpIsa^b	Isaiah Pesher 2
4QpIsa^c	Isaiah Pesher 3
4QpIsa^d	Isaiah Pesher 6
4QpNah	Nahum Pesher
4QpPs^a	Psalm Pesher 1
11QMelch	Melchizedek
11QTemple	Temple Scroll
CD	Damascus Document

PHILO

Abr.	*De Abrahamo*
Agr.	*De agricultura*
Cher.	*De cherubim*
Conf.	*De confusione linguarum*
Congr.	*De congressu eruditionis gratia*

Decal.	De decalogo
Det.	Quod deterius potiori insidari soleat
Deus	Quod Deus sit immutabilis
Fug.	De fuga et inventione
Gig.	De gigantibus
Her.	Quis rerum divinarum heres sit
Ios.	De Iosepho
Leg.	Legum allegoriae
Legat.	Legatio ad Gaium
Migr.	De migratione Abrahami
Mos.	De vita Mosis
Mut.	De mutatione nominum
Opif.	De opificio mundi
Post.	De posteritate Caini
Praem.	De praemiis et poenis
QE	Quaestiones et solutiones in Exodum
QG	Quaestiones et solutiones in Genesin
Sacr.	De sacrificiis Abelis et Caini
Somn.	De somniis
Spec.	De specialibus legibus
Virt.	De virtutibus

RABBINIC SOURCES

Mek.	Mekilta
Pesiq. Rab.	Pesiqta Rabbati
Pirqe R. El.	Pirqe Rabbi Eliezer
Rab.	Rabbah
Sem.	Semaḥot

Tg. Neof.	Targum Neofiti
Tg. Onq.	Targum Onqelos
Tg. Ps.-J.	Targum Pseudo-Jonathan

SECONDARY SOURCES

AB	Anchor Bible
ABD	*Anchor Bible Dictionary.* Edited by David Noel Freedman. 6 vols. New York: Doubleday, 1992
ABR	*Australian Biblical Review*
AcT	*Acta Theologica*
AGJU	Arbeiten zur Geschichte des antiken Judentums und des Urchristentums
ALGHJ	Arbeiten zur Literatur und Geschichte des hellenistischen Judentums
ANRW	*Aufstieg und Niedergang der römischen Welt: Geschichte und Kultur Roms im Spiegel der neueren Forschung.* Part 2, *Principat.* Edited by Hildegard Temporini and Wolfgang Haase. Berlin: de Gruyter, 1972–
ANTC	Abingdon New Testament Commentaries
ASTI	Annual of the Swedish Theological Institute
AzK	Arbeiten zur Kirchengeschichte
BA	*Biblical Archaeologist*
BAGD	Bauer, Walter, William F. Arndt, F. Wilbur Gingrich, and Frederick W. Danker. *Greek-English Lexicon of the New Testament and Other Early Christian Literature.* 2nd ed. Chicago: University of Chicago Press, 1979 (Bauer-Arndt-Gingrich-Danker)
BAR	*Biblical Archaeology Review*
BBR	*Bulletin for Biblical Research*

BEATAJ	Beiträge zur Erforschung des Alten Testaments und des antiken Judentum
BECNT	Baker Exegetical Commentary on the New Testament
BeO	*Bibbia e oriente*
BEvT	Beiträge zur evangelischen Theologie
BGBH	Beiträge zur Geschichte der biblischen Hermenutik
BHT	Beiträge zur historischen Theologie
Bib	*Biblica*
BibInt	Biblical Interpretation Series
BiPa	*Biblia Patristica: Index des citations et allusions bibliques dans la littérature.* Paris: CNRS, 2000
BJRL	*Bulletin of the John Rylands University Library of Manchester*
BNP	*Brill's New Pauly: Encyclopaedia of the Ancient World.* Edited by Hubert Cancik. 22 vols. Leiden: Brill, 2002–2011
BNTC	Black's New Testament Commentaries
BSac	*Bibliotheca Sacra*
BTB	*Biblical Theology Bulletin*
BZAW	Beihefte zur Zeitschrift für die alttestamentliche Wissenschaft
BZNW	Beihefte zur Zeitschrift für die neutestamentliche Wissenschaft
CAD	*The Assyrian Dictionary of the Oriental Institute of the University of Chicago.* Chicago: The Oriental Institute of the University of Chicago, 1956–2006
CBET	Contributions to Biblical Exegesis and Theology
CBQMS	Catholic Biblical Quarterly Monograph Series
CCF	Commentaries for Christian Formation
Comm	*Communio*
CQ	*Church Quarterly*

CR		*Classical Review*
CRINT		Compendia Rerum Iudaicarum ad Novum Testamentum
CTJ		*Calvin Theological Journal*
DJD		Discoveries in the Judaean Desert
DSD		*Dead Sea Discoveries*
DTT		*Dansk teologisk tidsskrift*
EDSS		*Encyclopedia of the Dead Sea Scrolls.* Edited by Lawrence H. Schiffman and James C. VanderKam. 2 vols. New York: Oxford University Press, 2000
EJL		Early Judaism and Its Literature
EstBib		*Estudios bíblicos*
EvQ		*Evangelical Quarterly*
ExpTim		*Expository Times*
FAT		Forschungen zum Alten Testament
FRLANT		Forschungen zur Religion und Literatur des Alten und Neuen Testaments
GTJ		*Grace Theological Journal*
HNT		Handbuch zum Neuen Testament
HTR		*Harvard Theological Review*
HTS		Harvard Theological Studies
HUCA		*Hebrew Union College Annual*
IB		*Interpreter's Bible.* Edited by George A. Buttrick et al. 12 vols. New York: Abingdon, 1951–1957
ICC		International Critical Commentary
IDS		*In die Skriflig*
Int		*Interpretation*
JBL		*Journal of Biblical Literature*
JEA		*Journal of Egyptian Archaeology*
JQR		*Jewish Quarterly Review*
JR		*Journal of Religion*

JRT	*Journal of Religious Thought*
JSJ	*Journal for the Study of Judaism in the Persian, Hellenistic, and Roman Periods*
JSNT	*Journal for the Study of the New Testament*
JSNTSup	Journal for the Study of the New Testament Supplement Series
JSOT	*Journal for the Study of the Old Testament*
JSOTSup	Journal for the Study of the Old Testament Supplement Series
JSP	*Journal for the Study of the Pseudepigrapha*
JSPL	*Journal for the Study of Paul and His Letters*
JTI	*Journal of Theological Interpretation*
JTS	*Journal of Theological Studies*
KAV	Kommentar zu den Apostolischen Vätern
LASBF	*Liber Annuus Studii Biblici Franciscani*
LCL	Loeb Classical Library
LNTS	The Library of New Testament Studies
LSJ	Liddell, Henry George, Robert Scott, Henry Stuart Jones. *A Greek-English Lexicon.* 9th ed. with revised supplement. Oxford: Clarendon, 1996
MH	*Museum Helveticum*
MilS	*Milltown Studies*
NA[28]	*Novum Testamentum Graece*, Nestle-Aland, 28th ed.
NAC	New American Commentary
NCBC	New Cambridge Bible Commentary
NCLLL	Leverett, Frederick. *A New and Copious Lexicon of the Latin* Language. Philadelphia: J. B. Lippincott Co., 1850
Neot	*Neotestamentica*
NICNT	New International Commentary on the New Testament

NIDNTT	*New International Dictionary of New Testament Theology.* Edited by Colin Brown. 4 vols. Grand Rapids: Zondervan, 1975–1978
NIGTC	New International Greek Testament Commentary
NovT	*Novum Testamentum*
NovTSup	Supplements to Novum Testamentum
NPNF¹	*Nicene and Post-Nicene Fathers*, Series 1
NTL	New Testament Library
NTS	*New Testament Studies*
OBT	Overtures to Biblical Theology
OTL	Old Testament Library
PRSt	*Perspectives in Religious Studies*
RB	*Revue biblique*
RevQ	*Revue de Qumran*
RHPR	*Revue d'histoire et de philosophie religieuses*
RQ	*Römische Quartalschrift für christliche Altertumskunde und Kirchengeschichte*
RRJ	*Review of Rabbinic Judaism*
RSR	*Recherches de science religieuse*
SBLDS	Society of Biblical Literature Dissertation Series
SBS	Stuttgarter Bibelstudien
ScrTh	*Scripta Theologica*
SCS	Septuagint and Cognate Studies
SDSS	Studies in the Dead Sea Scrolls and Related Literature
SJLA	Studies in Judaism in Late Antiquity
SJSJ	Supplements to the Journal for the Study of Judaism
SJT	*Scottish Journal of Theology*
SNTSMS	Society for New Testament Studies Monograph Series
SP	Sacra Pagina
SPhiloA	Studia Philonica Annual

SSEJC	Studies in Scripture in Early Judaism and Christianity
ST	*Studia Theologica*
StC	Studia Catholica
STDJ	Studies on the Texts of the Desert of Judah
StPatr	Studia Patristica
StPB	Studia Post-biblica
SVTQ	*St. Vladimir's Theological Quarterly*
SymS	Symposium Series
TBN	Themes in Biblical Narrative
TDNT	*Theological Dictionary of the New Testament*. Edited by Gerhard Kittel and Gerhard Friedrich. Translated by Geoffrey W. Bromiley. 10 vols. Grand Rapids: Eerdmans, 1964–1976
Text	*Textus*
Th	*Theology*
TQ	*Theologische Quartalschrift*
TRu	*Theologische Rundschau*
TSAJ	Texte und Studien zum antiken Judentum
TTE	*The Theological Educator*
TUGAL	Texte und Untersuchungen zur Geschichte der altchristlichen Literatur
VC	*Vigiliae Christianae*
VCS	Variorum Collected Studies (formerly Variorum Reprints)
VTSup	Supplements to Vetus Testamentum
WAW	Writings from the Ancient World
WBC	Word Biblical Commentary
WMANT	Wissenschaftliche Monographien zum Alten und Neuen Testament
WTJ	*Westminster Theological Journal*

WUNT	Wissenschaftliche Untersuchungen zum Neuen Testament
WW	*Word and World*
ZKG	*Zeitschrift für Kirchengeschichte*
ZNW	*Zeitschrift für die neutestamentliche Wissenschaft und die Kunde der älteren Kirche*
ZTK	*Zeitschrift für Theologie und Kirche*
ZWT	*Zeitschrift für wissenschaftliche Theologie*

Introduction

GALATIANS 4:21–31 HAS INTERESTED interpreters of Paul since the post-apostolic period. In these eleven verses, Paul contrasts themes that he employs throughout Galatians (e.g., flesh and spirit, slavery and freedom, law and promise) by engaging the characters and events found in Gen 16–21. Also, Paul uses two Greek words not found elsewhere in texts later included in the New Testament: ἀλληγορούμενα (Gal 4:24) and συστοιχεῖ (Gal 4:25). If these characteristics were not enough to secure our interest, Paul addresses a central question for believers in the first century CE: What customs must gentiles observe in order to be included in this formerly Jewish-only movement? For all these reasons, Gal 4:21–31 has a rich history of interpretation. One issue that warrants further investigation is the interpretive practice behind Paul's use of ἀλληγορούμενα in Gal 4:24. It warrants further investigation for three reasons. First, prior scholarship has explained it in numerous, sometimes mutually exclusive, ways. Second, these explanations appeal to a complex set of criteria (i.e., facticity, terminology, geographical location) and schemata (i.e., Alexandrian, Palestinian, and Hellenistic; typology), sometimes stated explicitly and sometimes not. Third, these explanations often are influenced by a variety of perspectives regarding Paul as an interpreter of Scripture. For these reasons, there is an unresolved state of scholarship on this interpretive issue, including its impact on our understanding of Paul as an interpreter of Scripture.[1]

In this project, the first book-length study on the interpretive practice behind Paul's use of ἀλληγορούμενα in Gal 4:24, I proffer a resolution

---

1. This current unresolved state of scholarship was acknowledged as early as 1995. See Borgen, "Some Hebrew and Pagan Features," 153.

for the current state of scholarship by providing a more precise understanding of Paul's practice within the ancient interpretive practice of allegory that answers the questions "What does Paul do, and why does it matter?" This project provides a more precise understanding of Paul's practice in four ways: (1) It defines Paul's interpretive work—Paul understood Gen 16–21 to have prior meanings that he believed to be authoritative and yet insufficient, and he used the interpretive practice of allegory—by means of source entities and meanings alongside their corresponding allegorical entities and meanings—to change those prior meanings of Gen 16–21 without completely denying or replacing them. (2) It explains how Paul used his allegorical practice to accomplish this interpretive work; he used it on two levels (i.e., rhetorical and functional) that stood in a contrasting relationship. (3) It reveals that Paul's practice is a part of his own repertoire as an interpreter of Scripture (i.e., he uses it elsewhere) and therefore the practice should not be relegated as atypical for Paul or as forced upon him by his circumstances. (4) It reveals that Paul's practice is a part of his repertoire as a Jewish interpreter of Scripture in the Second Temple period because others used it who shared the same milieu, beliefs, and authorial assumptions as Paul; therefore, Paul's allegorical practice is a means by which we can understand him within a Jewish context.

1. COMPARATIVE ANALYSIS

This project regularly employs the scholarly construct of comparative analysis and engages others' analyses. Comparative analysis, as a methodology, is defined and used in various ways. My use of comparative analysis is influenced heavily by the work of Jonathan Z. Smith.[2] Smith's approach—presented later in his career as "four moments in the comparative enterprise"[3]—is widely accepted as useful parameters for comparative analysis, and a summary of each is as follows:

1. Description—A double process. One process is locating an example within its own "social, historical, and cultural environments that

---

2. Influential are J. Z. Smith's "In Comparison," "'End' of Comparison," and his well-known work *Drudgery Divine*.

3. J. Z. Smith, "'End' of Comparison," 239.

invest it with its local significance."[4] The second process is to report how scholarly tradition has engaged with that example.

2. Comparison—Once the double process of description is complete for two examples, then they are compared "both in terms of aspects and relations held to be significant, and with respect to some category, question, theory, or model of interest to us."[5]

3. Redescription—The examples are redefined using information from the comparison.

4. Rectification—The ways in which scholarly tradition engaged with the examples must be reworked (i.e., rectified) to consider the redescriptions that resulted from the comparison of the two doubly-described examples.

This project participates in each moment at the appropriate times, and its methodology is informed by the continuing scholarly discussions both of Smith's perspectives and of comparative analysis.[6]

Four additional notes are helpful for clarifying the role of comparative analysis in this project. First, I neither make claims for nor am interested in proving cases of "borrowing"—that is, arguments such as "Paul did this because he knew Philo did something similar" or "Philo copied Paul." Such claims remain common in comparative analysis, and such arguments are not in this project. Second, I view differences between comparative examples to be as important as similarities. Differences make similarities interesting, or as Smith stated when evaluating Alfred Loisy's 1911 article "The Christian Mystery": "From such a parataxis of 'likeness,'

---

4. J. Z. Smith, "'End' of Comparison," 239.

5. J. Z. Smith, "'End' of Comparison," 239.

6. One significant contribution is the collection of essays in Barclay and White, *New Testament in Comparison*. In the introduction, the editors present five challenges facing scholars who use comparative analysis: (1) choosing what to compare, (2) selecting for the purpose of comparison, (3) categorizing the items compared, (4) determining the purpose of comparison, (5) and measuring degrees of similarity or difference (Barclay and White, "Posing the Questions," 5–7). These five challenges complement Smith's four moments as additional parameters for comparative analysis, and I provide responses to each within the scope of this project. The editors also dutifully note that these challenges require scholarly decisions about which not everyone will agree (and this is reflected in their project's essays). The result of these scholarly decisions is that one scholar's comparative analysis will be different than another's analysis. This situation requires that scholars present their own analyses honestly and—of equal importance—evaluate others' analyses based on the analyses' merit and not by whether they are identical to their own.

little of value can be learned."⁷ Third, my methodology is what Smith calls "triadic." He explains, "There is always an implicit 'more than,' and there is always a 'with respect to.'" Put another way, "*x* resembles *y* more than *z* with respect to . . ."⁸ Accordingly, my contributions in this project take into consideration all the comparative examples that I engage. Last, my analysis examines interpretive practices that are similar in lieu of how an ancient author described them. I discuss this distinction at length in chapters 2–3, but a brief example can be useful here. Aristobulus, as recounted by Eusebius, uses the Greek root μεταφορ- for an interpretive practice that is similar to the one Paul describes as ἀλληγορ-.⁹ This project examines these practices because they are similar, and I do not reject the comparison simply because the two interpreters use different Greek roots to describe their practices.

2. TERMINOLOGY

Because of the various definitions for and uses of allegory, as well as the various ways it is compared to other practices,¹⁰ it is essential to clarify terminology. Of greatest relevance are the distinctions "allegory" and "allegoresis." On the one hand, both involve two levels of meaning: one stated and another one intended. On the other hand, they are distinguished methodologically. *Brill's New Pauly: The Encyclopedia of the Ancient World* defines each as follows:

---

7. J. Z. Smith, *Drudgery Divine*, 43.
8. J. Z. Smith, *Drudgery Divine*, 51.
9. Eusebius, *Praep. ev.* 8.10.7–9. This is quoted and engaged below in ch. 2, sect. 2.1.2.
10. Today, the relationship of allegory to metaphor, as well as to typology or simile or analogy, can be defined differently across disciplines and differently by scholars within each discipline. The interest in this relationship is ancient, as some Greek and Roman rhetorical handbooks also distinguished some of them. Characteristics that have been used to distinguish them include (1) length; (2) if there is a complete plot—however defined; (3) if the entities involved are related to each other; (4) the scope of its application—that is, is it making a point about a single situation or a broader claim; and (5) if it is historical—however defined. Explanations of these practices also add complexity because the practices have been described as extensions, subtypes, subgenres, wider uses, et al. The variety of terms and explanations necessitate each project provide its own definition for "allegory" and other terms used, for which I provide my definitions in this section.

> Allegory is a technique used in producing texts, allegoresis (or allegorical exegesis) is a technique used in responding to texts; it plays an important role in the exegesis of Holy Scripture.[11]

From this perspective, the distinction between these two terms amounts to the difference between *producing* a new text and *responding* to a prior text. The usefulness of this distinction is limited for our purposes. To demonstrate how it is limited, let us consider Plato's famous allegory of the cave. Although one of the most influential allegories (i.e., a production of a new text) from the ancient world, Plato's allegory also is a response to a "text": elements of the human experience (e.g., caves, light, eyesight).[12] Without Plato's response to a prior text (i.e., allegoresis)—that is, his imbuing of philosophical ideas upon elements of the human experience—his production of a new text (i.e., allegory) could not exist. In other words, Plato's interpretive practice can be described accurately as allegory and allegoresis because he both responds and produces simultaneously. The limited usefulness of the distinction between allegory and allegoresis also can be observed in a pericope from Second Corinthians.

> Since, then, we have such a hope, we act with great boldness, not like Moses, who put a veil over his face to keep the people of Israel from gazing at the end of the glory that was being set aside. But their minds were hardened. Indeed, to this very day, when they hear the reading of the old covenant, that same veil is still there, since only in Christ is it set aside. Indeed, to this very day whenever Moses is read, a veil lies over their minds; but when one turns to the Lord, the veil is removed. (2 Cor 3:12–16)

Because Paul responds to Exod 34:33–35 by imbuing it with a new meaning, his technique can be described as allegoresis. However, Paul also produces an allegory by using "veil" to symbolize the situation in which some Jews reject Jesus. These allegorical expressions of Plato and Paul indicate that the distinction between allegory and allegoresis is in the toolbox of a modern reader more so than in the mind of an ancient author. Put simply, the line between allegory and allegoresis in the ancient world can be blurred.[13] I affirm this interrelationship and label it

---

11. Hildegard Cancik-Lindemaier and Dorothea Sigel, "Allegoresis," *BNP* 1:511.

12. By using "text" in this way, I affirm its broader definition that includes anything that conveys meaning (in contrast to the mindset that "text" applies only to written material).

13. This blurred line is reflected in how the ancient Greek root ἀλληγορ- was used. Here, LSJ is helpful. For ἀλληγορέω, it lists (1) "interpret allegorically," (2) "to be

the "ancient interpretive practice of allegory." Therefore, when I examine Paul's interpretive practice of allegory, this examination includes both his response to a text (i.e., his response to Gen 16–21) and his production of a new text (i.e., Gal 4:21–31).

The blurred line between allegory and allegoresis, however, does not render this distinction useless. When used with precision, each concept can be a heuristic tool that is helpful for better understanding Paul's interpretive practice of allegory (and I use each concept accordingly). What must be resisted is the tendency, which I demonstrate pervades prior scholarship on the interpretive practice behind Paul's use of ἀλληγορούμενα, to define Paul's practice *as one of these two interpretive acts at the exclusion of the other*. Accordingly, I use terminology as follows:

General Terms

- Ancient interpretive practice of allegory—The interpretive acts of allegoresis (i.e., responding to a prior text) and allegory (i.e., producing a new text) together
- Allegorical expression—An occurrence of the ancient interpretive practice of allegory
- Allegorist—Someone who uses the ancient interpretive practice of allegory
- Entities—characters, events, and ideas, within a prior text (i.e., source entities) or within a new text (i.e., allegorical entities) that an allegorist responds to or produces in the ancient interpretive practice of allegory

---

spoken allegorically," (3) "to speak figuratively or metaphorically," (4) "to speak allegorically"; for ἀλληγορητής, (1) "allegorical expounder"; for ἀλληγορία, (1) "allegory, veiled language," (2) "allegorical exposition," (3) "figurative, metaphorical language"; for ἀλληγορικός, (1) "figurative"; for ἀλληγορος (1) "allegorical"; for ἀλληγορως, (1) "allegorically." See LSJ, s.v. "ἀλληγορέω."

Terms Related to Responding to a Prior Text

- Allegoresis—A response to a text that imbues new meanings upon entities found within that text
- Source entity—An entity, within a prior text, upon which allegoresis is used
- Source meaning—The meaning that an allegorist places upon the source entity within the context of the prior text

Terms Related to Producing a New Text

- Allegory; an allegorical interpretation—The production of a new text that contains new entities and meanings corresponding to source entities and meanings within a prior text
- Allegorical entity—The entity within an allegory that corresponds to its source entity within a prior text
- Allegorical meaning—The meaning that an allegorist places upon the allegorical entity within the context of the allegory

3. CHAPTER SUMMARIES

I have organized the presentation of my arguments into seven chapters. In chapter 1, I arrange prior scholarship on Gal 4:21–31 into six interpretive issues and provide a history of research. The history of research (1) locates the interpretive practice behind Paul's use of ἀλληγορούμενα within the interpretive issues of Gal 4:21–31, (2) explains how and why its current state of scholarship is unresolved, and (3) indicates when a more precise understanding of Paul's practice also can benefit the state of scholarship on other interpretive issues. In chapter 2, I examine the ancient interpretive practice of allegory up to the time of Paul. The examination demonstrates that prior scholarship's criteria for selecting comparative examples—those interpretive practices of allegory used to explain Paul's practice—do not enable an analysis of Paul's practice within the ancient interpretive practice of allegory because they do not distinguish ancient allegorical expressions in terms of their similarities and differences. In chapter 3, I examine those ways that the interpretive schemata based on those criteria (examined in chapter 2) misrepresent not only how the ancient interpretive practice of allegory operated but also how Paul's practice fits within it. Additionally, I present different criteria and a different approach—each based on the analytical work of chapters 2–3—that situate an analysis of Paul's practice appropriately within the ancient interpretive practice of allegory. These criteria are (1) milieu, (2) assumptions as an author, (3) perception of the situation for which the interpretive practice is used, and (4) the hermeneutical purpose of the interpretive practice of allegory. The different approach is first establishing allegorists as suitable comparative examples (instead of interpretive practices) using the four criteria above, and only then examining their practices comparatively.

Chapters 4–6 analyze Paul's practice comparatively with the practices of three Jewish interpreters of Scripture who were roughly contemporary to Paul: those who composed the sectarian texts of the Dead Sea Scrolls, Philo, and the author of the Epistle of Barnabas.[14] I begin each chapter by demonstrating an interpreter—not an interpretive practice—is a suitable comparative example. Then, I examine the allegorical practice of the interpreter separately from Paul's practice. Next, I compare the interpreter's allegorical practice with Paul's practice. Last, I discuss the significance of the comparison for understanding Paul's practice more precisely. In chapter 7, the conclusion, I bring together the contributions from each comparative analysis and provide a more precise understanding of Paul's interpretive practice (and I summarized this understanding earlier in the introduction). I then discuss (1) the implications of this understanding for the state of scholarship on other interpretive issues within Gal 4:21–31 and (2) the opportunities for future research that my contributions reveal, including the implications of my contributions for current conversations within Pauline scholarship.

---

14. There is disagreement whether the author of the Epistle of Barnabas was a Jew or gentile. I affirm a Jewish authorship and explain this position in ch. 6, sect. 1.2.

1

Paul's Interpretive Practice of Allegory in the Context of Galatians 4:21–31

IN THIS CHAPTER, I situate Paul's interpretive practice of allegory within Gal 4:21–31 and explain how and why its state of scholarship remains unresolved. Additionally, I indicate how a better understanding of Paul's practice will contribute to the state of scholarship on other interpretive issues within 4:21–31. I have organized this chapter into three parts: introductory comments, six interpretive issues in 4:21–31, and towards a more precise understanding of Paul's interpretive practice.

1. INTRODUCTORY COMMENTS

I introduce this history of research with four essential discussions: methodological concerns, Gal 5:1, the structure of 4:21–31, and the function of 4:21–31 in the letter.

1.1. Methodological Concerns

Any discussion of this pericope must begin with the basic acknowledgment that we read only Paul's perspectives (and not his opponents' or the Galatians'). Accordingly, "Um es bildlich zu sagen: vor uns liegt ein Schachbrett mit nur schwarzen Figuren, und wir sollen aus der Position von Schwarz eruieren, wie Weiß gespielt hat."[1] This creates the potential

---
1. Bouwman, "Hagar- und Sara-Perikope," 3137.

for a number of methodological problems and dangers. These problems and dangers already have been summarized elsewhere.[2]

1. Undue selectivity—The requirement of a reader to make decisions about which of Paul's statements are the most important for the interpretation of a specific issue.
2. Overinterpretation—The inclination to draw themes and motivations from Paul's letter that may not be supported by his statements. For example, "that every statement by Paul is a rebuttal of an equally vigorous counter statement by his opponents."[3]
3. Mishandling polemics—The danger of attributing more (or less) meaning to Paul's statements than is actually indicated in the text. For example, interpreting Paul's polemical descriptions as the real situation in Galatia. Additionally, there is a danger to interpret Paul's words in accordance with our own theological views.
4. Latching onto particular words or phrases—A specific manifestation of "undue selectivity," one that understands Paul's phrases as "direct echoes of the opponent's vocabulary" and then hangs "a whole thesis on those flimsy pegs."[4]

These problems and dangers threaten the examination of many pericopes in Galatians. However, two characteristics of Gal 4:21–31 add additional layers of complexity. First, Paul is reinterpreting Jewish Scriptures (i.e., Gen 16–21) whose prior interpretations are foundational for Judaism.[5] Second, Paul exerts a tremendous amount of "hermeneutical jujitsu"[6]—discussed later in this chapter—when interpreting Gen 16–21. Accordingly, understanding some of the interpretive issues within Gal 4:21–31 is a challenging task.

Acknowledging these problems and dangers is significant because prior scholarship sometimes suffers from them. In section 2 of this

---

2. Barclay, "Mirror-Reading a Polemical Letter," 79–83.
3. Barclay, "Mirror-Reading a Polemical Letter," 79.
4. Barclay, "Mirror-Reading a Polemical Letter," 81–82.

5. For a discussion of the patriarchal narrative's role in Judaism, see Harrisville, *Figure of Abraham*. In this comprehensive study, Harrisville catalogues and discusses how the patriarchal narrative was used in the Jewish Scriptures, Paul's writings, other New Testament texts, late first-century Jewish literature (e.g., 4 Ezra, Josephus), Philo's writings, the Dead Sea Scrolls, the Pseudepigrapha, and the Apocrypha. He describes Gal 4:21–31 as "the last round from [Paul's] Abrahamic arsenal" (20).

6. For the phrase "hermeneutical jujitsu," see Hays, *Echoes of Scripture*, 112.

chapter,[7] I point out those occasions and their impact on understanding the interpretive issues within Gal 4:21–31.

1.2. Galatians 5:1

A substantial amount of scholarship is focused on the structure of Gal 4:21–31. One fundamental question is whether 5:1 should be included with 4:21–31: "For freedom Christ has set us free. Stand firm, therefore, and do not submit again to a yoke of slavery" (Gal 5:1). Prior scholarship typically excludes 5:1 from the unit,[8] regularly without comment.[9] However, some scholarship includes it.[10] One explanation given for including 5:1 is that 4:31 repeats themes found earlier in the letter; therefore, 4:31 cannot be the end of the pericope.[11] Another explanation is that 5:1 is a "bridge verse" or "transition paragraph" that serves both to summarize 4:21–31 and introduce chapter 5.[12]

This discussion is significant not only because a range of verses must be defined for this project but also because it highlights a characteristic of Gal 4:21–31 that is critical for my engagement with the six interpretive issues in this pericope in section 2: in 4:21–31, Paul employs various

---

7. Unless a chapter is listed before a referenced section (e.g., ch. 2, sect. 1), a referenced section refers to the section within the current chapter.

8. Amoit, *Épitre aux Galates*, 206; Betz, *Galatians*, 253–54; Blackwelder and Stamm, "Epistle to the Galatians," 544–45; Bonnard, *Épitre*, 100; Burton, *Epistle to the Galatians*, 269; Buscemi, *Lettera ai Galati*, 448; Das, *Galatians*, 277; DeSilva, *Letter to the Galatians*, 390; Dunn, *Epistle to the Galatians*, 259–60; George, *Galatians*, 348; Hendriksen, *Galatians*, 179; Lagrange, *Saint Paul*, 132–33; Lietzmann, *An die Galater*, 83–84; Longenecker, *Galatians*, 219–20; Lührmann, *Galatians*, 93–94; Matera, *Galatians*, 179; Moo, *Galatians*, 292; Oepke, *Brief des Paulus*, 117; Rhode, *Brief des Paulus*, 210–11; Ridderbos, *Epistle of Paul*, 172; Schlier, *Brief an die Galater*, 215; S. Williams, *Galatians*, 124.

9. One scholar who provides an explanation for the exclusion of Gal 5:1 is Ernest Burton. He argues both the language and message of Gal 4:31 indicate that "it is more probable that we should take [Gal 4:31] as the summation of the whole allegorical argument" (*Epistle to the Galatians*, 268–69). In particular, he points out the presence of παιδίσκη and ἐλεύθερος, both of which do not occur after Gal 4:31. For a similar defense based on διό in Gal 4:31, see Mußner, *Galaterbrief*, 334.

10. De Boer, *Galatians*, 208–10; Bring, *Commentary on Galatians*, 218; Bruce, *Epistle to the Galatians*, 226–27; Fung, *Epistle to the Galatians*, 204; Keener, *Galatians*, 211; Lémonon, *Épitre aux Galates*, 157; Lightfoot, *Saint Paul's Epistle*, 185; Martyn, *Galatians*, 446–47; Schreiner, *Galatians*, 292; Witherington, *Grace in Galatia*, 340; Wright, *Galatians*, 290.

11. De Boer, *Galatians*, 308.

12. Fung, *Epistle to the Galatians*, 216. Fung is followed by Malan, "Strategy," 425.

themes found throughout the letter. Because of this characteristic, I am not convinced by arguments based solely on thematic development. Accordingly, I affirm the majority position and do not include 5:1 in the analysis.

1.3. The Structure of Galatians 4:21–31

Although some prior scholarship discusses Gal 4:21–31 as a single unit, the pericope also has been divided into subsections. The various divisions I found—seventeen, to be exact—are significant for two reasons. First, all demonstrate a general agreement that this pericope follows a specific progression of ideas.[13] For all but two, this progression includes an introduction, an interpretation, and some type of real-life application for those who live in Galatia.[14] The second reason these divisions are significant is their classifications for the section that includes 4:24 demonstrate the unresolved state of scholarship on its interpretive issue. For example, some label the section as allegory[15] while others use terms such as figurative meaning,[16] spiritual meaning,[17] explanation,[18] analysis,[19] interpretation,[20] commentary,[21] and midrash.[22] The state of scholarship is further complicated by those who label this practice as allegory yet define it as a form of historical interpretation (i.e., typology). I discuss this label below in section 2.2.1.

---

13. One notable exception is O'Neill, "This Is Mount Sinai." O'Neill argues that the pericope is not a single unit, but that Gal 4:25–27 was composed by a first-century monastic community who then edited Gal 4:28–5:1.

14. The two who interpret the progression differently are Perriman, "Rhetorical Strategy," 30–32; and Tedder, "Children of Laughter," 60.

15. Blackwelder and Stamm, "Epistle to the Galatians," 539–44; De Boer, *Galatians*, 288; Das, *Galatians*, 490; Malan, "Strategy"; Matera, *Galatians*, 174; Perriman, "Rhetorical Strategy," 30–32; Sellin, "Hagar und Sara," 61; Tedder, "Children of Laughter," 60; Tolmie, *Persuading the Galatians*, 170; also, Tolmie, "Allegorie," 168; Willitts, "Isa 54,1," 198.

16. George, *Galatians*, 334–38; Keener, *Galatians*, 217.

17. Fung, *Epistle to the Galatians*, 204–15.

18. Harmon, *She Must and Shall*, 174.

19. Wright, *Galatians*, 304.

20. DeSilva, *Letter to the Galatians*, 396; DeYoung, "But As Then," 5; Moo, *Galatians*, 296.

21. Borgen, "Hebrew and Pagan Features," 156.

22. Buscemi, *Lettera ai Galati*, 457–58.

1.4. The Function of Galatians 4:21–31 in the Letter

The final essential discussion is to ask how Gal 4:21–31 functions in the letter. One nineteenth-century answer that some still follow today divides Galatians into three sections of two chapters each.[23] In this schema, 4:21–31 ends the second section and seeks to demonstrate "the law indeed bears witness against itself."[24] Over one hundred years later, a different schema was introduced, which has become a standard that all subsequent rhetorical analyses must engage.[25]

1:1–5	Epistolary prescript
1:6–11	*Exordium*
1:12—2:14	*Narratio*
2:15–21	*Propositio*
3:1—4:31	*Probatio*
5:1—6:10	*Exhortatio*
6:11–18	Epistolary postscript

In this schema, 4:21–31 is the end of the *probatio*. According to the scholar who proposed this schema, the *probatio* "determines whether or not the speech as a whole will succeed."[26] The reception of this schema is mixed[27] and its debate raises an important question for interpreters of Paul: Did Paul intend for this pericope to stand as a strong argument,[28]

---

23. Lightfoot, *Saint Paul's Epistle*, 67. He is followed by Burton, *Epistle to the Galatians*, lxxii–lxxiv; and George, *Galatians*, 74. C. K. Barrett also follows Lightfoot's divisions but renames them as follows: "history" (Gal 1–2), "theology" (Gal 3–4), and "ethics" (Gal 5–6). See Barrett, *Freedom and Obligation*, 3.

24. Lightfoot, *Saint Paul's Epistle*, 67.

25. Betz, *Galatians*, 16–23.

26. Betz, *Galatians*, 128.

27. Those who have placed this pericope at the end of an important section are as follows: Bruce, who placed it at the end of "Faith Receives the Promise" (*Epistle to the Galatians*, 57); Burton, at the end of the "Refutatory Portion of the Letter" (*Epistle to the Galatians*, lxxiv); George, at the end of the theological section (*Galatians*, 74); Martyn, who classifies it as a second exegetical argument before the transition to the pastoral section (*Galatians*, 26); Rhode, at the end of "Die Übereinstimmung des Paulinischen Evangeliums mit den Verheißungen des Alten Bundes" (*Brief des Paulus*, 126). Those who have not placed this pericope at the end of an important section are as follows: De Boer, *Galatians*, 14; Fung, *Epistle to the Galatians*, v–vii; Hansen, *Abraham in Galatians*, 27; Longenecker, *Galatians*, 184–87, 199; Matera, *Galatians*, 13; Mußner, *Galaterbrief*, vii–viii; Schlier, *Brief an die Galater*, 8.

28. Those who interpret this pericope as a strong argument are as follows: Barrett,

or did he add it as a supplementary addition[29] or afterthought?[30] This question is significant because much of prior scholarship explains the interpretive practice behind Paul's use of ἀλληγορούμενα based on judgments about what really mattered to Paul—this is discussed in chapter 2. In this project, I clarify the role Paul's interpretive practice can serve in determining how Paul intended this pericope to function in Galatians. I return to this topic at the conclusion of this project.

2. SIX INTERPRETIVE ISSUES IN GALATIANS 4:21–31

Prior scholarship on Gal 4:21–31 can be categorized heuristically into six interpretive issues. Some of these interpretive issues still are debated and a few have not seen any significant progress since their inception. Additionally, there is a tendency for prior scholarship on this pericope to use categorical (e.g., all, every) and superlative (e.g., most, very many) descriptors to support argumentative claims. This section reveals only a few arguments warrant such descriptors.

The six interpretive issues as they arise sequentially in the text are as follows: (1) the contrast between flesh and promise, (2) the interpretive practice behind Paul's use of ἀλληγορούμενα, (3) columns and a contrasting pair, (4) the function of Isa 54:1, (5) the climax of the pericope, and (6) why Paul interpreted Gen 16–21.

2.1. Galatians 4:21–23

²¹Λέγετέ μοι, οἱ ὑπὸ νόμον θέλοντες εἶναι, τὸν νόμον οὐκ ἀκούετε. ²²γέγραπται γὰρ ὅτι Ἀβραὰμ δύο υἱοὺς ἔσχεν, ἕνα ἐκ τῆς παιδίσκης καὶ ἕνα ἐκ τῆς ἐλευθέρας. ²³ἀλλ᾽ ὁ μὲν ἐκ τῆς παιδίσκης

"Allegory of Abraham," 157; De Boer, *Galatians*, 286; Borgen, "Hebrew and Pagan Features," 162–64; Broer, "'Vertreibe die Magd,'" 181; Cosgrove, "Law Has Given Sarah," 221–22; DeSilva, *Letter to the Galatians*, 391; Ebeling, *Truth of the Gospel*, 232; Gignilliat, "Paul, Allegory," 146; Hogeterp, "Hagar," 356; Van Kooten, "Philosophical Criticism," 362; Schwemer, "Himmlische Stadt," 198; Tolmie, "Allegorie," 164; Witherington, *Grace in Galatia*, 327; Woollcombe, "Biblical Origins," 55; Wright, *Galatians*, 292.

29. Those who interpret this pericope as a supplementary addition are as follows: Amoit, *Épitre aux Galates*, 201; Bruce, *Epistle to the Galatians*, 214; Dunn, *Epistle to the Galatians*, 243; Liao, "Meaning of Galatians 4:21–31," 117; Luther, "Lectures on Galatians, 1519," 26:310–13; Luther, "Lectures on Galatians, 1535," 26:435–37.

30. Those who interpret this pericope as an afterthought are as follows: Burton, *Epistle to the Galatians*, 251; Mußner, *Galaterbrief*, 316; Oepke, *Brief des Paulus*, 110.

κατὰ σάρκα γεγέννηται, ὁ δὲ ἐκ τῆς ἐλευθέρας δι' ἐπαγγελίας. (Gal 4:21–23)[31]

> [21]Tell me, you who desire to be subject to the law, will you not listen to the law? [22]For it is written that Abraham had two sons, one by a slave woman and the other by a free woman. [23]One, the child of the slave, was born according to the flesh; the other, the child of the free woman, was born through the promise. (Gal 4:21–23)

Paul begins by addressing the entire Galatian community,[32] which not yet has been won over by the opponents' arguments.[33] Paul uses the same word (νόμος) twice to foreshadow the new interpretation of Gen 16–21 that he provides. Additionally, he uses νόμος in two different ways: the first representing requirements of the Torah and the second representing what he reinterprets. To understand how Paul viewed the law in the first sense, we can recall Paul's earlier comments in Gal 3:23–26.[34]

> Now before faith came, we were imprisoned and guarded under the law until faith would be revealed. Therefore, the law was our disciplinarian until Christ came, so that we might be justified by faith. But now that faith has come, we are no longer subject to a disciplinarian, for in Christ you are all children of God through faith. (Gal 3:23–26)

Paul viewed the law as a disciplinarian (παιδαγωγός) until Jesus came. Paul believed that Jesus changed the function of the law and therefore

---

31. I provide the Greek text of Gal 4:21–31 as it is found in the NA[28] because I accept the text-critical decisions of this edition. This includes the rendering within NA[28] of the complex textual situation in Gal 4:25, which I discuss in sect. 2.2.2.1.

32. This is widely accepted, although nuances have been proposed. Wilhelm Lütgert (*Gesetz und Geist*, 88) and later J. H. Ropes argued that Paul responds to two different opponents in Galatia (*Singular Problem*, 43–46). This is no longer considered a viable position, yet scholars still engage it (e.g., Barclay, "Mirror-Reading a Polemical Letter," 87; Bonnard, *Épitre*, 95; Mußner, *Galaterbrief*, 217; Oepke, *Brief des Paulus*, 110; Schlier, *Brief an die Galater*, 216). Additionally, W. Schmithals's argument that Paul is responding to gnostic opponents is treated similarly in scholarship ("Häretiker in Galatien").

33. The present participle in Gal 4:21 (οἱ ὑπὸ νόμον θέλοντες εἶναι) indicates that the Galatians were not yet convinced by the opponents' arguments. Others who share this interpretation are as follows: Burton, *Epistle to the Galatians*, 252; Matera, *Galatians*, 168; Rhode, *Brief des Paulus*, 193. This interpretation was expressed as early as Origen (as found in Jerome, *Comm. Gal.* 4:28).

34. For this specific discussion, I need to reference only Paul's earlier use of the law in Gal 3:23–25. For a few in-depth analyses of the law in all of Galatians, see these four substantial works: Hong, *Law in Galatians*; Hübner, *Law in Paul's Thought*, 15–50; Theilman, *From Plight to Solution*, 46–86; Wilson, *Curse of the Law*.

could speak of a second νόμος in 4:21. Paul emphasized the second νόμος by the use of ἀκούω. "Hearing" in Judaism also could invoke an internalization that led to obedience.[35] If Paul intended this, then he wanted the Galatians not only to hear his interpretation but also to take action (cf. 4:30). Paul's second use of νόμος, in contrast to the first, is positive.[36]

In Gal 4:22–23, Paul begins his interpretive practice of allegory by summarizing Gen 16–21. The enormous effort Paul exerts to interpret Gen 16–21 is evident in these verses. First, Paul discusses two sets of Abrahamic descendants, earlier having envisioned only one (cf. Gal 3:6–7).[37] Second, this is one of the few occasions when Paul follows his use of an introductory formula with a summary.[38] Third, within his summary, Paul omits various details from Gen 16–21. Although Paul makes these three interpretive choices for the benefit of his argument, those choices also alter or remove characteristics of Gen 16–21 that were both profound and relevant for Judaism. I discuss the impact of these choices in section 2.3.2.

2.1.1. *Interpretive Issue 1: The Contrast between Flesh and Promise*

At the end of his summary of Gen 16–21, Paul contrasts one son who was born according to the flesh (σάρξ) with the other born according to the promise (ἐπαγγελία).[39] In other words, he contrasts two different statuses of birth.[40] When reading Gen 16–21, an apparent inconsistency comes to mind: Ishmael also was born with a promise.

---

35. Corsani, "Interpretazione tipologica," 214; Longenecker, *Galatians*, 206; Mußner, *Galaterbrief*, 327; Rhode, *Brief des Paulus*, 192, who also points to Gen 11:7 LXX; Deut 28:49 LXX; Matt 13:13; Luke 16:29; and 1 Cor 14:2. Many others assume this line of reasoning in their argumentation without specific reference to ἀκούω.

36. Martyn points out that this is the first positive use of the law in Galatians (*Galatians*, 433).

37. "Just as Abraham 'believed God, and it was reckoned to him as righteousness,' so, you see, those who believe are the descendants of Abraham" (Gal 3:6–7).

38. Ellis, *Paul's Use*, 22. In Gal 4:21–31, Paul uses introductory formulas three times. In Gal 4:22 and 4:27, he uses γράφω (used elsewhere twenty-eight times). In Gal 4:29, he uses λέγω γραφή (used elsewhere five times). For a larger discussion of Paul's introductory formulas, see 22–37.

39. In Galatians, Paul's only other discussion of promise (ἐπαγγελία) is in Gal 3.

40. Those who frame Paul's contrast in Gal 4:23 as two statuses are as follows: Burton, *Epistle to the Galatians*, 252; Fung, *Epistle to the Galatians*, 205; George, *Galatians*, 337; Lightfoot, *Saint Paul's Epistle*, 180.

The angel of the LORD also said to [Hagar], "I will so greatly multiply your offspring that they cannot be counted for multitude." And the angel of the LORD said to her, "Now you have conceived and shall bear a son; you shall call him Ishmael, for the LORD has given heed to your affliction. (Gen 16:10–11)[41]

This inconsistency[42] necessitates we go beyond the simple explanation of Paul's contrast described above (i.e., he contrasts two statuses of birth) and ask *what* Paul is contrasting by means of these statuses of birth. One interpretation is that Paul describes two ways of planting churches.[43] Although the initial evidence for this position is problematic,[44] it later focuses on Paul's use of γεννάω. The evidence proposed are (1) Paul's use of γεννάω in Phlm 10 and 1 Cor 4:14–15 to describe his missionary work and (2) Paul's use of γεννάω in Gal 4:23 and in 4:29 when τίκτω could be a more appropriate choice.[45] A closer examination demonstrates this position oversimplifies the meaning of γεννάω (cf. latching onto particular words or phrases) and overemphasizes its role in Gal 4:21–31 (cf. overinterpretation) for two reasons. First, Paul's use of γεννάω is not consistent across his letters and one use (cf. Rom 9:11) contradicts this position.[46] Second, Paul does not develop this interpretation in Gal 4:24–27 (i.e., Paul focuses on the mothers) or in 4:28–31 (i.e., Paul shifts his attention back to the sons).[47]

---

41. "And God heard the voice of the boy; and the angel of God called to Hagar from heaven, and said to her, 'What troubles you, Hagar? Do not be afraid; for God has heard the voice of the boy where he is. Come, lift up the boy and hold him fast with your hand, for I will make a great nation of him.'" (Gen 21:17–18).

42. Jerome was the first to recognize this inconsistency (cf. Jerome, *Comm. Gal.* 4:22–23). Also, Anthony Hanson proposes that this may explain why Paul did not include a similar argument within Rom 4 (*Studies in Paul's Technique*, 91).

43. In this section, I engage J. L. Martyn's argument. His argument is based on F. C. Baur's famous argument that there were two competing missions to the gentiles: one taught that gentiles who believe in Christ should observe the law (i.e., Petrine Christianity) and the other did not (i.e., Pauline Christianity). See Baur, *Paul the Apostle*.

44. Problematic is Martyn's use of the Pseudo-Clementine literature the Ascent of James and the Preachings of Peter—both written over a century after Galatians—as the only evidence ("Law-Observant Mission," 310–12).

45. Martyn, *Galatians*, 451–54; see also Martyn, "Covenants," 177–84.

46. "Even before they had been born [Μήπω γὰρ γεννηθέντων] or had done anything good or bad" (Rom 9:11). Context indicates that Paul uses the verb γεννάω in Rom 9:11 only to refer to the process of childbirth.

47. For another critique of Martyn that focuses on Paul's broader views of covenant, see Byrne, "Jerusalems Above and Below."

Another interpretation is that Paul intends for flesh to represent circumcision. The evidence proposed for this position is that the author of Genesis mentions flesh only in the context of circumcision.[48] Like the first interpretation, this one places too much emphasis on one word (i.e., circumcision; cf. latching onto particular words or phrases) and assumes Paul is using it in the same way as the author of Genesis (cf. overinterpretation). In Galatians, Paul previously has mentioned circumcision only once in relation to a group of Jews at Antioch (cf. Gal 2:12). Additionally, if Paul had this interpretive goal, another scriptural reality would complicate Paul's argument: both Isaac and Ishmael were circumcised.[49] For these reasons, it is difficult to accept this second interpretation.[50]

A third interpretation is that Paul contrasts the time at which promises were made in relation to when the children were conceived. Jerome was the first to proffer this position: "Concerning Ishmael after he was conceived, either an angel or God spoke; but concerning Isaac before he was conceived in Sarah's womb, God made a promise" (*Comm. Gal.* 4:22–23 [Scheck]). Luther supported this interpretation by contrasting Sarah's words with God's voice: "Therefore, Ishmael was born without the word, solely at the request of Sarah herself. Here was no word of God that commanded or promised Abraham a son."[51] If this contrast is what Paul intended, then Paul informed the Galatians that God initiated their spiritual birth in the same way that he initiated Isaac's physical birth (i.e., beforehand by his divine decree). Although it is not possible to recover Paul's exact meaning, this interpretation is attractive because it aligns with Paul's claim in Gal 4:28: "Now you, my friends, are children of the promise, like Isaac."

---

48. De Boer, *Galatians*, 292. He references Gen 17:11, 13, 14, 24–25.

49. Gen 17:25, as noted by Lührmann, *Galatians*, 89; Perriman, "Rhetorical Strategy," 33.

50. Also problematic is the position that circumcision is discussed because Anatolian religion involved castration (see Elliott, "Choose Your Mother," 678–79). We do not know enough about the context of Paul's audience to make this claim (cf. my critique of Elliott in sect. 2.2.2.3). Also, the view that Paul's opponents taught circumcision brought about perfection as patterned after mystery religions (cf. R. Jewett, "Agitators and Galatian Congregation," 207) is problematic for the same reason.

51. Luther, "Lectures on Galatians, 1535," 26:434.

2.2. Galatians 4:24–27

>²⁴ἅτινά ἐστιν ἀλληγορούμενα· αὗται γάρ εἰσιν δύο διαθῆκαι, μία ἀπὸ ὄρους Σινᾶ εἰς δουλείαν γεννῶσα, ἥτις ἐστὶν Ἁγάρ. ²⁵τὸ δὲ Ἁγὰρ Σινᾶ ὄρος ἐστὶν ἐν τῇ Ἀραβίᾳ· συστοιχεῖ δὲ τῇ νῦν Ἰερουσαλήμ, δουλεύει γὰρ μετὰ τῶν τέκνων αὐτῆς. ²⁶ἡ δὲ ἄνω Ἰερουσαλὴμ ἐλευθέρα ἐστίν, ἥτις ἐστὶν μήτηρ ἡμῶν. ²⁷γέγραπται γάρ·
>
> εὐφράνθητι, στεῖρα ἡ οὐ τίκτουσα,
> ῥῆξον καὶ βόησον, ἡ οὐκ ὠδίνουσα·
> ὅτι πολλὰ τὰ τέκνα τῆς ἐρήμου
> μᾶλλον ἢ τῆς ἐχούσης τὸν ἄνδρα. (Gal 4:24–27)

> ²⁴Here is an interpretive practice of allegory![52] These women are two covenants. One woman, in fact, is Hagar, from Mount Sinai, bearing children for slavery. ²⁵Now Hagar is Mount Sinai in Arabia and corresponds to the present Jerusalem, for she is in slavery with her children. ²⁶But the Jerusalem above is free,[53] and she is our mother. ²⁷For it is written,
>
> Rejoice, you childless one, you who bear no children,
> burst into song and shout, you who endure no birthpangs;
> for the children of the desolate woman are more numerous
> than the children of the one who is married. (Gal 4:24–27)

Within this section, there are three interpretive issues: the interpretive practice behind Paul's use of ἀλληγορούμενα, columns and a contrasting pair, and the function of Isa 54:1. Before the survey of these issues, it is important to acknowledge that Paul begins this section with a forthright statement: ἅτινά ἐστιν ἀλληγορούμενα· αὗται γάρ εἰσιν δύο διαθῆκαι.[54]

---

52. Based on the analysis in this project, I proffer this new translation of ἅτινά ἐστιν ἀλληγορούμενα. I discuss this translation in ch. 7, including why it does not follow the Greek text more closely.

53. I translate this phrase differently than the NRSV. See n93 below.

54. It is widely accepted that διαθῆκαι represents two contrasting systems of salvation. However, scholarship disagrees over which two systems Paul is contrasting. Some argue that Paul is contrasting the Abrahamic covenant with a new covenant in Jesus (Betz, *Galatians*, 244; Burton, *Epistle to the Galatians*, 258; Fung, *Epistle to the Galatians*, 207; George, *Galatians*, 340; Longenecker, *Galatians*, 211). Others argue that Paul contrasts the Abrahamic and Sinaitic covenants (De Boer, *Galatians*, 296; Bruce, *Epistle to the Galatians*, 218; DeSilva, *Letter to the Galatians*, 396; Hays, *Echoes of Scripture*, 114–15; Keener, *Galatians*, 221; Matera, *Galatians*, 169; Witherington, *Grace in Galatia*, 330). For another position that argues for only one covenant, see Dunn, *Epistle to the Galatians*, 294. I agree with Witherington's critique of Dunn when he states, "Dunn

Despite the straightforwardness of this statement, understanding it has proven to be one of the most difficult tasks in scholarship on Gal 4:21–31.

2.2.1. Interpretive Issue 2: The Interpretive Practice behind Paul's Use of ἀλληγορούμενα

Both ancient and subsequent exegetes, when discussing Gal 4:21–31, have given considerable attention to the interpretive practice behind Paul's use of ἀλληγορούμενα. Although ἀλληγορούμενα means *to speak something other*,[55] an understanding of the interpretive practice behind Paul's use of the term is elusive for several reasons. First, the Greek term has a rich history in Hellenistic literature that represents a diverse practice with no standardization (cf. ch. 2, sect. 2.2). Second, 4:24 is the only place in his extant letters where Paul uses the term, and it does not appear elsewhere in New Testament texts. Third, Paul's contemporary Philo uses the same term to allegorize Gen 16–21 as the progression of the human soul towards wisdom.[56] Last, Paul uses a similar interpretive practice elsewhere without ἀλληγορούμενα (cf. 1 Cor 3:1–3; 5:6–7; 9:9–10; 10:1–11; 12:12–25; 2 Cor 3:12–18).[57] For all these reasons, it is no surprise that the earliest extant commentary on this pericope—in the fourth century CE—sought to define what Paul meant by using ἀλληγορούμενα: "when one thing is said and another is meant" (Marius Victorinus, *In Galat.* 322).[58] Earlier in the third century CE, Origen and others (who often are labeled as the

---

has failed to grasp the radical character of Paul's argument when he says, 'what Paul describes as two covenants for the purposes of his exegesis are in effect two ways of understanding the one covenant purpose of God through Abraham and for his seed.' It is the argument of the agitators, not Paul, that the Mosaic covenant is an extension of the Abrahamic covenant" (*Grace in Galatia*, 330). For an interesting position in which Samuel Tedder finds two covenants already expressed in Gen 17, see Tedder, "Children of Laughter," 83–92.

55. LSJ, s.v. "ἀλληγορέω." ἀλληγορέω is the combination of ἄλλος, "other" (LSJ, s.v. "ἄλλος") and ἀγορεύω, "to speak" (LSJ, s.v. "ἀγόρευσις").

56. This theme runs throughout many of Philo's writings (e.g., Philo, *Congr.* 5–6; and Philo, *QG* 3.13–32). In the extant works of Philo, he uses the Greek root ἀλληγορ- forty-five times.

57. I discuss these pericopes in ch. 2, sect. 2.4.2.3.

58. For commentators roughly contemporary to Marius who also commented on the meaning of ἀλληγορούμενα, see Chrysostom, *Hom. Gal.* 4:24; Jerome, *Comm. Gal.* 4:24; Theodore of Mopsuestia, *Commentaries*, 73–79; Severian of Gabala, "Severian von Gabala," 302–3. I also engage these authors in this chapter.

"Alexandrian School")[59] began to embrace an interpretive practice of allegory that some considered too similar to Philo's practice.[60] In response, especially from those often labeled as the "Antiochene School," a concern emerged over whether the characters and events of Gen 16–21 were historical.[61] For example, Theodore of Mopsuestia (fourth to fifth century CE) wrote in his *Commentaries on the Minor Epistles of Paul* that those who disregard the history of a text "invert the meaning of everything since they wish the whole narrative of divine Scripture to differ in no way from dreams of the night. For they say that not even Adam actually existed as Adam" (115 [Greer]).

This concern for the characters and events of Gen 16–21 (as found in Gal 4:21–31) reemerged during the sixteenth century in the works of Martin Luther and John Calvin.[62] In the mid-nineteenth century, it emerged again in the seminal work of J. B. Lightfoot's commentary on Galatians:

> St Paul uses ἀλληγορία here much in the same sense as τυπικῶς in 1 Cor X. II ταῦτα δὲ τυπικῶς συνέβαινεν, not denying the historical truth of the narrative, but superposing a secondary meaning.[63]

The most influential manifestation of this concern, however, came in the mid-twentieth century when K. J. Woollcombe—building upon the

---

59. In recent decades, some have reevaluated the distinctions of Alexandrian and Antiochene schools. For a list of scholars and discussions, see Mitchell, *Paul, the Corinthians*, 122n48.

60. Philo and Origen allegorize similarly. Some argue there is a Philonic background to Origen's exegesis. For one example, see Trigg, *Origen*.

61. For more information on the exegesis of Gal 4:21–31 by those included in the Antiochene School, see Kepple, "Analysis of Antiochene Exegesis." For more information on the Patristic discussion of Gal 4:21–31, see Demura, "Origen and Exegetical Tradition"; Gil-Tamayo, "Todo esto"; Heldt, "Delineating Identity"; Heldt, "Epistle of Paul." Heldt, who provides the most thorough analysis in her dissertation, summarizes her findings as follows: "There are, properly speaking, no discussions of the passage as a whole, but rather only discussions focusing on individual verses or at most a group of verses" ("Delineating Identity," 163–64). I have found her assessment to be correct, except for a few discussions by Augustine (cf. Helleman, "Abraham Had Two Sons," 58–59). For a discussion of later gnostic interpretations of this pericope, see Van Os, "Children of Slave Woman."

62. Neither favored allegory because they understood it to betray history (Calvin, *Commentaries*, 135–36; Luther, "Lectures on Galatians, 1519," 6:310–13; Luther, "Lectures on Galatians, 1535," 6:435–37). For a thorough analysis of Luther's views, see Maschke, "Authority of Scripture."

63. Lightfoot, *Saint Paul's Epistle*, 180.

works of John Chrysostom,[64] Daniélou,[65] and Lightfoot—distinguished between what he called "allegorism" and "typological exegesis":

> Typological exegesis is the search for linkages between events, persons or things *within the historical framework of revelation*, whereas allegorism is the search for a secondary and hidden meaning underlying the primary and obvious meaning of the narrative. This secondary sense of a narrative, discovered by allegorism, does not necessarily have any connection at all with the historical framework of revelation.[66]

Since that time, many scholars[67] have used Woollcombe's definition to label the interpretive practice behind Paul's use of ἀλληγορούμενα as typology rather than allegory.[68] In response, other scholars have maintained that it is allegory.[69] Other scholars, unwilling to dismiss allegory but still concerned over Paul's view of Gen 16–21 as historical, have argued that typology is a subgenre of allegory.[70] This concern for historical characters and events has been so influential that some scholars even have classified Paul's interpretive practice as allegory, yet defined it as typology.[71] Another influential set of distinctions related to discussing Paul's practice is Alexandrian, Palestinian, and Hellenistic Allegory.[72] Despite these three

---

64. In the fourth century CE, John Chrysostom claimed that, "Contrary to usage, [Paul] calls a type an allegory" (Chrysostom, *Hom. Gal.* 4:24 [Alexander]).

65. Daniélou, *Lord of History*.

66. Woollcombe, "Biblical Origins," 40; emphasis original.

67. Bonnard, *Épitre*, 97; Bonsirven, *Exégèse rabbinique*, 275; Bouwman, "Hagar- und Sara-Perikope," 3144; Bring, *Commentary on Galatians*, 221; Dunn, *Epistle to the Galatians*, 248; George, *Galatians*, 340; Ebeling, *Truth of the Gospel*, 233; Gerber, "Ga 4,21–31," 174–76; Goppelt, *Typos*, 139; A. T. Hanson, *Studies in Paul's Technique*, 94; R. Jewett, *Paul's Anthropological Terms*, 100; Kepple, "Analysis of Antiochene Exegesis," 249; Lightfoot, *Saint Paul's Epistle*, 180; Mußner, *Galaterbrief*, 319–20; Oepke, *Brief des Paulus*, 111; Pastor, "A Propósito de Gal 4,25a," 206.

68. Others' use of Woollcombe's definition is ironic because Woollcombe himself argues that Gal 4:24 is not typological but an example of allegorical exegesis ("Biblical Origins," 42).

69. Barker, "Allegory and Typology," 209; Betz, *Galatians*, 238; Boyarin, *Radical Jew*, 35; Cosgrove, "Law Has Given Sarah," 221; Gräßer, *Alte Bund im Neuen*, 70; P. Jewett, "Concerning Allegorical Interpretation," 4; Martyn, *Galatians*, 436.

70. De Boer, *Galatians*, 296; Bruce, *Epistle to the Galatians*, 217; Buscemi, *Lettera ai Galati*, 454; Hansen, *Abraham in Galatians*, 214–15; Hendriksen, *Galatians*, 182.

71. Hermann Martin Friedrich Büchsel, "ἀλληγορέω," *TDNT* 1:260–61; Longenecker, *Galatians*, 209; Warren, "Paul's Hermeneutical Method," 121–24; Witherington, *Grace in Galatia*, 326–27.

72. R. P. C. Hanson, *Allegory and Event*, 82–83. Here, Hanson invokes geographical

terms being abandoned by much of recent scholarship, the assumptions behind these distinctions remain very influential in scholarship on Gal 4:21–31 (cf. ch. 2, sects. 1 and 3). I evaluate these distinctions in chapter 3 after engaging their assumptions in chapter 2.

The classifications of Paul's practice discussed above are the result of various theological perspectives regarding allegory and allegoresis. For example, Ben Witherington has quipped that those "trained in the historical critical method have something of an allergic reaction whenever they encounter allegory or allegorizing."[73] These various classifications of Paul's practice elicit a feeling expressed by Andrew Perriman, that "one is rather left with the impression that it has been understood despite itself."[74] By "it," Perriman means Paul's allegorical practice. Is it possible that this feeling is the result of prior scholarship trying to understand the interpretive practice behind Paul's use of ἀλληγορούμενα within prior scholarship's own context instead of within Paul's context? In chapters 2 and 3, I demonstrate this indeed is what has happened.

The various translations of ἅτινά ἐστιν ἀλληγορούμενα also reflect various interpretations of Paul's practice. Additionally, the present tense of the participle[75] and the plural forms add to the complexity of translating it. Published translations and various scholars' translations can be categorized into two groups: (1) those who use the word "allegory" and its cognates and (2) those who do not. Those who use the word "allegory" and its cognates can be subdivided into (1) those who translate it as a product[76] (e.g., as "allegory") and (2) those who translate it as a process[77]

---

location as one means by which Paul's interpretive practice can be explained. In ch. 2, I investigate whether geographical location can serve Hanson's purpose.

73. Witherington, *Grace in Galatia*, 138.

74. Perriman, "Rhetorical Strategy," 27.

75. In classical Greek, participles—except for future tense—outside of indirect statement communicated only the point in time when an action took place (Smyth, *Greek Grammar for Colleges*, §2043). By the time of the New Testament, however, participles outside of indirect statement could indicate a relationship in time between a participle and the main verb as in indirect statement (Funk, *Beginning-Intermediate Grammar*, §849.3). In the case of Gal 4:24, a present participle could indicate that an action is ongoing at the same time as the main verb. This also is noted by De Boer, *Galatians*, 294; Bruce, *Epistle to the Galatians*, 253; Longenecker, *Galatians*, 210.

76. Scripture translations include the AMP, AV, JB, KJV, LSG, NAB, NEB, NJB, NRSV, and RSV. Scholars' translations include Amoit, *Épitre aux Galates*, 199; Burton, *Epistle to the Galatians*, 253; Fung, *Epistle to the Galatians*, 206; Martyn, *Galatians*, 431; Witherington, *Grace in Galatia*, 321.

77. Scripture translations include the ESV and NASB. Scholars' translations include

(e.g., as "allegorical interpretation"). Those who do not use allegory and its cognates can be subdivided into (1) those who describe it as figurative[78] and (2) those who describe it in other non-allegorical ways.[79] It is my position that these thirty-nine translations—many of which reflect inappropriate assumptions about the ancient interpretive practice of allegory—do not describe Paul's interpretive practice appropriately within the context of the ancient interpretive practice of allegory or within the context of Second Temple Judaism. Accordingly, I return to this issue after the analyses and argue in the conclusion of this project that the most contextually appropriate translation for ἅτινά ἐστιν ἀλληγορούμενα is as follows: "Here is an interpretive practice of allegory!"

2.2.2. Interpretive Issue 3: Columns and a Contrasting Pair

In Gal 4:24–26, Paul sets up columns and a contrasting pair. Paul presents this structure by means of another New Testament *hapax legomenon*: συστοιχεῖ. The uniformity found within its ancient usage is helpful for determining its meaning in Gal 4:25. Aristotle (fourth century BCE), in *Metaphysics*, uses the noun form to designate a "*column* or *series* of things or ideas."[80] Additionally, the Greek historian Polybius (second century BCE) uses the verb form to describe soldiers who were standing in the same line.[81] These definitions correspond to Paul's well-defined message in 4:25: Mount Sinai (i.e., Hagar) aligns with the present Jerusalem. Some prior scholarship, however, has extended Paul's use of συστοιχεῖ to the entire pericope, arguing that Paul's use also sets up "a series of co-ordinate

---

Betz, *Galatians*, 238; De Boer, *Galatians*, 289; Broer, "Vertreibe die Magd," 182; Bruce, *Epistle to the Galatians*, 214; Dunn, *Epistle to the Galatians*, 242; Lagrange, *Saint Paul*, 123; Longenecker, *Galatians*, 198; Matera, *Galatians*, 167; Moo, *Galatians*, 299; Mußner, *Galaterbrief*, 317; Oepke, *Brief des Paulus*, 109; Rhode, *Brief des Paulus*, 192; Wagner, "Enfants d'Abraham," 290.

78. Scripture translations include the NIV and NKJV. Scholars' translations include Das, *Galatians*, 477; George, *Galatians*, 338; Söding, "Sie ist unsere Mutter," 236.

79. Scripture translations include the BDS, CEV, CJB, HCSB, LUT, and NLT. Scholars' translations include DeSilva, *Letter to the Galatians*, 394 ("These things are communicating something else"); and A. T. Hanson, *Studies in Paul's Technique*, 94 ("These things are intended to convey a deeper meaning").

80. LSJ, s.v. "συστοιχέω"; emphasis original. Cf. Aristotle, *An. pr.* 66b; *Metaph.* $1004^{b}27$; $1066^{a}15$; $1072^{a}31$.

81. LSJ, s.v. "συστοιχέω." Cf. Polybius, *Hist.* 10.23.7.

pairs, as *odd* and *even*, *one* and *many*, *right* and *left*."⁸² Lists of columns and coordinating pairs can be found in much scholarship.⁸³ Below is the most extensive published list.⁸⁴

Hagar	Sarah
son of the slave woman (Ishmael)	son of the free woman (Isaac)
"according to the flesh"	"through the promise"
old covenant	new covenant
Sinai	—
present Jerusalem	heavenly Jerusalem
slavery	freedom
"according to the flesh"	"according to the Spirit"
Judaism	Christianity

This application of συστοιχεῖ to the entire pericope has yet to receive any criticism in scholarship. However, I suggest that extending συστοιχεῖ to the entire pericope both misrepresents Paul's use of the term and complicates the interpretation of 4:21–31 for the following reasons. First, Paul used συστοιχεῖ only to connect Hagar with the present Jerusalem. When scholarship creates extensive columns and contrasting pairs, this does not allow the text to determine those entities that were most meaningful for Paul's argument. This is evident by the fact that many lists *supply* missing counterparts or *add* additional entities. Put simply, in the section where συστοιχεῖ is used, Paul never provides contrasts for Hagar, the first covenant, Mount Sinai, slavery, or "our mother." The second reason why it misrepresents Paul's use of συστοιχεῖ is because there is a distinction between Paul's content outside and inside 4:24–27. In 4:21–23 and 4:28–31, Paul focuses on the two sons of Abraham and their counterparts. In 4:24–27, however, he focuses on the two mothers and their covenantal counterparts. For these reasons, I limit συστοιχεῖ to what is stated in the

---

82. LSJ, s.v. "συστοιχέω"; emphasis original. Cf. Aristotle, *Metaph.* 986ᵃ23.

83. Betz, *Galatians*, 245; Blackwelder and Stamm, "Epistle to the Galatians," 539; De Boer, *Galatians*, 297; Das, *Galatians*, 498; Dunn, *Epistle to the Galatians*, 244; Fung, *Epistle to the Galatians*, 213; George, *Galatians*, 342; Keener, *Galatians*, 214; Lightfoot, *Saint Paul's Epistle*, 181; Martyn, "Apocalyptic Antinomies," 419; Martyn, *Galatians*, 450; Vouga, *An die Galater*, 116; Witherington, *Grace in Galatia*, 326; Wright, *Galatians*, 294. For an alternate list with three columns, see Elliott, "Choose Your Mother," 679; with four columns, see De Boer, *Galatians*, 262.

84. Betz, *Galatians*, 245.

text and accordingly discuss only the columns and coordinating pair presented by Paul. My list is as follows:

Hagar	—
Mount Sinai	—
Present Jerusalem	Jerusalem above
—	Our mother

2.2.2.1. Column 1: One woman, in fact, is Hagar, from Mount Sinai, bearing children for slavery. Now Hagar is Mount Sinai in Arabia (Gal 4:24–25).

In aligning the first column, Paul invokes his first proper name in this pericope: Hagar.[85] The surrounding context reveals Paul's message: "The identification of Hagar with Sinai means simply that she and her descendants represent the law, which holds men and women in bondage."[86] What is unclear, however, is how such a connection between Hagar and Sinai could be made. This undoubtedly accounts for the scribal variations in Gal 4:25.[87] There are three general explanations for this connection.

---

85. In scholarship on Gal 4:21–31, attitudes towards Hagar found in other Jewish literature are rarely engaged. Two exceptions are Miller, "Surrogate, Slave and Deviant"; and Zucker and Brinton, "Other Woman." These two works provide useful insights by examining the various ways Hagar was viewed by the writers of Genesis, Josephus, Philo, Paul, the rabbis, and the church fathers. From these studies, it is clear that Paul used Hagar as we would expect from a Jewish interpreter of Scripture in the Second Temple period: "Conspicuously absent in the cadre of Jewish traditions on the figure of Hagar is any normative set of details. Each writing records its own unique set, some fuller and some slimmer, based on variations within or alterations to the traditions. Paul's relating of the Hagar story in Gal 4:21–31 is no exception. He offers a very brief and stylized account" (Miller, "Surrogate, Slave and Deviant," 50). These studies balance out the more extreme positions, such as Borgen's argument that Paul presents Hagar as a foreigner transformed into a law-abiding Jew ("Hebrew and Pagan Features," 153–54); Mary Callaway's claim that "[Hagar] is always equated with the 'wrong' people, whether it is slaves, sophists, Egyptians, or Jews" ("Mistress and the Maid," 97); and Raquel Echeverría's claim that "Agar sí fue una mujer libre . . . su regreso a la casa de Abraham no fue un acto de humillación sino que lo hizo partiendo de su propia decisión, de su propio criterio e inteligencia" ("Re-lectura de la alegoría," 25).

86. Bruce, *Epistle to the Galatians*, 220. For a similar argument, see Martyn, *Galatians*, 439.

87. Manuscripts that exclude "Hagar" are P^{46} ℵ C F G 1241. 1739 lat (sa; Ambst). Manuscripts that include "Hagar" (with γάρ) are K L P Ψ 062. 33. 81. 104. 630. 1505. 1881 M sy bo^{mss} and (with δέ) are A B D 0278. 323. 365. 1175. 2464 sy^{hmg} bo^{pt}. The

Paul's Interpretive Practice of Allegory in the Context of Galatians 4:21–31

The first is that Paul references the Arabic word for rock (حجر).[88] The second is that Mount Sinai was actually called "Hagar" by the Arabs.[89] Although these two explanations are possible, both assume the Galatians knew information that likely was unavailable to them.[90] The third explanation is that Paul intends to make a geographical connection.[91] Again, although possible, Paul does not mention Mount Sinai's location again or assign it a counterpart. Therefore, it is unclear how this information would support his argument. Ultimately, Paul's reasoning "wird uns dunkel bleiben."[92] Fortunately, the surrounding context clarifies the purpose of the connection even when it is not possible to recover how it was made.

2.2.2.2. COORDINATING PAIR: AND CORRESPONDS TO THE PRESENT JERUSALEM, FOR SHE IS IN SLAVERY WITH HER CHILDREN. BUT THE JERUSALEM ABOVE IS FREE (GAL 4:25–26).[93]

Next, Paul aligns Mount Sinai (i.e., Hagar) with the present Jerusalem and then contrasts the present Jerusalem with the Jerusalem above. In

---

longer and more difficult reading typically is accepted. For exceptions, see Betz, *Galatians*, 245; Bouwman, "Hagar- und Sara-Perikope," 3142; Burton, *Epistle to the Galatians*, 259; Carlson, "Sinai Is a Mountain," 100–101; Lightfoot, *Saint Paul's Epistle*, 192–93; Mußner, "Hagar, Sinai, Jerusalem," 60.

88. Betz, *Galatians*, 245; A. T. Hanson, *Studies in Paul's Technique*, 95–96; Lietzmann, *An die Galater*, 31.

89. Bring, *Commentary on Galatians*, 230; Chrysostom, *Hom. Gal.* 4:25; Ellicott, *Epistle to the Galatians*, 111; Lührmann, *Galatians*, 90; Di Mattei, "Paul's Allegory," 111–12; Schlier, *Brief an die Galater*, 219. For nuances within this interpretation, see Tolmie, *Persuading the Galatians*, 172–73.

90. For similar and other critiques, see Bruce, *Epistle to the Galatians*, 219–20; Burton, *Epistle to the Galatians*, 259–61; Fung, *Epistle to the Galatians*, 208; Lightfoot, *Saint Paul's Epistle*, 196; Longenecker, *Galatians*, 211.

91. The first proponent of this explanation was Theodore of Mopsuestia, *Commentaries*, 115. For recent supporters, see George, *Galatians*, 341; Gese, "Hagar Is a Mountain"; Van Kooten, "Philosophical Criticism," 366; Lémonon, *Épitre aux Galates*, 164; Lührmann, *Galatians*, 90–91; Matera, *Galatians*, 170; McNamara, "(Hagar) Sina," 37; Montagnini, "Monte," 36; Moo, *Galatians*, 303; Mußner, "Hagar, Sinai, Jerusalem," 58; Pastor, "A Propósito de Gal 4,25," 206; Schwemer, "Himmlische Stadt," 200; Söding, "Mutter," 235; Steinhauser, "Gal 4,25a"; Tolmie, "Allegorie," 170–71; S. Williams, *Galatians*, 128.

92. Rhode, *Brief des Paulus*, 200.

93. I have translated Gal 4:26—ἡ δὲ ἄνω Ἰερουσαλὴμ ἐλευθέρα ἐστίν—differently than the NRSV. The NRSV's rendering, "But the other woman corresponds to the Jerusalem above; she is free," is one example of how the overextension of συστοιχεῖ inappropriately impacts translation.

contrasting Jerusalems, Paul contrasts two levels of meaning. First, Paul teaches about the religious significance of the present Jerusalem; in particular, that it is equated with the imposition of the law.[94] To our present knowledge, before Paul, Jewish traditions had not used the present Jerusalem's coordinating entity—the Jerusalem above—to distinguish between the law and freedom. Therefore, if Paul is contrasting the present Jerusalem and the Jerusalem above as a coordinating pair, what does he intend for the Jerusalem above to represent?[95] Paul's second level of meaning can answer this question when we recognize that Paul writes from an eschatological perspective.[96] Paul has mixed the spatial and temporal aspects[97] of Jerusalem to demonstrate the age of the Jerusalem

---

94. For those who interpret this as representing Judaism as a whole, see Ambrosiaster, "Commentary on Galatians," 25; Betz, *Galatians*, 246; Burton, *Epistle to the Galatians*, 261; Lightfoot, *Saint Paul's Epistle*, 181. See also the discussion of supersessionism in sect. 2.3.1. For those who interpret this as a specific Jewish-Christian institution ruling in Jerusalem, see Longenecker, *Galatians*, 213; Matera, *Galatians*, 170; Witherington, *Grace in Galatia*, 333. A similar position is that the leaders in Jerusalem had sanctioned Paul's opponents for their own law-observant mission to the gentiles (see Martyn, *Galatians*, 439; Martyn, "Law-Observant Mission"). Martyn is followed by De Boer, *Galatians*, 301–2; and Matera, *Galatians*, 170. It is important to recognize that a sanction by the leaders in Jerusalem does not demand Martyn's position. As Lührmann points out, "The new teachers in Galatia in some way or other presumably based their gospel on 'Jerusalem,' even if they could hardly be justified in basing it on the 'pillars' of the Christian church there" (*Galatians*, 91).

95. Some prior scholarship has argued that the Jerusalem above is related to the idea expressed in Revelation's "new Jerusalem," but I do not understand Paul to be using such highly developed imagery here. For discussions and various positions, see Blackwelder and Stamm, "Epistle to the Galatians," 541; De Boer, *Galatians*, 301; Burton, *Epistle to the Galatians*, 263; Dunn, *Epistle to the Galatians*, 253; Fung, *Epistle to the Galatians*, 210; Lincoln, *Paradise*, 9–33; Longenecker, *Galatians*, 214; Matera, *Galatians*, 170; Schlier, *Brief an die Galater*, 221–25; Witherington, *Grace in Galatia*, 335.

96. "Paul reads the Bible in light of a central conviction that he and his readers are those upon whom the ends of the ages have come. They are God's eschatological people who, in receiving the grace of God through Jesus Christ, become a living sign, a privileged clue to the meaning of God's word in Scripture. This hermeneutical conviction demands a fresh reading of Scripture" (Hays, *Echoes of Scripture*, 121). For others who affirm this eschatological interpretation, see Betz, *Galatians*, 247; De Boer, *Galatians*, 301–2; Brandenburger, *Fleisch und Geist*, 51–52; Bruce, *Epistle to the Galatians*, 221; Burton, *Epistle to the Galatians*, 263; Dunn, *Epistle to the Galatians*, 252–54; George, *Galatians*, 343; Gräßer, *Alte Bund im Neuen*, 75; Martyn, *Galatians*, 441; Schlier, *Brief an die Galater*, 221; Scott, *Apocalyptic Letter*; Silva, *Explorations in Exegetical Methods*, 180–81; Still, "Once upon a Time," 133; Witherington, *Grace in Galatia*, 334; Wright, *Galatians*, 304. For an exception who argues that Paul was not influenced by eschatology, see Kwon, *Eschatology in Galatians*, 93–100.

97. This mix is common in apocalyptic thought. An excellent summary is found in De Boer, "Paul's Quotation," 373–74. For recent studies on Paul's eschatology, see J.

Paul's Interpretive Practice of Allegory in the Context of Galatians 4:21–31

above already has arrived.[98] Accordingly, this coordinating pair communicates to the Galatians that Jesus inaugurated a new eschatological age, one in which the Galatians have a new identity as a part of God's people even though they are free from the law.[99]

2.2.2.3. COLUMN 2: AND SHE IS OUR MOTHER (GAL 4:26).

Paul now aligns the Jerusalem above with the phrase "our mother." Prior scholarship typically recognizes that Paul takes up a famous Jewish dictum[100] in order to bridge Gal 4:24–26 to his subsequent quotation of Isa 54:1. A few other positions, however, have been proposed.[101] One of these positions seeks to locate Paul's use of "mother" within the context of Anatolian religion. Argued by Susan Elliot, it claims Paul was connecting Hagar with one of Anatolian religion's central figures: the mountain mother of the gods.[102] Building upon the work of William Ramsey,[103] she argues that the goddess was associated both with a mountain and with the law.[104] For Elliott, this association provides the proper context for understanding Paul's claim that the Jerusalem above is "our mother," as well as for the identification of Hagar as Mount Sinai. She summarizes her argument as follows:

Davies, *Paul among the Apocalypses*; and Gaventa, *Apocalyptic Paul*.

98. Fung, *Epistle to the Galatians*, 210. Also, "Neu ist aber die Verbindung einer zeitlichen Kategorie (jetzt) mit einer lokalen (von oben)" (Bouwman, "Hagar- und Sara-Perikope," 3149).

99. George, *Galatians*, 343–44. Additionally, Jeremy Punt recently has written four articles that focus on the role of identity in this pericope. Although beyond the scope of this project, most interesting are his application of social identity theory to this pericope ("Hermeneutics in Identity Formation") and his comparison of Gal 4 with 1 Pet 3 ("Subverting Sarah"). For his other works, see Punt, "Revealing Rereading," pts. 1–2. For another study of identity formation in Gal 4:21–31, see Sänger, "Sara, die Freie."

100. On the use of "our mother" in Jewish tradition, see Betz, *Galatians*, 247–48; Bruce, *Epistle to the Galatians*, 221; Dunn, *Epistle to the Galatians*, 254; Longenecker, *Galatians*, 215. For primary sources, see 2 Bar. 3:1; 2 Esd 10:7; 14:4; Hos 2:4; Isa 50:1; 51:18; 66:7–11; Jer 50:12.

101. De Boer argues that Paul's use of "our mother" could refer to James ("Paul's Quotation," 382). Martyn uses this interpretation to support his position that there was a Jerusalem sanctioned law-observant mission to the gentiles (*Galatians*, 439). The critique of Elliott's position below also applies to these two positions.

102. Elliott, "Choose Your Mother." Elliott is followed only by Russell, "Twists and Turns," 90–91.

103. Ramsay, *Epistle to the Galatians*, 35–44.

104. Elliott, "Choose Your Mother," 676–82.

> Paul could hardly make such a link in the Anatolian context without simultaneously identifying Hagar with the Mother of the Gods. We thus have the basic key to explain not only how the configuration of images was associated with Hagar but also how Paul could present this configuration as if it should be self-evident to the audience. . . . By use of the allegory of Hagar, Paul can bring the Mother of the Gods, in all her manifestations, down to the level of slave concubine.[105]

Elliott's argument, although novel, is unpersuasive for the following reasons. First, it is not possible to verify her foundational assumptions.[106] We simply do not know enough about the prior beliefs of Paul's audience.[107] Second, Elliott argues that Paul intended to remove both the Sinai covenant and the mountain mother from positions of power with "one single rhetorical-allegorical swipe."[108] However, it is unclear whether Paul intends Sinai to indicate the Sinai covenant and if he does, then he is not arguing for its removal in the way Elliott proffers (cf. sect. 2.3.1). Finally, she overlooks that Paul's broader focus in Gal 4:21–31 is not on the mothers but on the sons; the two mothers are contrasted only in 4:24–27. Accordingly, Elliott overemphasizes and overinterprets μήτηρ, and it is unlikely that Paul intended to communicate what she attributes to him. The more likely interpretation is to understand this dictum as Paul's preparation for referencing Isa 54:1 at the end of this section (cf. Gal 4:27). In 4:26, Paul transforms the Jerusalem above (to which the Galatians belong as free from the law) so that it functions as the mother of the Galatians in opposition to the present Jerusalem. After this transformation, Paul moves on to the conclusion of this section.

2.2.3. Interpretive Issue 4: The Function of Isaiah 54:1

> For it is written:
> Sing, O barren one who did not bear;
> > burst into song and shout,

---

105. Elliott, "Choose Your Mother," 677.

106. Interestingly, Elliott does not respond to Ramsay's argument that Anatolian religion transformed into a more male-centered system before Paul's time, evident by the neighboring worship of Zeus the Charioteer and Zeus the Thunderer (Ramsay, *Epistle to the Galatians*, 41).

107. Joel Willitts shares my critique ("Isa 54,1," 189n4).

108. Elliott, "Choose Your Mother," 681.

Paul's Interpretive Practice of Allegory in the Context of Galatians 4:21–31

> you who have not been in labor!
> For the children of the desolate woman will be more
> than the children of her that is married, says the LORD.
> (Isa 54:1)

In Gal 4:27, Paul gives additional meaning to the Jewish dictum "our mother" through the use of Isa 54:1. A few characteristics of Isa 54:1 in its own historical context can help us to better understand its function in Gal 4:27. First, it is widely accepted that this verse describes the pre- and post-exilic Jerusalem.[109] Second, it is possible that Second Isaiah references Gen 16–21 in Isa 54:1, already having mentioned Sarah in Isa 51:2.

> Look to Abraham your father
> and to Sarah who bore you;
> for he was but one when I called him,
> but I blessed him and made him many. (Isa 51:2)

Isa 51:2 not only is the only reference to Sarah in the Jewish Scriptures outside Genesis but also shares the theme of motherhood with Isa 54:1. Third, if Second Isaiah is referencing Sarah in the patriarchal narrative, then she represents law-abiding Jews who had returned after the exile. These characteristics make it difficult to comprehend why Paul used Isa 54:1,[110] especially since Paul is equating the law-abiding Jews in Isa 54:1 with a gentile audience whom he claims does not have to observe the law. Nevertheless, whatever his logic,[111] Paul must have believed that Isa 54:1 had come to fulfillment, thus transforming it into an eschatological

---

109. Baltzer, *Deutero-Isaiah*, 435; Blenkinsopp, *Isaiah 40–55*, 360–61; Childs, *Isaiah*, 428; Goldingay and Payne, *Isaiah 40–55*, 2:341; G. Smith, *Isaiah 40–66*, 477–78. For those writing on Galatians who affirm this interpretation, see Blackwelder and Stamm, "Epistle to the Galatians," 542; Blessing, "Desolate Jerusalem," 53–54; Burton, *Epistle to the Galatians*, 264; Bruce, *Epistle to the Galatians*, 222; Dunn, *Epistle to the Galatians*, 255; Fung, *Epistle to the Galatians*, 210. One exception is De Boer, who argues that the second woman is Babylon (*Galatians*, 302).

110. There is no precedent for a Jesus-centric application of Isa 54:1 to Gen 16–21 (De Boer, *Galatians*, 303). An application of Isa 54:1 to the life of Jesus, however, may be forming during this time (Bruce, *Epistle to the Galatians*, 222). This application is attested later in Christian literature (e.g., 2 Clem. 2:1–3 as noted by Dunn, *Epistle to the Galatians*, 255) and in Jewish literature (e.g., the haftarah for Gen 16 as noted by Barrett, "Allegory of Abraham," 169n29; De Boer, "Paul's Quotation," 386–87, 387n68; Callaway, "Mistress and the Maid," 97; Di Mattei, "Paul's Allegory," 114–20; Willitts, "Isa 54,1," 202n40).

111. Some have argued that Paul employs Gezerah Shavah via the word "barren" (cf. Gen 11:30): Longenecker, *Galatians*, 215; Warren, "Paul's Hermeneutical Method," 120; Witherington, *Grace in Galatia*, 336.

statement.¹¹² Accordingly, Isa 54:1 supplied Paul with the opportunity to emphasize the Galatians' membership in God's family.¹¹³

Prior scholarship typically limits the influence of Isa 54:1 to Gal 4:24–27. However, some have argued that Isa 54:1 influences the entire pericope. Karen Jobes, the first to argue for this interpretation, lays out her position as follows:

> Most of these treatments of the text are based not on exegeting Paul's use of Isa 54:1 in place, but by completing the implied parallels between Hagar and Sarah (although Paul himself leaves the parallel unspecified) and simply identifying the barren one with Sarah and the new covenant. The resulting connection between Sarah and the Christian church is understood from biblical theology, not from Paul's use of Isa 54:1.¹¹⁴

Others have joined Jobes in her quest for re-evaluating the impact of Isa 54:1. Each argues that Paul frames Gal 4:24–27, perhaps even the entire pericope or letter, through the lens of Isa 54:1.¹¹⁵ Jobes's argument, which

---

112. This is the typical interpretation for Isa 54:1 in Gal 4:27. See Betz, *Galatians*, 248–49; De Boer, *Galatians*, 304; Bruce, *Epistle to the Galatians*, 222; Burton, *Epistle to the Galatians*, 264; Cosgrove, "Law Has Given Sarah," 221; Dunn, *Epistle to the Galatians*, 255; Fung, *Epistle to the Galatians*, 211; George, *Galatians*, 344; Lightfoot, *Saint Paul's Epistle*, 182; Longenecker, *Galatians*, 216. Witherington offers a nuanced position, "that Paul is exhorting himself, as the barren woman, to rejoice over what God has already done among the Gentiles" (*Grace in Galatia*, 336).

113. As Martyn notes specifically, *"barrenness versus fecundity"* (*Galatians*, 442; emphasis original) and *"having a husband versus having no husband"* (443; emphasis original). Martyn acknowledges that this interpretation does not fit his two-missions thesis and he responds by saying "such, inconsistency, however, is characteristic of allegorical exegesis" (443).

114. Jobes, "Jerusalem, Our Mother," 303.

115. Martinus C. de Boer analyzes in what ways Paul's eschatological view is both Christological and apocalyptic, applying that analysis to the role of Isa 54:1 in Gal 4:21–31 ("Paul's Quotation"). He recycles much of the material presented by Jobes and other scholars. M. S. Harmon's position is that Second Isaiah's sphere of influence extends to the entirety of chs. 3–4, and he provides numerous examples where he believes that Paul is using Second Isaiah as a framework (*She Must and Shall*, 185–86). His argument, upon closer inspection, reveals a tendency for overinterpretation (e.g., Gal 3:13 alludes to the entirety of Isa 53 [186]) and for latching onto particular words or phrases (e.g., Gal 3:2's ἡ ἐξ ἀκοῆς πίστεως alludes to Isa 53:1's לשמעתנו [186]). Joel Willitts focuses on the placement of Isa 54:1 in the pericope: "moving out from the center, the quotation is the basis for the contrast between Jerusalem 'present' and 'above' (4.25–26a), which is the basis for the contrasting covenants (4.24a) and in turn is the theological basis for Paul's imperatival application (4.30–5.1)" ("Isa 54,1," 201–2). Willitts, like De Boer, provides few arguments beyond what Jobes already has provided. Unlike the other three, Samuel Tedder has proposed a new interpretation in his recent dissertation, that "Isa 54:1 is not introduced to

Paul's Interpretive Practice of Allegory in the Context of Galatians 4:21–31   25

undoubtedly influenced the later positions, is that Paul was attracted to Isa 54:1 not because it directly supported the argument he was trying to make but because of the interpretive work Isaiah already had done.[116] In other words, Isaiah laid a foundation that enabled Paul's application of Isa 54:1. Paul needed only to take the next interpretive step and apply Isaiah's work to the Galatian situation.[117] Jobes summarizes this application as follows:

> Sarah's identity as the barren woman to whom God promises a miraculous birth merges with that of the barren one of Isa 54.1 at only one point in history—when Jesus, the seed of Abraham

---

support that Sarah is the mother of the Galatian believers, but rather that it is the 'Jerusalem above' (4:26–27)" ("Children of Laughter," 167). He argues that Paul used Isa 54:1 to frame not only the message of Gal 4:21–31 but also Paul's entire theology: "I dare to suggest that the coherent core in Paul's theology is his conviction that the divine promise to Abraham, as understood by its re-appropriation in the vision of Isaiah, is the Creator God's commitment to humanity and the whole cosmos that blessing and restoration will have the final word over curse and alienation, and that the promise is designed to generate the 'children of laughter'—a regenerated people of God from both Jews and Gentiles who depend on Christ and the Spirit in their life together as the re-created humanity" (243). The difficulty with accepting Tedder's argument is that it relies too heavily on modern understandings of allegory (cf. 144–49; in particular, the extensive use of Dawson, *Allegorical Readers*) without much engagement with Paul or other ancient authors (e.g., the only other ancient allegorist engaged is Philo). Additionally, he makes numerous assumptions about Paul's motivations without significant corroborating evidence: e.g., "These correspondences *do not seem accidental but rather intended*, and thus indicate . . ." (184; emphasis added). For these reasons, without more supporting evidence, it is best to view these specific arguments of Tedder as suffering from overinterpretation.

116. Jobes, "Jerusalem, Our Mother," 309. It is unfortunate that Di Mattei claims the same position as his own with no reference to Jobes ("Paul's Allegory," 119).

117. Before Jobes, Cosgrove recognized that "what Paul secures from Isaiah is the suggestion that Sarah remained barren throughout history until the coming of her child, Christ, and with him her many children" ("Law Has Given Sarah," 231). While this position is not as developed as Jobes's argument, it is one examination that influenced Jobes's perspective (Jobes, "Jerusalem, Our Mother," 316).

(and hence the son of Sarah) arose from the grave to be the firstborn son of the New Jerusalem.... When Paul cites Isa 54:1, he is metaleptically announcing to the Galatians that when Jesus arose from death, all of the elect seed of Abraham were also born.[118]

Jobes offers a believable explanation for how Paul could use a text that benefits law-abiding Jews for the benefit of non-law-abiding gentiles. However, her assessment raises the question whether Paul's audience would understand such an argument steeped in Jewish Scripture and tradition. This question raises another: Would Paul take the risk that his audience might not understand him? We have observed that Paul explains his use of Gen 16–21 in Gal 4:24–27 but not his use of Isa 54:1. Jobes recognizes this counterargument and offers a solution: Paul used this text on a previous visit to the Galatians.[119] Using Richard Hays's seven criteria for intertextual echoes, Jobes attempts to validate her position.[120] Ultimately, her position does not meet multiple criteria because some of her evidence is conjectural.[121] Although it is unlikely that Paul applied Isa 54:1 as extensively as Jobes and others have argued, their interpretations have made an important contribution upon which I build: Paul used Isa 54:1 as a subordinate biblical lemma, more specifically as an eschatologically charged proof to support his interpretive practice of allegory.[122]

118. Jobes, "Jerusalem, Our Mother," 316.

119. Jobes, "Jerusalem, Our Mother," 318. Kamila Blessing, who agrees with Jobes, acknowledges this problem and argues that the Galatians likely were unaware of this tradition. Therefore, Paul "was really, first of all, writing to himself . . . [and] has also written to the Jewish opponents who are wreaking havoc in his Galatian mission" (Blessing, "Background of Barren Woman," 325–26).

120. Jobes, "Jerusalem, Our Mother," 319. Richard Hays's seven criteria for intertextual echoes are (1) availability of the source text, (2) volume of the echo, (3) recurrence, (4) thematic coherence, (5) historical probability, (6) history of interpretation, and (7) satisfaction (*Echoes of Scripture*, 29–32).

121. In her discussion of Hays's seven criteria, Jobes also makes multiple concessions ("Jerusalem, Our Mother," 319–20). In the criteria "volume of the echo," she states, "Although no one lexical or syntactical pattern from Isaiah is repeated again and again in Galatians, the presence of several coherent echoes within a unified pericope suggests they are really there" (319). In "recurrence," she states, "Paul does not quote Isa 54:1 elsewhere, but he does use the theme of Sarah's barrenness in Rom 4:17ff to associate childlessness with death, miraculous birth with resurrection, and Abraham's faith with faith in Christ's resurrection" (319). Most telling, however, are her comments in "historical plausibility": "As suggested, it is plausible that Paul previously taught the Galatians from the Greek text of Isaiah and that his citation of Isa 54:1 is intended to evoke memories of that previous teaching" (319).

122. For the term "subordinate biblical lemma," see Runia, "Structure," 238. Runia defines this term as the invocation of "other biblical texts in order to cast more light

Paul's Interpretive Practice of Allegory in the Context of Galatians 4:21–31

The examinations in chapters 4–6 highlight how other Jewish allegorists roughly contemporary to Paul also used subordinate biblical lemmata to support their interpretive practices of allegory. In the conclusion of this project, I discuss the evidence collectively and its implications for understanding the use of Isa 54:1 in Gal 4:21–31.

2.3. Galatians 4:28–31

²⁸ὑμεῖς δέ ἀδελφοί, κατὰ Ἰσαὰκ ἐπαγγελίας τέκνα ἐστέ. ²⁹ἀλλ᾽ ὥσπερ τότε ὁ κατὰ σάρκα γεννηθεὶς ἐδίωκεν τὸν κατὰ πνεῦμα, οὕτως καὶ νῦν. ³⁰ἀλλὰ τί λέγει ἡ γραφή; ἔκβαλε τὴν παιδίσκην καὶ τὸν υἱὸν αὐτῆς· οὐ γὰρ μὴ κληρονομήσει ὁ υἱὸς τῆς παιδίσκης μετὰ τοῦ υἱοῦ τῆς ἐλεθέρας. ³¹διό, ἀδελφοί, οὐκ ἐσμὲν παιδίσκης τέκνα ἀλλὰ τῆς ἐλευθέρας. (Gal 4:28–31)

²⁸Now you, my friends, are children of the promise, like Isaac. ²⁹But just as at that time the child who was born according to the flesh persecuted the child who was born according to the Spirit, so it is now also. ³⁰But what does the scripture say? "Drive out the slave and her child; for the child of the slave will not share the inheritance with the child of the free woman." ³¹So then, friends, we are children, not of the slave but of the free woman. (Gal 4:28–31)

Beginning in Gal 4:28, Paul returns to the themes of sonship that he developed in 4:21–23. Up to this point, Paul has yet to lay his hermeneutical cards on the table. In 4:28, Paul reveals his hand, making very clear what he had only intimated previously: the Galatians are children of the promise, even without circumcision. How preposterous! It was precisely Gen 16–21—the very tradition that Paul uses to support his claim that gentiles do not have to be circumcised—that established those who belong to God's covenant *must* be circumcised.[123] Boldly, Paul continues his application by offering another scriptural proof based on Gen 21:9:

---

on the main text." Then, "secondary exegesis" may or may not follow, which Runia defines as "exegesis of subordinate biblical lemmata to the extent the exegete deems fit for the full understanding of the main biblical text" (238). I employ Runia's terms in this project as he defines them.

123. Paul's position would have been "very disturbing to any patriotic Jew" (George, *Galatians*, 342). For similar sentiments, see Amoit, *Épitre aux Galates*, 205; Bruce, "Abraham Had Two Sons," 76; Eckstein, *Verheißung und Gesetz*, 247; Hays, *Echoes of Scripture*, 115; Lambrecht, "Abraham and His Offspring," 528–29; Lim, *Holy Scripture*,

> But Sarah saw the son of Hagar the Egyptian, whom she had borne to Abraham, playing with her son Isaac. (Gen 21:9)

> But just as at that time the child who was born according to the flesh persecuted the child who was born according to the Spirit, so it is now also. (Gal 4:29)[124]

Although צחק (play) in Gen 21:9 may or may not indicate hostility, it is clear that Paul intends for it to be hostile in Gal 4:29 both by the surrounding context[125] and his use of the Greek verb διώκω.[126] Additionally, Paul makes sure that his audience does not miss his application by changing "the son of Hagar the Egyptian" (Gen 21:9) to "the child who was born according to the flesh" (Gal 4:29) and "her son Isaac" (Gen 21:9) to "the child who was born according to the Spirit" (Gal 4:29). By these changes, Paul communicates to the Galatians that history now repeats itself and that they should view his opponents' teachings as a form of persecution. Paul's interpretive practice here—the use of ἀλλ' ὥσπερ τότε to claim that the situation he perceived in Galatia was similar to another historical situation—often has been used to support the classification of the interpretive practice behind Paul's use of ἀλληγορούμενα as typology.[127] However, Paul's interpretive practice in Gal 4:24–27 and his interpretive practice here are different. In 4:24–27, Paul employs women and covenants as corresponding source and allegorical entities. Then, he

---

54; Löfstedt, "Allegory," 479; Perriman, "Rhetorical Strategy," 36; S. Williams, *Galatians*, 125.

124. Paul now contrasts flesh and spirit, having changed from his earlier contrast of flesh and promise in Gal 4:23. It is possible that Paul makes this shift because of his focus on themes in chs. 5–6 (De Boer, *Galatians*, 306; George, *Galatians*, 346; Longenecker, *Galatians*, 217). It also is possible that Paul intimated more, such as it is the spirit that has made Isaac's promise effectual (Fung, *Epistle to the Galatians*, 214) or that it is to further emphasize "Isaac represents a different kind of or line of descent, one of the spirit" (Dunn, *Epistle to the Galatians*, 257) (cf. sect. 2.1.1).

125. Baasland, "Persecution." Also, if one accepts that rabbinic literature can reflect earlier ideas, then it is possible that a similar interpretation of Gen 21:9 already was current in Paul's time (Betz, *Galatians*, 250n116; Bruce, *Epistle to the Galatians*, 223–24; Bruce, "Abraham Had Two Sons," 76–78; Longenecker, *Galatians*, 217). See Gen. Rab. 53.11; Pesiq. Rab. 48.2; Pirqe R. El. 30; Sotah 6:6; Tg. Ps.-J. Gen 21:9–11; Tg. Onq. Gen 21:9; Tg. Neof. Gen 21:9. Also, Paul's contemporary Josephus frames Sarah's request to expel Hagar as a reaction to the possibility of Ishmael's future persecution of Isaac after Abraham died (Josephus, *Ant.* 1.215).

126. The Septuagint of Gen 21:9 uses the Greek root παίζ-. This verb more appropriately embodies the meaning of the Hebrew צחק.

127. For examples, see ch. 2, sect. 1.1.

elaborates on the allegorical entities. In 4:28–31, Paul does not use source and allegorical entities, but he points out that the situation he perceives in Galatia is similar to what happened in Gen 16–21. Accordingly, what Paul does in Gal 4:24–27 and what he does in 4:28–31 should not be understood or evaluated as the same practice.[128]

2.3.1. Interpretive Issue 5: The Climax of the Pericope

Prior scholarship typically considers the Greek imperative ἔκβαλε in Gal 4:30 to be the climax of this pericope and to embody the full force of Paul's message. Paul, continuing the story from Genesis that he began in 4:29, quotes Gen 21:10 in Gal 4:30.

> So she said to Abraham, "Cast out this slave woman with her son; for the son of this slave woman shall not inherit along with my son Isaac." (Gen 21:10)

> But what does the scripture say? "Drive out the slave and her child; for the child of the slave will not share the inheritance with the child of the free woman." (Gal 4:30)

In Gen 21:10, Sarah requests that Abraham cast out (גרש) Hagar because of the events in 21:9. Abraham is not comfortable with this request,[129] but agrees once God affirms Sarah's request in 21:12. Here, Paul uses Sarah's command as the means to connect both his developed theme of sonship and his allegorical expression of the two mothers. To make this point clear, Paul again changes the Genesis text in two ways. First, Paul raises Sarah's request to the authoritative level of Scripture by replacing "So she said to Abraham" (Gen 21:10) with "But what does the scripture say?" (Gal 4:30). Second, Paul replaces the final phrase "along with my son Isaac" (Gen 21:10) with the phrase "with the child of the free woman" (Gal 4:30). Paul's changes raise an important question: What does Paul mean by the Greek imperative ἔκβαλε?

---

128. The inaccurate blending here of two separate practices is similar to how scholarship on Gal 4:21–31 has treated 1 Cor 10:1–11, in which the interpretive practice of allegory (cf. 1 Cor 10:4) is blended with Paul's reference to past events (cf. 1 Cor 10:6, 11). I discuss 1 Cor 10:1–11 in greater detail in ch. 2, sect. 2.4.2.3.

129. Gen 21:10–11. One possible explanation for Abraham's hesitancy is that the customs of his day may not have allowed for him to dismiss Ishmael. For discussions of the code of Hammurabi and marriage contracts from Nuzu, see Bruce, "Abraham Had Two Sons," 73; Bruce, *Epistle to the Galatians*, 216; Miller, "Surrogate, Slave and Deviant," 140n4.

Prior scholarship offers three answers to this question. The most widely attested position is that Paul teaches Christians have replaced Jews as God's people. This supersessionist interpretation is evident as early as Marcion in the second century.[130] Even Tertullian, who argues against Marcion, acknowledged the merit of this interpretation.[131] Some church fathers upheld this interpretation.[132] It continues in modern scholarship,[133] having been described as an arrow that "sails through the patristic, medieval, and modern periods."[134] The example quoted most often in scholarship on Gal 4:21–31 is the claim of J. B. Lightfoot.

> The Apostle thus confidently sounds the death-knell of Judaism at a time when one-half of Christendom clung to the Mosaic law with a jealous affection little short of frenzy, and while the Judaic party seemed to be growing in influence and was strong enough, even in the Gentile churches of his own founding, to undermine his influence and endanger his life.[135]

Fortunately, as the understanding of Second Temple Judaism and of the issues surrounding early believers has grown, this interpretation no longer is sustainable. We now understand Paul was engaging in an inter-Jewish debate. He was not pitting a form of "Christianity" against a form of "Judaism."[136]

---

130. Tertullian, *Marc.* 5.4.

131. Martyn, "Covenants," 166. I find Martyn's argument convincing that Tertullian's reaction, one of surprise for Marcion's inclusion of this pericope in his version of Galatians, was an attempt to hide that "no part of [Galatians] was more friendly to Marcion's theological programme than the paired opposites of 4:21–5:1" (165).

132. For the Latin fathers, see Ambrosiaster, "Commentary on Galatians," 26; Augustine, *Commentary on Galatians*, 193–99; Jerome, *Comm. Gal.* 4:29–31; Marius Victorinus, *In Galat.* 326. For the ninth century, see "Commentary on Galatians," in Photius of Constantinople, "Photius von Constantinople," 609. For the thirteenth century, see Aquinas, *Epistle to the Galatians*, lecture 9.

133. Amoit, *Épitre aux Galates*, 205; Betz, *Galatians*, 250–51; Bring, *Commentary on Galatians*, 232; Burton, *Epistle to the Galatians*, 267; Fung, *Epistle to the Galatians*, 214–15; Lietzmann, *An die Galater*, 33; Liao, "Meaning of Galatians 4:21–31," 223; Lightfoot, *Saint Paul's Epistle*, 184; Löfstedt, "Allegory," 488; Oepke, *Brief des Paulus*, 115; Perriman, "Rhetorical Strategy," 41. Broer provides a lengthy discussion of this issue and concludes as follows: "Es führt daher nach meinem Urteil kein Wed daran vorbei, daß im brief des Paulus an die galater genau das vorliegt, wa heute häufig die Enterbungs-Theorie genannt wird, insofern das Judentum hier als nicht mehr erbberechtigt bezeichnet wird" ("Vertreibe die Magd," 192).

134. Martyn, "Covenants," 168.

135. Lightfoot, *Saint Paul's Epistle*, 184.

136. De Boer, *Galatians*, 287; Hays, *Echoes of Scripture*, 109; Longenecker, *Galatians*,

Paul's Interpretive Practice of Allegory in the Context of Galatians 4:21–31   31

If this long-standing interpretation is incorrect, then how did Paul intend for the Galatians to understand ἔκβαλε? Two positions remain. The first position (of the two remaining) is that Paul commands practical action. In this way, he commands the Galatians to remove the opponents from their midst physically.[137] Although this position typically is assumed *de facto* without supporting arguments, it has been noted that Paul's hostile attitude towards his opponents (cf. Gal 1:8–9; 4:17; 5:10) supports this interpretation.[138] The last position is that Paul does not give practical advice but a solemn warning either to the Galatians[139] or to angelic agents.[140] One argument proposed in favor of this position is that if Paul intended for the Galatians to expel the opponents, then Paul is no different than the opponents.[141] This specific argument is not convincing for methodological reasons.[142] More problematic, however, is that this

217; Matera, *Galatians*, 173, 178–79; Miller, "Surrogate, Slave and Deviant," 153; Mußner, *Galaterbrief*, 332; Rhode, *Brief des Paulus*, 204–6; Schlier, *Brief an die Galater*, 227; Sellin, "Hagar und Sara," 72–73; Wright, *Paul and the Faithfulness*, 1135.

137. De Boer, *Galatians*, 307–8; Buckel, *Free to Love*, 185; Dunn, *Epistle to the Galatians*, 258; George, *Galatians*, 347; Hansen, *Abraham in Galatians*, 145–46; Keener, *Galatians*, 227; Longenecker, *Galatians*, 217; Malan, "Strategy," 437; Martyn, *Galatians*, 446; Matera, *Galatians*, 178; McClane, "Hellenistic Background," 132–33; Mußner, *Galaterbrief*, 332; Witherington, *Grace in Galatia*, 338–39.

138. Hansen, *Abraham in Galatians*, 145–46. Paul's anathema is particularly revealing: "But even if we or an angel from heaven should proclaim to you a gospel contrary to what we proclaimed to you, let that one be accursed! As we have said before, so now I repeat, if anyone proclaims to you a gospel contrary to what you received, let that one be accursed!" (Gal 1:8–9).

139. Bruce, *Epistle to the Galatians*, 225; Cosgrove, "Law Has Given Sarah," 233; DeSilva, *Letter to the Galatians*, 405; Kwon, *Eschatology in Galatians*, 98; Ridderbos, *Epistle of Paul*, 182. One scholar even has argued that it was a solemn warning to avoid living under the "Roman master order," which was disguised "through practices of separation that appear to conform to God's law" (Kahl, "Hagar's Babylonian Captivity," 269).

140. Barrett, "Allegory of Abraham," 165. He is followed by Bachmann, *Anti-Judaism in Galatians*, 93.

141. Eastman, "Cast Out Slave Woman," 313.

142. Eastman bases her argument on the relationship between scriptural citations and imperatives in Romans. She states, "Taken together, all the examples from Romans show that imperatives within scriptural citations may function as witnesses, as sources of encouragement and as illustrations of Paul's claims about the law. But taken by themselves, the singular imperatives do not seem to speak directly to Paul's auditors; rather, they are accompanied by second person plural imperatives that clarify Paul's commands to the letters' recipients" ("Cast Out Slave Woman," 323). Unfortunately, she does not seek to answer key methodological questions that undermine her conclusions. (E.g., How do we account for the different situations in these cities and the different dates of composition? How do we know that Paul's views did not change? What consistency can be demonstrated in the texts beyond the use of imperatives?)

third position dismisses Paul's hostile attitude towards his opponents as unimportant (cf. undue selectivity)—especially the religious anathema in Gal 1:8–9 (cf. mishandling polemics). Of these two remaining positions, I support the majority position that Paul commands practical action.

In the final line of this pericope, Paul strongly affirms the Galatians' new identity both to support his previous imperative and to bring this section to its end: "So then, friends, we are children, not of the slave but of the free woman." (Gal 4:31).[143]

2.3.2. Interpretive Issue 6: Why Paul Interpreted Genesis 16–21

Throughout the discussion of the five preceding interpretive issues, we have observed the enormous effort that Paul exerted in order to interpret Gen 16–21. As noted previously, Paul alters or removes characteristics of Gen 16–21 that make these chapters both profound and relevant for Judaism. Martyn has summarized Paul's changes in a helpful way, and the summary warrants a full citation.

> a. God makes his covenant with Abraham and with his multiple descendants, but there is no thought that its being passed from one generation causes it to be several covenants (cf. Gen 15:18; 17:7).
>
> b. God provides Abraham with a simple and clear definition of the covenant. God's covenant is both the promise and the nomistic commandment (the circumcision of the flesh), the two being indissolubly connected to one another (cf. Gen 17:10–13).
>
> c. Abraham observed God's covenant without exception. He circumcised himself, his sons, and every male in his household (cf. Gen 17:23–27; 21:4).

---

143. In this pericope, slavery appears only here (although it appears elsewhere in Gal 3:28; 4:7; and in Paul's other letters). Paul's use of slavery in Galatians has been used to undermine Paul's message of freedom (e.g., "Hagar's rejection seems to deny Paul's earlier argument for unity. . . . It undermines Paul's understanding that the use of difference to reinforce subordination is no longer valid in the messianic community" [Russell, "Twists and Turns," 86]). Recently two scholars have argued that Paul's use of slavery did not undermine his message. First, Peter Balla has argued that Paul used slavery to create a point of contact with his audience so that he can use Sarah and Hagar as symbols for man's relationship to God ("Paul's Use"). Second, Brigitte Kahl has argued that Paul used slavery in order to institute a mutual slave service towards Christ ("Hagar").

d. Although, responding to God's command, Abraham circumcised Ishmael, just as he circumcised every other male in his house, God established his covenant with Isaac and emphatically not with Ishmael as the exchange concerning the birth of Isaac shows (cf. Gen 17:18–21).

With regard to every one of these four points Paul departs dramatically from the stories in Genesis. He announces two covenants; he separates promise and nomistic commandments, defining one covenant as that of promise, the other as that of Sinai; he omits altogether the solemn definition of God's covenant as the commandment of circumcision; having spoken of two covenants, he identifies the first of them as the covenant of Hagar and her son, ignoring the absence in Genesis of a covenant with Ishmael.[144]

The culmination of the previous discussions and this well-defined outline raise a very important question: Why did Paul use Gen 16–21? Although some have argued that Paul chose this narrative of his own free will,[145] most believe he was responding to his opponents' prior use of it. C. K. Barrett was the first to proffer this explanation in 1982.[146] This posi-

---

144. Martyn, "Covenants," 185–86.

145. Most notable is Cosgrove's argument that Gen 17 does not support the opponents' teachings because circumcision failed to incorporate Ishmael into the family of God: "The story would not have been the most natural one from which to make the case that *circumcision* is determinative for joining the right branch of the family, since Abraham circumcises *all* his sons. Indeed Ishmael is the first son to be circumcised (Gen. 17:23; cf. *Jub* 15:23)" ("Law Has Given Sarah," 223; emphasis original). In response—as noted in much scholarship—the circumcisions of Isaac and Ishmael also could be used to support the opponents' argument by demonstrating circumcision was a requirement for both children. Cosgrove is followed by Kwon, *Eschatology in Galatians*, 93; Löfstedt, "Allegory," 478; Perriman, "Rhetorical Strategy," 33; Tolmie, "Allegorie," 165; Tolmie, *Persuading the Galatians*, 166–67; Watson, *Paul and the Hermeneutics*, 206–7.

146. Barrett, "Allegory of Abraham," 158. For his followers, see Barclay, "Mirror-Reading a Polemical Letter," 79, 88, 91n13; De Boer, *Galatians*, 287; De Boer, "Paul's Quotation," 375n18; Borgen, "Hebrew and Pagan Features," 163; Bouwman, "Hagar- und Sara-Perikope," 3145; Broer, "Vertreibe die Magd," 178; Corsani, "Interpretazione tipologica," 221; Dunn, *Epistle to the Galatians*, 243; Fowl, "Who Can Read," 82; Fung, *Epistle to the Galatians*, 204n1; George, *Galatians*, 334; Hansen, *Abraham in Galatians*, 143; Hays, *Echoes of Scripture*, 111–12; Hogeterp, "Hagar," 345; Keener, *Galatians*, 213; Löfstedt, "Allegory," 477–78; Longenecker, *Galatians*, 207–8; Malan, "Strategy," 429; Matera, *Galatians*, 174; Perriman, "Rhetorical Strategy," 28; Rhode, *Brief des Paulus*, 192; Tamez, "Hagar and Sarah," 267; Witherington, *Grace in Galatia*, 324; Wright, *Galatians*, 304. Additionally, four scholars affirm it without reference to Barrett, presumably because they assume it is common knowledge: Fee, "Abraham's True Children," 132;

tion is attractive because it explains how Paul could present a detailed allegorical expression of a foundational Jewish tradition to a gentile audience without any explanation of the context or main characters. If the Galatians already had heard this story from Paul's opponents, they would have been familiar with its content. Additionally, this explanation may be supported by the fact that Paul does not use this particular argument elsewhere. If Paul had selected Gen 16–21, perhaps he also would have used it elsewhere. In the conclusion, I return to this interpretive issue and discuss how Paul's interpretive practice of allegory supports the majority position.

3. TOWARDS A MORE PRECISE UNDERSTANDING OF PAUL'S INTERPRETIVE PRACTICE

The preceding analysis reveals a rich history of interpretation for Gal 4:21–31. Within this history, prior attempts to explain the interpretive practice behind Paul's use of ἀλληγορούμενα have resulted in an unresolved state of scholarship on this interpretive issue. Additionally, this history reveals how a more precise understanding of Paul's practice can inform our understanding of other interpretive issues in 4:21–31.

In the section on the interpretive practice behind Paul's use of ἀλληγορούμενα (sect. 2.2.1), I stated that prior scholarship has understood Paul's practice within scholarship's own context and not within Paul's. In chapters 2 and 3, I (1) evaluate what criteria and interpretive schemata have been used to explain Paul's interpretive practice and (2) demonstrate how the criteria and schemata do not enable an analysis of Paul's practice that situates it appropriately within the ancient interpretive practice of allegory. At the end of chapter 3, I proffer different criteria and a different approach that enables us to understand Paul's interpretive practice more precisely. Then, I apply my criteria and approach in chapters 4–6 in order to discover this more precise understanding.

Jobes, "Jerusalem, Our Mother," 300; Martyn, *Galatians*, 433; Wolter, "Israelproblem nach Gal 4,21–31," 3.

2

Evaluating the Criteria Used by Prior Scholarship
When Examining Paul's Interpretive Practice of Allegory

THE INITIAL TASKS REQUIRED for understanding the interpretive practice behind Paul's use of ἀλληγορούμενα more precisely are (1) to examine how the ancient interpretive practice of allegory up to the time of Paul has been used to explain Paul's practice and (2) to determine if those uses enable an analysis of Paul's practice that situates it appropriately within the ancient interpretive practice of allegory. Both tasks must begin by recognizing that most attempts to explain Paul's interpretive practice—including this project—are based on the same general methodology: comparative analysis (cf. sect. 1 of the introduction). This is significant because it means that explanations for Paul's practice are distinguished by (1) the criteria used to find comparative examples and (2) the resultant interpretive schemata used when engaging Paul's practice with those examples. In this chapter, I examine—task 1—the criteria that prior scholarship has used to select the comparative examples for explaining Paul's practice and determine—task 2—if they enable an appropriate analysis. Chapter 3 completes these two tasks for the resultant interpretive schemata.

In this chapter, I extract three criteria from prior scholarship, examine those criteria within the ancient interpretive practice of allegory up to the time of Paul, and argue that the criteria do not situate an analysis of Paul's practice—or of any ancient allegorist's practice—appropriately within his context because the criteria *do not distinguish one ancient interpretive practice of allegory from another in terms of their similarities or differences.* I demonstrate one criterion did not influence the ancient interpretive practice of allegory and two others function only as organizational tools. This chapter, as well as the first two sections of chapter 3, set the stage for the different criteria and approach I proffer in chapter 3, section 3. This chapter is divided into three sections: the criteria used in prior scholarship for selecting comparative examples, examining the criteria within the ancient interpretive practice of allegory, and results of the examination.

1. THE CRITERIA USED IN PRIOR SCHOLARSHIP FOR SELECTING COMPARATIVE EXAMPLES

An examination of prior scholarship reveals three criteria have been used for selecting comparative examples: facticity, terminology, and geographical location.

1.1. Facticity

The criterion "facticity" designates a nuanced position within the distinction between abstract entities (e.g., freedom, truth, sin, spiritual maturity) and concrete entities (e.g., characters, events, creatures, objects). Facticity is the belief that concrete entities existed in the past. *In scholarship on Gal 4:21–31, this criterion is discernible when scholars argue that Paul viewed his source entities as actual people who walked the earth or as events that were real occurrences.* For some scholars, facticity defines Paul's practice. Twenty-two scholars from 1870 to 2021 explicitly state a concern for facticity.[1] Below are six examples.

1. These scholars are listed in chronological order. I also include dates to demonstrate the pervasiveness of this concern. Those who demonstrate this concern are as follows: Lightfoot, *Saint Paul's Epistle*, 180 (1870); Blackwelder and Stamm, "Epistle to the Galatians," 540 (1953); Woollcombe, "Biblical Origins," 42 (1957); Daniélou, *Lord of History*, 140 (1958); Hendriksen, *Galatians*, 182 (1968); R. Jewett, *Paul's Anthropological Terms*, 100 (1971); Cothenet, "A l'arrière-plan de l'allégorie," 462; Goppelt, *Typos*, 139 (1982); Rhoers, "Typological Use," 211 (1984); George, *Galatians*, 339–40 (1994); Martyn, *Galatians*, 436 (1997); Fung, *Epistle to the Galatians*, 217 (1998); Gerber, "Ga 4,21–31," 170 (2002); Buscemi, *Lettera ai Galati*, 455 (2004); Gil-Tamayo, "Todo esto,"

St Paul uses ἀλληγορία here much in the same sense as τύπος in 1 Cor X. II ταῦτα δὲ τυπικῶς συνέβαινεν, not denying the historical truth of the narrative, but superposing a secondary meaning. (1870)[2]

When Paul says that these things are "allegorical utterances," he does not mean that the Genesis story is unhistorical myth, but he sees in it a religious meaning that ranges far beyond the literal history. (1953)[3]

Paul does, however, definitely go beyond the historical to the hidden and underlying meaning. But at the same time he seems to be merely drawing out the spiritual principles underlying the actual events, so that the deeper, spiritual meaning is in full harmony with, although additional to, the historical meaning. (1998)[4]

Quoi qu'il en soit, il est admis pour Paul qu'elle supporte une lecture qui, sans en nier l'historicité, permet de clarifier le présent différencié d'Israël et de l'Église dans leur rapport à la Loi. (2002)[5]

The modern interpreter must recognize that Paul is not dismissing but rather assuming the factual nature of the Genesis account. He explains his interpretive approach in 4:25: Hagar "is aligned with" or "corresponds to" (συστοιχεῖ) the present Jerusalem. The translation "taken figuratively" in 4:24 (instead of "spoken allegorically") helps avoid the mistaken notion that Paul does not take Genesis at face value. (2014)[6]

In Philo's hands, the story really does "communicate something else," something quite divorced from the historical dynamics of the narrative. Paul's allegorical reading is more reserved, insofar

---

39 (2008); De Boer, *Galatians*, 296 (2011); Moo, *Galatians*, 295–96 (2013); Das, *Galatians*, 485 (2014); Barclay, *Paul and the Gift*, 415–16; Tedder, "Children of Laughter," 156 (2017); DeSilva, *Letter to the Galatians*, 395 (2018); Wright, *Galatians*, 303 (2021).

2. Lightfoot, *Saint Paul's Epistle*, 180.
3. Blackwelder and Stamm, "Epistle to the Galatians," 540.
4. Fung, *Epistle to the Galatians*, 217.
5. Gerber, "Ga 4,21–31," 170.
6. Das, *Galatians*, 485.

> as he is not seeking to eliminate the historical specificity of the story in favor of some timeless philosophical principle. (2018)[7]

Although prior scholarship never has labeled facticity to be a criterion for selecting comparative examples, it has served this purpose in two ways. First, it has been used to exclude as comparative examples the interpretive practices of allegorists who were roughly contemporary to Paul. Of particular significance is Philo's allegorical practice—described by Barclay, De Boer, Cothenet, DeSilva, Tedder, and Wright as not helpful for understanding Paul's practice due to facticity (cf. n1)—about whom Woollcombe's explanation stands as a representative example.

> In the Pauline interpretation [of Sarah and Hagar], *the historical pattern* of the story of Sarah and Hagar is used as a parable of the historical pattern of God's dealings with the Old and New Israel. In the Philonic interpretation, however, the historical pattern of the story plays no part at all: Philo used only the names of Sarah and Hagar, interpreted allegorically, as a key wherewith to open the door to his own notion of the undersense of the narrative.[8]

Second, when this vein of prior scholarship uses comparative examples, it either explains Paul's interpretive practice by means of a malnourished view of Paul's interpretive practices elsewhere (discussed in sect. 2.4.2.3) or by means of retrojecting later rabbinic interpretive practices—viewed by these scholars as demonstrating facticity—back into Paul's milieu. The latter explanation has brought about the tendency to distinguish Paul's practice from other practices by using the label "Palestinian."

> It seems reasonable to conclude, then, that St. Paul was quite ready to use allegory, and even to use it in order to evacuate the ordinances of the Torah of their literal meaning on occasion, but that he *employed this allegory in a Palestinian rather than an Alexandrian tradition*, and that in practice the bent of his thought lay so much towards typology rather than what we

---

7. DeSilva, *Letter to the Galatians*, 395.

8. Woollcombe, "Biblical Origins," 53; emphasis original. Other scholars who do not consider Philo's interpretive practice helpful for understanding Paul's interpretive practice—based on the criterion of facticity—are as follows: Balla, "Paul's Use," 123; Barrett, "Allegory of Abraham," 169n24; Betz, *Galatians*, 239n11; Bruce, *Epistle to the Galatians*, 217; Ellis, *Paul's Use*, 52; Fung, *Epistle to the Galatians*, 217; George, *Galatians*, 26; Hansen, *Abraham in Galatians*, 212; R. P. C. Hanson, *Allegory and Event*, 82–83; A. T. Hanson, *Studies in Paul's Technique*, 103; Lightfoot, *Saint Paul's Epistle*, 199; Löfstedt, "Allegory," 491; Longenecker, *Galatians*, 209–10; Perriman, "Rhetorical Strategy," 29.

should strictly call allegory that he had in the course of his extant letters few occasions to indulge in allegory.⁹

Although some scholars have abandoned Hanson's language of "Palestinian" and "Alexandrian," the concern for facticity demonstrates one assumption behind these terms remains very influential in scholarship on Gal 4:21–31. Accordingly, chapter 3 engages Hanson's interpretive schema because some assumptions driving it—facticity and geographical location (cf. sect. 1.3)—still are pervasive.

1.2. Terminology

The criterion "terminology" designates any linguistic term that ancient allegorists used to signal their interpretive practices of allegory. *In scholarship on Gal 4:21–31, this criterion is discernible when scholars argue that suitable comparative examples are ancient authors who, like Paul, used the root ἀλληγορ- (cf. Paul's use of ἀλληγορούμενα in 4:24).* This has brought about the tendency to offer explanations of Paul's practice based on the use of ἀλληγορ- within Greek literature. Eight scholars from 1921 to 2018 explicitly state this concern.¹⁰ Below are three examples.

> Paul specifies that the story of these two women, which he interprets in this manner, was told as an allegory (ἀλληγορούμενα, Gal 4:24) and, therefore, must be interpreted allegorically. (1982)¹¹

> Is the passage in question simply an allegory, or is it an exercise in typology? At the very least it must be said that some form of allegory is present. Otherwise, why would St Paul have used a word like ἀλληγορούμενα? (1994)¹²

---

9. R. P. C. Hanson, *Allegory and Event*, 82–83; emphasis added.

10. These scholars are listed in chronological order. I also include dates to demonstrate the pervasiveness of this concern. Those who demonstrate this concern are as follows: Burton, *Epistle to the Galatians*, 253 (1921); P. Jewett, "Concerning the Allegorical Interpretation," 9 (1954); Goppelt, *Typos*, 139 (1982); Barker, "Allegory and Typology," 207 (1994); McClane, "Hellenistic Background," 131 (1998); Witherington, *Grace in Galatia*, 326 (1998); Di Mattei, "Paul's Allegory," 105–6 (2006); De Boer, *Galatians*, 296 (2011); Keener, *Galatians*, 214–15 (2018).

11. Goppelt, *Typos*, 139.

12. Barker, "Allegory and Typology," 207.

> Paul's method in any case reflects the definition of "allegory" given by ancient writers. (2011)[13]

The assumption at the core of this criterion is that *Paul meant what the Greeks meant* when they used ἀλληγορ-. This is problematic because what the Greeks *meant*—examined below—varies. More importantly, even if we accept that Paul and the Greeks' shared terminology is significant for understanding Paul's practice in some way, there has been no thorough examination in order to determine (1) *to what extent* the shared terminology is significant or (2) *if* Greek interpretive practices are the most suitable comparative examples for examining Paul's practice. Ultimately, the criterion terminology projects Greek interpretive practices onto Paul without any examination beyond the basic recognition that Paul and some Greeks used the root ἀλληγορ-.

1.3. Geographical Location

The criterion "geographical location" designates allegorists' interpretive practices of allegory within a specific location that some scholars believe influenced other allegorists' interpretive practices. *In scholarship on Gal 4:21–31, this criterion is discernible when scholars argue that Paul's practice is explained best by means of other interpretive practices within a specific location.* Eight scholars from 1900 to 2008 explicitly state a concern for geographical location.[14] Below are four examples.

> It is too arbitrary to convince us, yet in view of v. 23 we can scarcely say that it is entirely arbitrary. It has some slender foundation in the Old Testament story.... If this type of argument is unreal to us we must remember that Paul is under the influence of his Rabbinic training. (1911)[15]

---

13. De Boer, *Galatians*, 296.

14. These scholars are listed in chronological order. I also include dates to demonstrate this concern's pervasiveness. Those who demonstrate this concern are as follows: Thackeray, *Relation*, 192 (1900); Allan, *Epistle of Paul*, 76; R. P. C. Hanson, *Allegory and Event*, 82–83 (1959); Barrett, "Allegory of Abraham," 163 (1982); King, "Paul and the Tannaim," 370; Bouwman, "Hagar- und Sara-Perikope," 3150 (1987); Di Mattei, "Paul's Allegory," 114 (2006); Gignilliat, "Paul, Allegory," 136 (2008).

15. Allan, *Epistle of Paul*, 76.

> Throughout Paul's response he purposefully utilized rabbinical exegetical methods, interpretive techniques, and arguments based upon Tannaitic conceptions. (1983)[16]

> Auch der Schriftbeweis in V.27 wird von Paulus mehr oder weniger usurpiert. In dem alten palästinischen Zyclus war Jes 54 die *haftara* (Abschnitt aus den Propheten) zu Gen 16. (1987)[17]

> Paul is reading the Genesis narrative via the lens of Isa 54:1, as the later *haftara* liturgical readings of the Palestinian rabbinic tradition attest. (2008)[18]

Two assumptions are at the core of this criterion. First, rabbinic interpretive practices accurately reflect the interpretive practices within Palestine during Paul's time. The late dating of the rabbinic sources makes this position difficult to support in many but not all situations (cf. sect. 2.4.2.4). Second, if rabbinic practices accurately reflect Palestinian practices at Paul's time, then this criterion assumes Paul used them because he was exposed to them there. Ultimately, this criterion and its assumptions reveal how another one of Hanson's claims remains pervasive: "[Paul] employed this allegory in a Palestinian rather than an Alexandrian tradition."[19] As such, those who use this criterion retroject rabbinic interpretive practices onto Paul no differently than those who use the criterion terminology to project Greek interpretive practices onto him.

2. EXAMINING THE CRITERIA WITHIN THE ANCIENT INTERPRETIVE PRACTICE OF ALLEGORY

The task of this section is to determine whether the criteria of facticity, terminology, and geographical location, can be used to distinguish one practice from another within the ancient interpretive practice of allegory *in a way that enables us to better understand Paul's practice by comparative analysis*. I argue that these criteria cannot be used in this way because (1) facticity does not influence how the ancient interpretive practice of allegory operated, and (2) the other two criteria function only as organizational tools when examining ancient allegorical practices because

16. King, "Paul and the Tannaim," 370.
17. Bouwman, "Hagar- und Sara-Perikope," 3150.
18. Gignilliat, "Paul, Allegory," 136.
19. R. P. C. Hanson, *Allegory and Event*, 82.

they do not distinguish one ancient allegorical practice from another regarding those practices' similarities and differences. To demonstrate my arguments, I now examine various expressions of the ancient interpretive practice of allegory in four locations: Egypt, Greece, Italy, and Palestine. My use of geographical location is for heuristic purposes only and does not indicate any argument for its significance within the ancient interpretive practice of allegory.

2.1. The Ancient Interpretive Practice of Allegory in Egypt

In Egypt, there are two collections of allegorical expressions: one from the middle and new kingdoms (2030–1070 BCE) and the other in the late centuries BCE to early CE.

2.1.1. In the Middle and New Kingdoms

Five allegorical expressions are useful for evaluating the criterion facticity.[20] First, "The Blinding of Truth" is an allegory about Truth personified, his younger brother Falsehood, and Truth's son. Falsehood harms Truth, but Falsehood ultimately is punished by means of Truth's son. In this expression, virtues and vices—that is, abstract entities—are allegorized into characters—that is, concrete entities. In two other expressions, "The Lion and the Mouse" and "The War of Cats and Mice," creatures and events are allegorized into abstract entities. In "The Lion and the Mouse," a mouse saves a lion's life because the lion had spared the mouse's life earlier in the story. In the end, a reader is taught that strength is circumstantial. In "The War of Cats and Mice," mice are described in situations that are impossible to endure (e.g., a mouse pharaoh unsuccessfully attacking a formidable cat fortress with his chariot). These events satirize the human effort to overcome difficult circumstances. Fourth, the Ramesseum Dramatic Papyrus includes various instructions for ritual proceedings in which non-ritual objects are given ritual meanings allegorically (e.g., "beer" for "Horus"). Finally, in the Egyptian Book of the Dead, objects in spell 99 are allegorized into abstract entities (e.g., a vessel for drawing water is called the "hand of Isis"), as well as objects in spell 153 (e.g., wood as the "hand of Osiris"). These five expressions reveal two important characteristics of the ancient interpretive practice of allegory regarding facticity.

20. These allegorical expressions can be found in Griffiths, "Allegory."

First, they reveal that Egyptians used source and allegorical entities with no observable concern for the facticity of the characters or events they used. Second, they reveal that concrete and abstract entities can be used interchangeably within the ancient interpretive practice of allegory with no observable concern for facticity.

The criterion of geographical location can be evaluated by examining "The Quarrel of the Body and the Head." This allegorical expression demonstrates how similar interpretive practices of allegory were not restricted to only one geographical location. The common expression of this allegorical practice has been summarized helpfully elsewhere.

> [This Egyptian allegory] appears in the speech of Menenius Agrippa as recorded by Livy, 2.32 and Plutarch, *Vita Coriolani* 6: the belly is accused of having an easy time, but replies by saying that it nourishes the whole body, the moral being that all the body's members need one another and that the senate, equated with the belly, is really helpful to the plebs. *That a form of this short allegory first appears in Egyptian literature, though in a severely fragmentary state, is a fact of some significance.*[21]

This expression reveals two important characteristics of the ancient interpretive practice of allegory regarding geographical location. First, it reveals that the same allegorical expression can be found in one culture and location and also appear much later in a different culture and location. Second, it reveals that the Egyptians used this interpretive practice earlier than the Greeks (who often are assumed to have used it first [cf. sect. 2.2]).

2.1.2. In the Late Centuries BCE to Early CE

The second collection of allegorical expressions is from allegorists who lived in Alexandria during the late centuries BCE to early CE. Around the second century BCE,[22] Pseudo-Aristeas allegorized Moses's teachings in order to defend Jews' special status among humanity:

> Everything pertaining to conduct permitted us toward these creatures and toward beasts has been set out symbolically. Thus the cloven hoof, that is the separation of the claws of the hoof,

---

21. Griffiths, "Allegory," 91–92; emphasis original. Griffiths also points to 1 Cor 12:12; Col 1:18; and Eph 1:22, all of which contain similar expressions.

22. For a discussion of the date of the Letter of Aristeas, see Charlesworth, *Old Testament Pseudepigrapha*, 2:8–9.

> is a sign of setting apart each of our actions for good, because the strength of the whole body with its action rests upon the shoulders and the legs. The symbolism conveyed by these things compels us to make a distinction in the performance of all our acts, with righteousness as our aim. This moreover explains why we are distinct from all other men. (Let. Aris. 150b–52a [Shutt])

In this expression, Pseudo-Aristeas allegorizes an object (i.e., the cloven hoof of an ox) into an abstract entity (i.e., the distinctiveness of the Jews). Aristobulus, recounted by Eusebius, similarly allegorized an object (i.e., a hand) into an abstract entity (i.e., power):

> As to hands, then, clearly they are thought of, even by us, in a more general way. For whenever you, as king, dispatch forces with the intention of accomplishing something, we say, "The king has a mighty hand." And those that hear this refer it to the power that you possess. Now Moses also indicates this through our law when he speaks to this effect: "God led you out of Egypt with a mighty hand." And again, "I will extend my hand," the Lord says to him, "and will strike the Egyptians." And on the death of the cattle and of the other beasts, Moses said to the king of the Egyptians, "Behold, the hand of the Lord shall be upon your cattle, and death shall be widespread in your fields." Consequently, the hands are thought of in terms of the power of God. For truly, it is possible to think metaphorically[23] that all men's strength and activities are in their hands. Thus, quite appropriately has the lawgiver spoken metaphorically in an expanded sense, in saying that the accomplishments of God are his hands. And the divine "standing," understood in this expanded sense, might well be called the constitution of the cosmos. (*apud* Eusebius, *Praep. ev.* 8.10.7–9 [Holladay])

Although these two authors shared similar cultic convictions[24] and allegorized similarly,[25] their practices are distinct in that Aristobulus's

---

23. For comments on the use of the root μεταφορ- here, see sect. 1 of the introduction.

24. Pseudo-Aristeas and Aristobulus share similar concerns for Moses and for the Law. Aristobulus takes his defense of Moses further than Pseudo-Aristeas by placing the blame of any errors upon himself: "So I will begin to take up in order each thing signified, insofar as I can. But if I shall fall short of the truth, and not be convincing, do not attribute the faulty reasoning to the lawgiver but to me and my inability to express distinctly the things which he thought out" (Eusebius, *Praep. ev.*, 8.10.6 [Holladay]). Additionally, in a later passage, Pseudo-Aristeas asserts that Homer, Hesiod, and Linus borrowed from Moses's teachings (13.12).

25. When these two authors are discussed in scholarship on Gal 4:21–31, they typically are grouped together with no discussion of their differences. For examples,

allegorical meanings are anti-anthropomorphic. This is significant because this anti-anthropomorphism also is evident in the rabbinic interpretive practice of allegory—discussed below in section 2.4.2.4. This demonstrates, in the same way as "The Quarrel of the Body and the Head," that similar practices can be found in different geographical locations; put simply, *one geographical location does not have a monopoly on one type of allegorical expression within the ancient interpretive practice of allegory.*[26]

The abundance of extant literature from the third allegorist, Philo of Alexandria, has generated a tremendous amount of scholarship. I give more attention to Philo's allegorical practice in chapter 5, and four characteristics of his practice help accomplish the task of this section. First, the ways in which Philo allegorized can be observed in other locations and time periods. Therefore, his practice should not be labeled as "Alexandrian" (cf. ch. 3, sect. 1; ch. 5, sect. 2) or "Philonian."[27] Second, Philo's understanding of facticity mirrors what is observed elsewhere: it does not impact the ancient interpretive practice of allegory. In *Migr.* 89, Philo argues against those who use a concern for facticity to deny allegorical meanings. However, he also argues against those who deny the actual commandments by focusing only on their allegorical meanings. For Philo, facticity and the ancient interpretive practice of allegory *operate in different interpretive domains.* Third, Philo is an "'exegete' who broadly proceeds according to the development of the scriptural text"[28]

see Büchsel, *TDNT* 1:260–61; Dawson, *Allegorical Readers*, 73–81; R. P. C. Hanson, *Allegory and Event*, 41–42; Longenecker, *Biblical Exegesis*, 32; Svendsen, *Allegory Transformed*, 6–17; Woollcombe, "Biblical Origins," 51.

26. This also is indicated when viewing the practices of Pseudo-Aristeas and Aristobulus alongside Philo's practice. Although Philo allegorized in the same location, with similar religious convictions (e.g., Philo defends Moses [*Ios.* 28; *Mos.* 2.190; etc.] and also used allegory to explain areas of Scripture that could be interpreted as potential contradictions [*Leg.* 3.4; 3.236; *Ios.* 28; et al.]), we observe in ch. 5, sect. 2, that Philo's interpretive practice of allegory was more diverse than what is found in the extant writings of his fellow Alexandrians and is similar to practices used by those in other locations.

27. Despite Philo's various statements about allegorical rules in which he uses different Greek words—φυσικός (*Post.* 7), κανών (*Somn.* 1.73; *Spec.* 1.287), and νόμος (*Somn.* 1.102; *Abr.* 68)—there is no distinctly Philonian set of rules. One substantial attempt to create such a set is Siegfried, *Philo von Alexandria*, 165–75.

28. Whitman, *Interpretation and Allegory*, 38. The pioneering work for this approach was Siegfried, *Philo von Alexandria*. A summary of works using this approach can be found in Borgen, *Philo of Alexandria*, 9–13. Borgen also follows this approach in his substantial contribution to the topic.

and not "simply delivering the God of the Old Testament into the hands of the Greeks."[29] This interpretation is supported not only by the analysis in chapter 5 but also by the similarities between Philo and the rabbis' interpretive practices (cf. sect. 2.4.2.4.). Fourth, we must resist the urge to consider the copious amount of extant Philonic literature—enough to fill twelve volumes of the Loeb Classical Library—to be an indication that Philo has a special role in our understanding of the ancient interpretive practice of allegory. As large as his corpus may be, Philo remains one allegorist among many others.

2.2. The Ancient Interpretive Practice of Allegory in Greece

In Greece, the earliest known allegorists lived in the sixth to fourth centuries BCE. Unfortunately, we know of these authors and their works only through references found in later extant literature. These allegorists included Theagenes of Rhegium,[30] Pherecydes of Syros,[31] and many other philosophers.[32] These allegorists used their interpretive practices either (1) to defend Homer's stories against accusations of sacrilege or (2) to unearth the stories' deeper meanings.[33] One early allegorist from Greece whose work has survived is Socrates. In the *Republic*, Plato recounts Socrates's explanation of the "Allegory of the Cave"[34] to Plato's brother:

> So then, my dear Glaucon, I said, we must fit this image in its entirety to what we were discussing before, comparing the place

---

29. Olsen, "Allegory, Typology, and Symbol," 173.

30. Porphyry, in the third century CE, tells us it was Theagenes of Rhegium who first allegorized Homer's writings (*Quaest. hom. Odd.* 20.67.1–75.7).

31. Jonathan Tate was the first to argue that Pherecydes of Syros was the first Greek allegorist. He bases his argument on Origen, *Cels.* 6.42 ("Beginnings of Greek Allegory"). Griffiths also points to Aristophanes, *Birds* 822, for a similar ancient statement about Porphyry's allegorical practice ("Allegory," 80).

32. Aeschylus (sixth century BCE), Anaxagoras (fifth century BCE), Cleanthes (fourth century BCE), Crates (fourth century BCE), Metrodorus of Lampsacus (third century BCE), and Chrysippus (third century BCE). Other less-known allegorists are summarized in Hersman, *Greek Allegorical Interpretation*, 10–16.

33. For two recent scholars who draw attention to this non-apologetic function, see McClane, "Hellenistic Background," 127; and Whitman, *Allegory*, 20. For pioneering works on this use of allegory in Greece, see Tate: "Beginnings of Greek Allegory"; "On History of Allegorism"; "Plato and Allegorical Interpretation"; "Plato and Allegorical Interpretation (Continued)."

34. Plato, *Republic* 7.514A–41B. Other works of Plato that include allegory are the *Symposium*, *Cratylus*, and *Phaedrus*.

that appeared through our sight to the dwelling in the prison chamber and the light of the fire there to the power of the sun. If you take the upward journey and the seeing of what is above as the upward journey of the soul to the intelligible realm, you will not mistake my intention, since you are keen to hear this. (*Republic* 7.517b [Jones and Preddy])

This expression is significant not only because a similar practice is used by Philo later in Alexandria[35] but also because it demonstrates how the interpretive practice of allegory was used for various hermeneutical purposes within Greece. In the *Republic*, Plato used allegory for non-apologetic purposes in contrast to those philosophers who apologetically defended Homer. This non-apologetic function (both here and in the allegorical expressions from Egypt) is overlooked often in modern scholarship. This oversight has led to arguments that misrepresent the ancient interpretive practice of allegory, such as "allegorical readings always begin as counterreadings, starting with denial or negation,"[36] or "a successful allegory displaces its antecedent, remakes it subject, and constitutes its own independent authority."[37] Although the hermeneutical purpose of an interpretive practice of allegory is not a criterion that prior scholarship has used to select comparative examples, chapter 3 discusses both why and how it should be used as one.

By the first century BCE, some Greek authors began to use the root ἀλληγορ- to indicate expressions within the ancient interpretive practice of allegory.[38] On the one hand, this development made it easier to identify some ancient expressions of allegorical practices. On the other hand, however, prior scholarship has misused this development in two ways. First, it has tended to consider only the uses of ἀλληγορ- as allegorical practices. However, this is myopic because the earliest allegorists in Greece did not use ἀλληγορ- in their expressions of the interpretive practice of allegory.[39] ἀλληγορ- indicated some but not all expressions of the ancient interpretive practice of allegory. Second, prior scholarship

---

35. Philo allegorizes the patriarchal narrative as the progression of the soul through different levels of knowledge just as Plato allegorizes the elements of the human existence.

36. Dawson, *Allegorical Readers*, 9.

37. Castelli, "Allegories of Hagar," 241.

38. Lexical discussions of the Greek root ἀλληγορ- can be found in Anderson, *Glossary*, 14–16; Büchsel, *TDNT* 1:260–63; BAGD, s.v. "ἀλληγορέω"; LSJ, s.v. "ἀλληγορέω"; Peisker, "Parable, Allegory, Proverb."

39. For example, some allegorists such as Plutarch used ὑπόνοια (*Mor.* 19e–f).

has treated the interpretive practices behind various allegorists' use of ἀλληγορ- as a standardized practice. A closer examination of both the nontechnical use and technical definitions of ἀλληγορ- does not support this position. Rather, the examination demonstrates that different Greek authors used the term in different ways.[40]

2.2.1. The Nontechnical Use of ἀλληγορ-

From the fourth century BCE to the second century CE, the use of the root ἀλληγορ- was widespread.[41] Orators, poets, philosophers, historians, and diviners within Greece used this term in a variety of ways. The allegorical expressions below are listed in chronological order (as are other lists that are similarly structured in this chapter).

Demetrius (second century BCE) records that Demades (fourth century BCE) used the interpretive practice of allegory, with the help of innuendo and hyperbole, to make forceful statements (*Eloc.* 282). He then provides sayings of Demades to support his claim, such as "Alexander is not dead, men of Athens; or the whole world would have smelled his corpse" (283 [Innes]).

Athenaeus (second century CE) records that Callimachus (third century BCE) allegorized the love of lettuce to signal sexual inadequacy: "Callimachus says that Venus hid Adonis under a lettuce, which is an allegorical statement of the poet's, intended to show that those who are much addicted to the use of lettuces are very little adapted for pleasures of love" (*Deipn.* 2.80 [Yonge]).

Plutarch (first century CE), in his argument against the Stoics, records one allegory of Chrysippus (a philosopher of the third century BCE). Chrysippus used the interpretive practice of allegory to illustrate the Stoic doctrine of "total blending"—a belief that two entities come to exist equally, although initially they might have been unequal:

---

40. As noted in the introduction, ἀλληγορ- was used in more than one way. For ἀλληγορέω, *LSJ* lists (1) "interpret allegorically," (2) "to be spoken allegorically," (3) "to speak figuratively or metaphorically," (4) "to speak allegorically." For ἀλληγορητής, "allegorical expounder." For ἀλληγορία, (1) "allegory, veiled language," (2) "allegorical exposition," (3) "figurative, metaphorical language." For ἀλληγορικός, "figurative." For ἀλληγορός, "allegorical." For ἀλληγορως, "allegorically." See LSJ, s.v. "ἀλληγορέω."

41. Aristotle may have expressed this concept earlier as separate words: "For instance, when Theodorus said to Nicon, the player on the cithara, 'you are troubled'; for while pretending to say 'something troubles you,' he deceives us; for he means something else [ἄλλο γὰρ λέγει]" (Aristotle, *Rhet.* 3.1412a–b).

"[Chrysippus] says that nothing keeps a single drop of wine from tempering the sea; and, no doubt in order that this may not amaze us, he says that the drop in the blending will extend to the whole universe. What could be manifestly more absurd than this I do not know" (*Comm. not.* 1078e [Cherniss]). Plutarch also states that the Egyptians, like the Greeks, use the names of gods to represent certain elements of the world allegorically: "These men are like the Greeks who say that Cronus is but a figurative name for Chronus (Time), Hera for Air, and that the birth of Hephaestus symbolizes the change of Air into Fire. . . . But the wiser of the priests call not only the Nile Osiris and the sea Typhon, but they simply give the name of Osiris to the whole source and faculty creative of moisture, believing this to be the cause of generation and the substance of life-producing seed; and the name of Typhon they give to all that is dry, fiery, and arid, in general, and antagonistic to moisture" (*Is. Os.* 363d–64a [Babbitt])

Strabo (first century CE) states that Homer used allegory for instruction, particularly in explaining the wanderings of Odysseus. He concludes: "But if there be some discrepancy we must ascribe it to the changes wrought by time, or to ignorance, or to poetic license—which is compounded of history, rhetorical composition, and myth" (*Geogr.* 1.2.7, 17 [Jones]). Here, we observe the same apologetic concern for Homer that was expressed by Greeks in earlier centuries, yet now expressed with the term ἀλληγορ-.

Artemidorus (second century CE) states that dreams are allegories to see what is in the soul (*Oneirocritica* 1.2, 11). He uses the ancient interpretive practice of allegory to reveal a person's thoughts and desires.

The preceding list of allegorical expressions is not exhaustive but is sufficient for an evaluation of the three criteria. Regarding the criterion of terminology, with the exception of Artemidorus, each author who uses the term ἀλληγορ- *in actuality* is describing others who do not use that terminology in their interpretive practice. Put simply, the author using ἀλληγορ- is projecting that term onto another's practice that the projector perceives to align with the projector's understanding of ἀλληγορ- (and not with the understanding of the author being described). These different perceptions of allegory demonstrate how the use of ἀλληγορ- was not standardized in Greece (and also will align with what we observe when examining the technical definitions of ἀλληγορ- below.). Therefore, the use of this term alone is not sufficient evidence to determine comparative examples for the purpose of examining different interpretive practices.

Regarding the criterion of facticity, there is no indication that it influenced these authors' presentations of others' practices or the practices themselves. Even Strabo, who comments on the historical accuracy of Homer's geographical explanations, indicates that poetic license allows Homer to work outside the bounds of facticity. Regarding the criterion of geographical location, some of these allegorical expressions are similar to those found in other locations. Plutarch's allegorical expression of wine and the sea to describe total blending is similar to Aristobulus's allegorical expression of a hand to describe the power of God. Artemidorus's allegorical expression of dreams is similar to the allegorical expression that Nathan told David in 2 Sam 11:26–12:15 (cf. sect. 2.4.1). These expressions reveal how similar expressions are found in different geographical locations.[42] Therefore, the nontechnical use of ἀλληγορ- provides no support for the use of geographical location as a criterion for selecting comparative examples.

Although ancient authors in Greece could use ἀλληγορ- to indicate a practice that they understood to be allegorical, the allegorical expressions in this section demonstrated how those understandings were not uniform. We also observe a variety of understandings when examining the technical definitions of ἀλληγορ-.

2.2.2. Technical Definitions of ἀλληγορ-

Around the first century BCE, Greek authors began to define ἀλληγορ- in a technical sense. In contrast to those authors in the previous section, these authors went beyond describing others' interpretive practices as allegorical. Some defined the practice and provided examples (cf. sect. 2.2.2.1). Others defined it, provided examples, and then discussed it within a system of rhetoric put forth within their own rhetorical handbooks (cf. sect. 2.2.2.2).

2.2.2.1. TECHNICAL DEFINITIONS OUTSIDE OF RHETORICAL HANDBOOKS

Tryphon (first century BCE) lists ἀλληγορ- as one of fourteen tropes (*Peri tropon*, introduction). He later defines it: "Allegory is a word revealing

---

42. Both Plutarch (*Is. Os.* 356a) and Porphyry (*Vit. Pyth.* 12) also recognize that the Egyptians and Greeks used the ancient interpretive practice of allegory in similar ways.

something else authoritatively, overshadowing the thought with another thing in a similar likeness to the former, such as: 'In which place the sword casts much corn straw on the ground'" (*Peri tropon* γ, my translation).[43] Tryphon provides no additional information.

Heraclitus (first century CE) states, "For the moment, it is probably essential to give a little technical account of allegory, quite briefly. The word itself, which is formed in a way expressive of truth, reveals its own significance. For the trope which says one thing but signifies something other than what it says receives the name 'allegory' precisely from this." Heraclitus continues by providing examples in which one poet compares tyranny to a stormy sea and another poet the arrogance of a woman to the wild spirit of a horse. He ends by saying that the true significance of the practice is understood from "the pair of contrasting opposites"(*Homeric Problems* 5 [Russell]).

Plutarch (first century CE) states, "Very close to these is allegory, which says one thing through another, as in 'Now you'll keep your watch all night, Melanthius, in the sort of soft bed you deserve' [*Od.* 22.195–96] for he is hanging in chains and the speaker says he will sleep in a soft bed" (*Vit. poes. Hom.* 70 [Keany and Lamberton]). Plutarch explains that the ancient interpretive practice of allegory enables Homer's description of Melanthius's situation to be understood in a more biting and sarcastic way, intensifying his polemic.

Tryphon II (first century CE) lists ἀλληγορ- as one of twenty-seven tropes and then gives an example in which an untamed horse can cause havoc in the games like a fire burning out of control. Later, he defines ἀλληγορ- as "a word making visible something else, having stood in place for the thought of another" (*De tropis* 216.1, my translation).[44]

2.2.2.2. Technical Definitions Inside of Rhetorical Handbooks

Demetrius (second century BCE) describes allegory as follows: "Allegory is also impressive, particularly in threats, for example that of Dionysius, 'their cicadas will sing from the ground.' If he had said openly that he would ravage the land of Locris, he would have shown more anger but less dignity. As it is, he has shrouded his words, as it were, in allegory.

---

43. For the Greek text, see Tryphon, *Peri tropon*.
44. For the Greek text, see Tryphon II, "De Tropis."

What is implied always strikes more terror, since its meaning is open to different interpretations, whereas what is clear and plain is apt to be despised, like men who are stripped of their clothes. . . . Here again in the case of allegory we should avoid a succession of them, or our words become a riddle. . . . This is why expressions which symbolise something else are forceful, since they resemble brevity in speech. We are left to infer a great deal from a short statement, as in the case of symbols. For example, the saying 'the cicadas will sing to you from the ground' is more forceful in this allegorical form than if it had been straightforwardly expressed, 'your trees will be cut down.'" (*Eloc.* 99–102, 243 [Innes]).

Hermogenes (second century CE) states, "Allegorical approaches, if they are maintained, also produce a solemn style, as Plato does in the *Phaedrus* when he says, 'Zeus, the great leader in heaven, rides his winged chariot,' etc. (246e). I should add, however, that this happens only when someone decides to create an allegory out of elements that are not trite or commonplace. Such allegories do not create solemnity but introduce a different sort of thought, often a vulgar one" (*Peri ideon* 246 [Wooten]).

Additionally, two Roman authors provide a perspective on the Greek use of ἀλληγορ-.[45] Cicero (first century BCE) states, "When there is a continuous stream of metaphors, a wholly different style of speech is produced; consequently the Greeks call it ἀλληγορία or 'allegory' [*translationes*]. They are right as to the name, but from the point of view of classification Aristotle does better in calling them all metaphors [*translationes*]" (*Orator* 94 [Hendrickson and Hubbell]).

Quintilian (first century CE) states, "Akin to these are the Figures [*schemata*] of which the Greeks are so fond, by which they soften the impact of unpleasant facts. Themistocles is thus believed to have persuaded the Athenians to make an offering of their city to the gods, because it was too brutal to tell them to abandon it. And the man who wanted the golden Victories to be melted down for war purposes toned down his words into 'We must make use of our victories.' But the whole process of saying one thing while wishing something else to be understood is akin to Allegory [*allegoriae*]" (*Inst.* 9.2.92 [Russell]).

The definitions in this section, alongside those in the previous section 2.2.2.1, reveal the different ways that Greeks understood ἀλληγορ- in a technical sense. For these eight authors who seek to define ἀλληγορ-, it

---

45. For a discussion of allegorists who lived in Italy, see sect. 2.3. Here, I discuss only those comments that directly address how Romans understood the interpretive practice of allegory to be used in Greece.

is evident that their attempts are descriptive of a practice already taking place in Greece. Each definition is the attempt of one author to describe how he understands a practice that he observes within his milieu. Olsen is correct when he states that ἀλληγορ- can mean "very different things from author to author, and not infrequently, within the writings of a single author."[46] This plurality of meaning is significant for evaluating the criterion of terminology. In the same way that the descriptions of others' practices as allegorical (cf. sect. 2.2.1) did not reflect a standardized understanding of ἀλληγορ-, so also do these technical definitions. *For this reason, using one author's practice or definition of ἀλληγορ- to explain another's practice becomes nothing more than a modern interpreter's preference.* Therefore, terminology itself is not a reliable criterion for determining suitable comparative examples. Regarding the criterion of geographical location, again we observe similar interpretive practices outside of Greece. For example, Heraclitus allegorized an abstract entity (i.e., tyranny) into an object (i.e., storm) just as Paul allegorized (discussed below) spiritual maturity into food in 1 Cor 3:1–3 (cf. sect. 2.4.2.3). Also, the polemical function of Demetrius's allegorical practice is mirrored in what Nathan tells David in 2 Sam 11:26–12:15 (cf. sect. 2.4.1). Similarities between the technical definitions of ἀλληγορ- in Greece and practices elsewhere demonstrate once more how geographical location is not a determinative criterion. Last, no technical definition demonstrates any concern for facticity.

2.3. The Ancient Interpretive Practice of Allegory in Italy

In Italy, two sets of allegorical expressions are useful for this analysis: (1) Roman authors' allegorical practices and (2) technical definitions of allegorical practices in Roman rhetorical handbooks.

2.3.1. Roman Authors' Allegorical Practices

Within this first set of evidence, the allegorical practices of first-century BCE writers Virgil, Ovid, Horace, and Lucretius are sufficient for the analysis. In his monumental work, the *Aeneid*, Virgil allegorizes the journey of the news of Aeneas and Dido's trysts as follows:

---

46. Olsen, "Allegory, Typology, and Symbol," 163.

> At once Rumour runs through Libya's great cities—Rumour the swiftest of all evils. Speed lends her strength, and she wins vigour as she goes; small at first through fear, soon she mounts up to heaven, and walks the ground with head hidden in the clouds. Mother Earth, provoked to anger against the gods, brought her forth last, they say, as sister to Coeus and Enceladus, swift of foot and fleet of wing, a monster awful and huge, who for the many feathers in her body has as many watchful eyes beneath—wondrous to tell—as many tongues, as many sounding mouths, as many pricked-up ears. By night, midway between heaven and earth, she flies through the gloom, screeching, and droops not her eyes in sweet sleep; by day she sits on guard on high rooftop or lofty turrets, and affrights great cities, clinging to the false and wrong, yet heralding truth. (*Aen.* 4.173–88 [Fairclough])

In the subsequent lines, Virgil makes clear the meaning of his allegorical entities:

> Now exulting in manifold gossip, she filled the nations and sang alike of fact and falsehood, how Aeneas is come, one born of Trojan blood, to whom in marriage fair Dido deigns to join herself; now they while away the winter, all its length, in wanton ease together, heedless of their realms and enthralled by shameless passion. These tales the foul goddess spreads here and there upon the lips of men. Straightway to King Iarbas she bends her course, and with her words fires his spirit and heaps high his wrath. (*Aen.* 4.189–97 [Fairclough])

A second author, Ovid, uses the interpretive practice of allegory in a similar way, allegorizing Envy as a horrible beast that Minerva seeks to turn against a daughter of Cecrops:

> The battered doors flew open; and there, sitting within, was Envy, eating snakes' flesh, the proper food of her venom. At the horrid sight the goddess turned away her eyes. But that other rose heavily from the ground, leaving the snakes' carcasses half consumed, and came forward with sluggish step. . . . Her eyes are all awry, her teeth are foul with mould; green, poisonous gall o'erflows her breast, and venom drips down from her tongue. She never smiles, save at the sight of another's troubles; she never sleeps, disturbed with wakeful cares; unwelcome to her is the sight of men's success, and with the sight she pines away; she gnaws and is gnawed, herself her own punishment. . . . Wherever she goes, she tramples down the flowers, causes the grass to wither, blasts the high waving trees, and taints with the foul

pollution of her breath whole peoples, cities, homes. (*Metam.* 2:768–95 [Miller])

These two allegorical expressions—including others found in those works[47]—have been labeled as examples of Augustan-age personification allegory.[48] However, Virgil also used the ancient interpretive practice of allegory in a different way. In the *Georgics*, he allegorized the life of a farmer to satirize the unending toil of human work.[49] Two other authors, Horace and Lucretius, did not use personification allegory. In Horace's *Epistle* 1, he claims that the story of Ulysses's refusal to succumb to the Sirens should be understood allegorically as a call to devote the mind to "honourable studies and pursuits" (*Ep.* 1:2.36; for context see 1:2.17–43 [Fairclough]).[50] Last, Lucretius claims that descriptions of Cybele are allegorical explanations of astronomy: "Seated in a chariot she drives a pair of lions, thus teaching that the great world is poised in the spacious air, and that earth cannot rest on earth" (*De rerum natura*, 2.601–603; for context see 2.600–643 [Rouse]).[51]

The previous allegorical expressions are significant for this analysis in the following ways. Regarding the criterion of facticity, there is no indication that these allegorists' practices were influenced by a concern for the historicity of their source entities. For example, Virgil and Ovid both allegorize abstract entities into concrete entities with no concern for facticity as is found in "The Blinding of Truth" in Egypt and in Heraclitus's allegorical expression in Greece. Regarding the criterion of terminology,

---

47. In Vergil, another allegorical expression is of Sleep (*somnus*), whom he portrays as speaking with humans (*Aen.* 5:834–71). For a discussion of Ovid's allegorical interpretations of *somnus*, as well as *fama* and *fames*, see Lowe, "Personification Allegory," 424–33.

48. Lowe, "Personification Allegory," 414. For the classification of these anthropomorphisms as "extended personification allegory," see Feeny, *Gods in Epic*, 241.

49. Kronenberg, *Allegories of Farming*, 132–55.

50. This is only one expression from Horace's interpretive practice of allegory. John Stevens summarizes Horace's expansive use of it as follows: "If it seems strange to speak of Horatian allegory, one need only consider the new demands of imperial poetry: Horace begins *Carm.* 3.1 with a comparison of Jupiter and Augustus; in 3.3 the deification of Romulus and the events of the Trojan war become a background against which to depict the new Augustan order; and in 3.1.7 and 3.4.42–68, the Gigantomachy points to the great battle at Actium that brought Octavian to single rule. In odes such as 1.5 and 1.14, Horace reveals openly that he is imitating Greek lyrics that are themselves allegorical. It was an allegorical era" (Stevens, "Seneca and Horace," 283).

51. As with Horace, Lucretius's practice is extensive. For a discussion of Lucretius's other allegories, see Gale, *Myth and Poetry*, 19–44.

we observe that the allegorists do not use any standardized terminology for indicating their interpretive practices of allegory. Regarding the criterion of geographical location, we observe that the ancient interpretive practice of allegory was used for similar purposes in other locations. Virgil's satire of human toil by means of allegorical expression is mirrored in the animal allegories of ancient Egypt. Lucretius's explanation of Cybele is similar to the practices of those early Greek philosophers who allegorized Homer's stories. For these reasons, these authors' allegorical practices reveal additional sets of expressions that demonstrate how geographical location is not a suitable criterion for selecting comparative examples.

2.3.2. Technical Definitions of Allegorical Practices

Around the time that the Greeks began to define ἀλληγορ- in a technical sense, so did Romans begin to define terms they used in the ancient interpretive practice of allegory. Also like the Greeks, some Roman authors defined these terms within a system of rhetoric put forth within their own rhetorical handbooks.[52]

Cicero (first century BCE)—in addition to his comments above in section 2.2.2.2—describes the ancient interpretive practice of allegory in the following way: "But there is no mode of speech more effective in the case of single words, and none that adds more brilliance to the style; for from this class of expression comes a development not consisting in the metaphorical use of a single word [*in uno verbo translato*] but in a chain of words linked together, so that something other than what is said has to be understood" (*De or.* 3.166 [Sutton]). Additionally, he lists that allegory (*immutatio oratione*) can have the hermeneutical purpose of enabling jests (*mutatis verbis*) to become delightful (*venusta*) (2.261–62).

Quintilian (first century CE)—in addition to his comments above in section 2.2.2.2—describes the Roman use of allegory in the following

---

52. Unlike the widespread use of the term ἀλληγορ- in Greek rhetorical handbooks, the Latin term *allegoria* is mentioned only by Quintilian in *Inst.* 8.6.44. Other terms used in Italy are *aenigmata, translatio, immutatio, inversio,* and *permutatio.* After investigation, I have chosen the most relevant examples for discussion. Additionally, *aenigmata* and *permutatio* also were used for purposes other than the ancient interpretive practice of allegory. On the Latin *figura*, see Auerbach, "Figura." After a lengthy analysis, Auerbach affirms the fourth century CE was when *figura* and "the method of interpretation connected with it are fully developed in nearly all the Latin Church writers" (34).

way: "Allegory [*allegoria*], which people translate as *inversio*, presents one thing by its words and either (1) a different or (2) sometimes even a contrary thing by its sense" (*Inst.* 8.6.44 [Russell]).[53]

The anonymous author of *Rhetorica ad Herennium* (first century CE) describes allegory in the following way. He describes three hermeneutical purposes of the ancient practice along with relevant examples:

> Allegory [*permutatio*] is a manner of speech denoting one thing by the letter of the words, but another by their meaning [*aliud verbis aliud sententia demonstrans*]. It assumes three aspects: comparison [*similitudio*], argument [*argumentum*], and contrast [*contrarium*]. It operates through a comparison when a number of metaphors originating in a similarity in the mode of expression are set together, as follows: "For when dogs act the part of wolves, to what guardian, pray, are we going to entrust our herds of cattle?" An Allegory is presented in the form of argument when a similitude is drawn from a person or place or object in order to magnify or minify, as if one should call Drusus a "faded reflection of the Gracchi." An Allegory is drawn from a contrast if, for example, one should mockingly call a spendthrift and voluptuary frugal and thrifty. Both in this last type, based on a contrast, and in the first above, drawn from a comparison, we can through the metaphor make use of argument. In an Allegory operating through a comparison, as follows: "What says this king—our Agamemnon, or rather, such is his cruelty, our Atreus?" In an Allegory drawn from a contrast: for example, if we should call some undutiful man who has beaten his father "Aeneas," or an intemperate and adulterous man "Hippolytus." (*Rhet. Her.* 4.34.46 [Caplan])

These three definitions align with what we have observed in the Greeks' technical definitions of ἀλληγορ-, chiefly that the Greeks—and here, the Romans—are attempting to corral the diverse allegorical practice that they observe in their own geographical locations. Additionally, we observe no standardized terminology being used in these discussions (cf. n52) and no concern for the facticity of either the source or allegorical entities. Ultimately, both the Romans' allegorical practices and their technical definitions of the interpretive practice of allegory demonstrate that facticity, terminology, and geographical location are not suitable criteria for selecting comparative examples because they do not distinguish

---

53. Quintilian goes on to divide allegory into two types—pure or mixed—(*Inst.* 8.6.47–49) and to list the common abuses to the allegorical method (*Inst.* 8.6.50–51).

2.4. The Ancient Interpretive Practice of Allegory in Palestine

In Palestine, there are five sets of allegorists that are useful for this analysis. I have organized them by time period: allegorists before Paul and those roughly contemporary to Paul.

2.4.1. *Allegorists before Paul*

In Palestine, the earliest set of allegorists are those who wrote the Jewish Scriptures. In 2 Sam 11:26—12:15, the Lord sends Nathan to speak an allegory to David. In this ancient interpretive practice of allegory, a rich man takes a lamb from a poor man and kills the animal for a guest, although the rich man himself had many animals he could have used. David becomes angry at this story, but Nathan replies with this explanation: "You are the man!" (2 Sam 12:7). In this allegorical expression, Nathan allegorized David as a rich man in order to force him to confront his sin regarding Uriah and Bathsheba.

In the vision of Ezek 37:1–14, the Lord shows a valley full of bones to Ezekiel and orders him to prophesy over it. When Ezekiel obeys, he sees the bones come together with flesh and skin. After a second prophecy, breath enters the bodies and they come alive. At the end of this vision, the Lord concludes, "Mortal, these bones are the whole house of Israel. They say, 'Our bones are dried up, and our hope is lost; we are cut off completely.' Therefore prophesy, and say to them, 'Thus says the Lord God: I am going to open your graves, and bring you up from your graves, O my people; and I will bring you back to the land of Israel'" (Ezek 37:11–12). In this expression, God allegorizes Israel as a valley of dry bones that comes alive under his command.

Ps 80:7–14 describes a vine that the Lord freed, planted, and then nourished. Then, the psalmist laments, "Why then have you broken down its walls, so that all who pass along the way pluck its fruit?" (80:12). He ends by asking the Lord to turn again towards the vine and to care for it (80:14). In this expression, the psalmist allegorizes the nation of Israel into a vine for the purpose of asking God's help in a difficult situation.

These three expressions exhibit practices that are similar to what we have observed elsewhere. Second Samuel's allegorical expression of concrete entities as concrete entities is similar to "The Quarrel of the Body and the Head." The allegorical expression of Israel as objects in Ezekiel (i.e., bones) and Psalms (i.e., a vine) is similar to what we observed in Aristobulus (i.e., a hoof) and to what we observe in Paul (cf. sect. 2.4.2.3). Additionally, we observe no specific terminology being used in these allegorical expressions from the Jewish Scriptures.

2.4.2. Allegorists Roughly Contemporary to the Time of Paul

Four sets of allegorists operated in Palestine roughly contemporary to the time of Paul: the authors of the sectarian texts of the Dead Sea Scrolls, Josephus, the authors of the New Testament, and the rabbis—the rationale for including the fourth group is discussed below.

2.4.2.1. Sectarian Texts of the Dead Sea Scrolls

The first set of allegorists is the authors of the sectarian texts from the Dead Sea Scrolls. I devote more attention to their allegorical practices in chapter 4, and a few expressions are useful for evaluating the criteria of terminology and geographical location. One helpful expression is the famous "Allegory of the Well":

> And God recalled the covenant with the first ones, and he raised up from Aaron men of discernment and from Israel wise men; and he allowed them to hear. And they dug the well (of which it is written,) "the well was dug by the princes and excavated by the nobles of the people, with a ruler" (Num 21:18). The "well" is the Torah and those who "dig" it are the penitents of Israel who depart from the land of Judah and dwell in the land of Damascus. God called them all "princes," for they sought him and their honor was not rejected by anyone's mouth. And the "ruler" is the interpreter of the Torah, of whom Isaiah said, "He takes out a tool for his work" (Isa 54:16). And the "nobles of the people" are those who come to excavate the well with the statutes which were ordained by the ruler to walk in them in the entire time of evil, and (who) will obtain no others until the rise of one who will teach righteousness in the end of days. (CD VI, 2b–11a)

In this allegorical expression, the author allegorizes the concrete source entities of Num 21:18 (i.e., the well, the diggers, the staff, and the nobles) into both abstract (i.e., the law) and concrete (i.e., the community and their leader) allegorical entities. We observe a similar interpretive practice in the Pesher Habakkuk.

> [....Look, O traitors, and] s[ee; and wonder (and) be amazed, for I am doing a deed in your days that you would not believe if] it were told (Hab 1:5). (VACAT) [The interpretation of the passage concerns] [פשר] the traitors together with the Man of the Lie, for (they did) not [...] the Righteous Teacher from the mouth of God. And it concerns the trait[ors to] the new [covenant,] f[o]r they were not faithful to the covenant of God [and they profaned] his holy name. (1QpHab I, 16—II, 4a)

> "Woe to the one who builds a city with blood and founds a town on iniquity. Are not these from Yahweh of Hosts? Peoples toil for fire and nations grow weary for nothing" (Hab 2:13–14). (VACAT) The interpretation of the passage [פשר] concerns the Spouter of the Lie, who caused many to err, building a city of emptiness with bloodshed and establishing a congregation with falsehood, for the sake of its glory making many toil in the service of emptiness and saturating them with w[o]rks of falsehood, with the result that their labor is for nothing; so that they will come to judgements of fire, because they reviled and reproached the elect of God. (1QpHab X, 5b–13)

In these expressions, the authors are allegorically interpreting characters described in the book of Habakkuk as the members of their community and their adversaries. In the Pesher Habakkuk, we also observe that the term פשר is used to indicate the ancient interpretive practice of allegory (similar to how some authors used ἀλληγορ-).⁵⁴ However, פשר is not

---

54. The interpretive practice behind the sectarian's use of פשר, pointed out by various scholars (cf. ch. 4n4), may be related in some way to the ancient use of the Akkadian *pišru* (Martha Roth, "*pasaru*," *CAD* 12:236–45). In recent years, one scholar has drawn attention to the fact that both terms in their respective contexts must be used exegetically when the interpretation "is required to agree with a specific element in reality" (Gabbay, "Akkadian Commentaries," 304). This exegesis can be allegorical. The operation behind the use of these terms aligns with the observation that similar interpretive practices of allegory can be found in different geographical locations and time periods. Gabbay summarizes his argument in the following way: "Taking the pesharim as an example, it is evident that the writers of the pesharim were surely not aware of the letters of scholars to the Assyrian king written over 500 years before their time, from which most of the information about the term *pišru* can be acquired. However, these

used in CD VI, 2b–11a above.⁵⁵ Regarding geographical location, Philo and the Aramaic targumim interpret Num 21:18 in a similar way as the authors of CD VI, 2b–11a ("Allegory of the Well").⁵⁶ Accordingly, these allegorical expressions are another set of evidence that indicates how terminology and geographical location are not useful criteria for selecting comparative examples.

2.4.2.2. Josephus

The second allegorist, Josephus, allegorizes in the following way:

> For if one reflects on the construction of the tabernacle and looks at the vestments of the priest and the vessels which we use for the sacred ministry, he will discover that our lawgiver was a man of God and that these blasphemous charges brought against us by the rest of men are idle. In fact, every one of these objects [in the tabernacle] is intended to recall and represent the universe, as he will find if he will but consent to examine them without prejudice and with understanding. Thus, to take the tabernacle, thirty cubits long, by dividing this into three parts and giving up two of them to the priests, as a place approachable and open to all, Moses signifies the earth and sea, since these too are accessible to all.... Again, by placing upon the bale the twelve loaves, he signifies that the year is divided into as many months.... The tapestries woven of four materials denote the natural elements. (*Ant.* 3.179–83 [Thackeray])

Josephus is profoundly instructive because, although writing from Rome, he was a Jew trained in Palestine.⁵⁷ However, his interpretive practice is

---

letters are one reflection of a more general notion of *pišru* which happens to come up in the letters, *but which surely also existed independently of them*" (312; emphasis added). For a more detailed analysis that leads to the same conclusion, see Machiela, "Qumran Pesharim."

55. One scholar has argued, "Sometimes, an ancient author (e.g., the author of CD) assumes that his readers will infer the *pesher* from mere reference to a biblical verse" (Kister, "Biblical Phrases," 38). There simply is no evidence here for this position. Rather, this chapter demonstrates that the variety found in the sectarian interpretive practice of allegory—as it relates to the use of terminology—aligns with the variety observed in other allegorical expressions within the ancient world.

56. Flusser, *Judaism of Second Temple*, 18–19.

57. Although Josephus likely wrote this allegory in Rome, we know that he traveled there later in life after receiving his education in Palestine (*Vita* 1–3). It is for this reason that I have included him in this section. It is important to remember that my use of

more akin to Philo's allegorical expression of objects into abstract entities.[58] For this reason, when Josephus's practice is engaged, often it is grouped with the Alexandrian authors' and given little attention.[59] This grouping is unfortunate because Josephus's allegorical expression is another example demonstrating how no single geographical location had a monopoly on one type of expression within the ancient interpretive practice of allegory.

2.4.2.3. The New Testament

The ancient interpretive practice of allegory is used often within the New Testament. For example, the Gospel writers present Jesus as allegorizing in parables.[60]

> Keep awake therefore, for you do not know on what day your Lord is coming. But understand this: if the owner of the house had known in what part of the night the thief was coming, he would have stayed awake and would not have let his house be broken into. Therefore you also must be ready, for the Son of Man is coming at an unexpected hour. (Matt 24:42–44)

---

geographical locations as categories is a heuristic tool only and does not indicate any argument for its significance within the ancient interpretive practice of allegory.

58. Josephus also shares Philo's concern for Moses and the law: "For, studying it in this spirit, nothing will appear to them unreasonable, nothing incongruous with the majesty of God and His love for man; everything, indeed, is here set forth in keeping with the nature of the universe; some things the lawgiver shrewdly veils in enigmas, others he sets forth in solemn allegory [ἀλληγοροῦντος]; but wherever straightforward speech was expedient, there he makes his meaning absolutely plain" (Josephus, *Ant.* 1.24 [Thackeray]).

59. Some examples include Anderson, *Ancient Rhetorical Theory*, 177; Barker, "Allegory and Typology," 204; De Boer, *Galatians*, 295; Di Mattei, "Paul's Allegory," 106; R. P. C.Hanson, *Allegory and Event*, 53–54; McClane, "Hellenistic Background," 132. One exception is Büchsel: "What we see in Josephus does not indicate, therefore, that there was any essential difference between Palestinian and Alexandrian allegorizing" (*TDNT* 1:263). As noted previously, I engage the categories of Palestinian and Alexandrian allegory in ch. 3.

60. In addition to Matt 24:42–44 (the thief in the night), see Matt 25:14–30 (the parable of the talents); Luke 10:30–35 (the good Samaritan); Luke 15:11–31 (the prodigal son); etc. Accordingly, despite the many claims that the some church fathers (often labeled as Antiochene) modeled their allegory after Philo, Young Min Hyun insightfully points out that the fathers could have been following Jesus's example (Hyun, "Bible, Allegory, and Poetry," 304).

Here, Jesus allegorizes his listeners as the owner of the house in order to exhort them to be ready for the Son of Man's arrival.[61] In Hebrews, the author uses allegory in many places similar to Philo of Alexandria.[62] The allegorical expressions in the New Testament most helpful for examining the criteria, however, are those found in Paul's other letters. Scholars who discuss Paul's interpretive practice of allegory point to one or more of five pericopes. I have included each here (with the exception of Gal 4:21–31):

> Your boasting is not a good thing. Do you not know that a little yeast leavens the whole batch of dough? Clean out the old yeast so that you may be a new batch, as you really are unleavened. (1 Cor 5:6–7)

> For it is written in the Law of Moses, "You shall not muzzle an ox while it is treading out the grain. Is it for oxen that God is concerned?" Or does he not speak entirely for our sake? It was indeed written for our sake, for whoever plows should plow in hope and whoever threshes should thresh in hope of a share in the crop. (1 Cor 9:9–10)

> I do not want you to be unaware, brothers and sisters, that our ancestors were all under the cloud, and all passed through the sea, and all were baptized into Moses in the cloud and in the sea, and all ate the same spiritual food, and all drank the same spiritual drink. For they drank from the spiritual rock that followed them, and the rock was Christ. Nevertheless, God was not pleased with most of them, and they were struck down in the wilderness. Now these things occurred as examples for us, so that we might not desire evil as they did. Do not become idolaters as some of them did; as it is written, "The people sat down to eat and drink, and they rose up to play." We must not indulge in sexual immorality as some of them did, and twenty-three thousand fell in a single day. We must not put Christ to

---

61. Some prior scholarship distinguishes between allegory and parable. Other scholarship does not distinguish. For a discussion of arguments supporting each position, see Blomberg, *Interpreting the Parables*, 29–49. Despite some differences between allegory and parable, they do share a similar method. Mikael Parsons describes it in this way: "In comparison to parable, however, allegory is reducible to a nonfigurative level and offers a much more limited range of interpretation than does parable. *It shares symbolic mode with parable but tends to be less open to true polyvalence*" ("Allegorizing Allegory," 152; emphasis added). John Dominic Crossan describes it in this way: "Allegory and parable agree in that both operate on two levels: they disagree in that allegory is reducible and parable is not" ("Parable and Example," 87).

62. Svendsen, *Allegory Transformed*, 55–69.

the test, as some of them did, and were destroyed by serpents. And do not complain as some of them did, and were destroyed by the destroyer. These things happened to them to serve as an example, and they were written down to instruct us, on whom the ends of the ages have come. (1 Cor 10:1–11)

Since, then, we have such a hope, we act with great boldness, not like Moses, who put a veil over his face to keep the people of Israel from gazing at the end of the glory that was being set aside. But their minds were hardened. Indeed, to this very day, when they hear the reading of the old covenant, that same veil is still there, since only in Christ is it set aside. Indeed, to this very day whenever Moses is read, a veil lies over their minds; but when one turns to the Lord, the veil is removed. Now the Lord is the Spirit, and where the Spirit of the Lord is, there is freedom. And all of us, with unveiled faces, seeing the glory of the Lord as though reflected in a mirror, are being transformed into the same image from one degree of glory to another; for this comes from the Lord, the Spirit. (2 Cor 3:12–18)

These four allegorical expressions demonstrate that Gal 4:21–31 is not the only place where Paul used the ancient interpretive practice of allegory. The fact that Paul used no terminology in these four expressions, but did in 4:24, reveals that his use of terminology aligns with what we have observed elsewhere. Regarding Paul's use of τύποι (cf. 1 Cor 10:6) and τυπικῶς (cf. 1 Cor 10:11), chapter 3, section 2, demonstrates there is no evidence within Paul's milieu to support (1) understanding the root τυπ- as a technical term or (2) interpreting the use of τυπ- as a concern for facticity. Additionally, scholars have misunderstood Paul's interpretive practice of allegory in 1 Cor 10:1–11. It is not expressed in 10:6 or 11, but in 10:4: "And the rock was Christ." In addition to these expressions, it is possible to point out two other expressions within Paul's writings that have not been identified previously within scholarship on Gal 4:21–31.

And so, brothers and sisters, I could not speak to you as spiritual people, but rather as people of the flesh, as infants in Christ. I fed you with milk, not solid food, for you were not ready for solid food. Even now you are still not ready, for you are still of the flesh. (1 Cor 3:1–3)

For just as the body is one and has many members, and all the members of the body, though many, are one body, so it is with Christ. For in the one Spirit we were all baptized into one body—Jews or Greeks, slaves or free—and we were all made to drink of one Spirit. Indeed, the body does not consist of one member but of many. If the foot would say, "Because I am not a hand, I do not belong to the body," that would not make it any less a part of the body. And if the ear would say, "Because I am not an eye, I do not belong to the body," that would not make it any less a part of the body. If the whole body were an eye, where would the hearing be? If the whole body were hearing, where would the sense of smell be? But as it is, God arranged the members in the body, each one of them, as he chose. If all were a single member, where would the body be? As it is, there are many members, yet one body. The eye cannot say to the hand, "I have no need of you," nor again the head to the feet, "I have no need of you." On the contrary, the members of the body that seem to be weaker are indispensable, and those members of the body that we think less honorable we clothe with greater honor, and our less respectable members are treated with greater respect; whereas our more respectable members do not need this. But God has so arranged the body, giving the greater honor to the inferior member, that there may be no dissension within the body, but the members may have the same care for one another. (1 Cor 12:12–25)

Paul allegorizing spiritual maturity as food in the first allegorical expression also is observable in Philo (e.g., *Migr.* 29; *Congr.* 19; *Agr.* 9). Paul allegorizing the community as parts of the body in the second expression also is observable in "The Quarrel of the Body and the Head" from Egypt, as well as in Livy, *Ab urbe cond.* 2.32; and Plutarch, *Cor.* 6, from Italy. More striking is that both the purpose and message for which Paul uses his interpretive practice in 1 Cor 12:12–25 are nearly identical to those in "The Quarrel of the Body and the Head."

The preceding analysis of Paul's practice is another demonstration of how prior scholarship's criteria cannot be used to distinguish individual allegorical practices from each other regarding their similarities or differences.

2.4.2.4. The Rabbis[63]

The final group of allegorists is the rabbis. Although the extant writings are later, there is evidence that some of the early Tannaim allegorized.[64] First, the later rabbis record two earlier groups that interpreted Jewish Scriptures allegorically: the *Dorshe Reshumot* and the *Dorshe Hamurot*.[65]

> "And the Lord showed him a tree, and he cast it into the waters, and the waters were made sweet" (Exod 15:25). The *Dorshe Reshumot* said, He showed him the words of the Torah, which are designated as a tree in a figurative sense, as it is said (Prov 3:18): "She (the Torah, or Wisdom) is a tree of life to them that lay hold of her." (Mek. de Rabbi Shimon, Exod 15:25 [Lauterbach])

> The *Dorshe Reshumot* said, Rephidim (mentioned in Exod 17:8 as the place where Amalek fought with Israel) means nothing else than "weakness of hands," because the Israelites relaxed in their keeping of the law, therefore came the enemy upon them, for the enemy comes only because of sin and transgression. (Mek. de Rabbi Shimon, Exod 17:8 [Lauterbach])

> The *Dorshe Hamurot* said (interpreting Deut 18:3), The shoulder corresponds to, or is a symbol for, the arm of a priest, as it is said of Phinehas, "and he took a javelin in his hand" (Num 25:7). (*Sifrei Devarim*, Deut, 165 [Lauterbach])

> The *Dorshe Hamurot* said (regarding the passage Deut 12:3), "And ye shall overthrow their altars." How have the wood and stones sinned that they should be destroyed? It is merely because some mishap came to man through them that the Scripture orders them to be destroyed. Now, if the law orders that pieces of wood and stones, which can possess neither merit nor guilt, neither goodness nor evil, only because they have caused

---

63. Although rabbinic literature was written later and some not in Palestine, my analysis discusses allegorical expressions that likely originated in Palestine. Nevertheless, it is important to remember that my use of geographical locations as categories is a heuristic tool only and does not indicate any argument for its significance.

64. In an article that has proven to be very influential, Joseph Bonsirven organizes Tannaitic rabbinic allegory into six categories ("Exégèse allégorique"). He uses various allegorical expressions from rabbinic literature to support his categories.

65. Lauterbach, "Ancient Jewish Allegorists" and "Ancient Jewish Allegorists (Continued)." Despite being written over a century ago, this work regularly is cited in scholarship on rabbinic allegory (if for no other reason than its useful collection of primary sources).

some moral harm to man, should by destroyed, then, how much more is a man to be punished who causes his fellow-man to sin, and leads him away from the path of life unto the path of death? (Sem. 8 [Lauterbach])

It has been argued that the rabbis grew uncomfortable with the *Dorshe Reshumot* and the *Dorshe Hamurot*.[66] If this was true, we should understand this response to be the result of the rabbis becoming more uncomfortable with the diverse ways in which the interpretive practice of allegory *already* was being used, not as these groups' practice becoming less concerned with facticity (as is argued).[67] This is supported by two pieces of evidence: (1) some interpretations of the *Dorshe Reshumot* are similar to Philo—Mek. de Rabbi Ishmael, 52b; and Philo, *Leg.* 2.21; Mek. de Rabbi Shimon, 53a; and Philo, *Post.* 14[68]—and (2) the rabbis' apologetic allegorical expression of the Song of Songs is similar to the way that the Greeks allegorized Homer. In fact, so many similarities exist between rabbinic allegory and allegory in Greece that one scholar has argued Rabbi Hillel based his seven principles of interpretation on Hellenistic rhetoric.[69] The second evidence is that the Tannaim allegorized the Song of Songs.[70]

> The Song of Songs, interpreted literally as a fine collection of love-lyrics, is of little or no spiritual value, and would certainly not have been admissible as canonical literature. But, interpreted as an allegory of the love of Yahweh for his people, it has constantly been used as an aid to devotion in both Jewish and Christian faiths.[71]

The final evidence is that innumerable allegorical expressions centered around twelve themes already have been identified in rabbinic literature.[72]

---

66. Lauterbach, "Ancient Jewish Allegorists," 304.

67. Lauterbach argued that the rabbis feared the method "might lead to the denial of the historic facts narrated in the Bible" ("Ancient Jewish Allegorists," 330). In other words, the rabbis were concerned with facticity.

68. For these examples, see Lauterbach, "Ancient Jewish Allegorists," 310–11.

69. Daube, "Rabbinic Methods of Interpretation."

70. The rabbinic practice of allegorizing the Song of Songs is acknowledged widely. For evidence that the Tannaim allegorized it, see Instone-Brewer, *Techniques and Assumptions*, 69–70, 169; Fields, "Jewish Interpretation"; R. P. C. Hanson, *Allegory and Event*, 33–34; Kaplan, *My Perfect One*; Kaplan, "Song of Songs"; Manns, "Jewish Interpretations."

71. Woollcombe, "Biblical Origins," 54.

72. Asher Feldman has thoroughly engaged twelve distinct themes that the rabbis

It is unlikely this expansive allegorical practice of the rabbis originated only with later rabbis.

The rabbis' allegorical practices are one final set of practices that belonged to a diverse ancient interpretive practice of allegory and that cannot be distinguished from other practices in meaningful ways by the criteria of facticity, terminology, and geographical location.

3. RESULTS OF THE EXAMINATION

Now that we have completed the analyses of the three criteria within the ancient interpretive practice of allegory up to the time of Paul, it is possible to fully coalesce the results and demonstrate how the use of these criteria to select comparative examples does not enable an analysis of Paul's practice that situates it appropriately within the ancient interpretive practice of allegory.

3.1. Facticity

Regarding facticity, the analysis demonstrates that a concern for facticity did not influence the ancient interpretive practice of allegory. It is not that ancient allegorists were unable to distinguish between fiction and nonfiction—they could, and a concern for facticity could be the reason why they are allegorizing (e.g., those who defended Homer, such as Strabo)—but *there is no indication that facticity impacted what took place when the allegorical practice is used*. We observe this same scenario in Paul. Paul's use of concrete and abstract entities was no different than his contemporaries' uses of them. In 1 Cor 9:9–10, Paul allegorized a creature (i.e., an ox) into a character (i.e., someone who preaches the gospel). In 1 Cor 12:12–25, he allegorized characters (i.e., the community in Corinth) into objects (i.e., parts of the body). In 1 Cor 10:1–11, we observed the reverse: Paul allegorized an object (i.e., a rock) into a character (i.e., Jesus). Additionally, despite some scholars having argued otherwise (cf. n1), Paul did use abstract entities within his interpretive practice of allegory. He allegorized objects into abstract entities: food into spiritual maturity in

---

allegorized. These include (1) the fields, their cultivation and ducts; (2) the garden; (3) trees; (4) viticulture; (5) the fig; (6) the olive; (7) the palm; (8) the nut tree; (9) the thorn and the reed; (10) the lily; (11) the myrtle; (12) pastoral allegories. See Feldman, *Parables and Similes*, 26–226.

1 Cor 3:1–3 and yeast into sin in 1 Cor 5:6–7. Most important, however, is that he allegorized characters into abstract entities: "These women are two covenants" (Gal 4:24). This allegorical expression is very important because it demonstrates *how Paul in Gal 4:24 can do exactly what Philo did* in his interpretive practice (i.e., Sarah as "virtue" and Hagar as "education" [*Congr.* 23]). Regarding the historical sense, there is no difference between Paul and Philo.[73] For all these reasons, to claim that Paul's practice is influenced by facticity is to misrepresent both Paul and the ancient interpretive practice to which he belongs. Accordingly, examples chosen based on the criterion of facticity do not enable a more precise understanding of Paul's practice.

3.2. Terminology

Regarding terminology, the analysis demonstrates the use of terminology was variegated among ancient allegorists. Different allegorists used different terms; sometimes, the same allegorist used different terms. Other times, no terms were used. These circumstances were observed across various locations and within the same location. In Greece, we observed that allegorists sometimes used ἀλληγορ- to indicate their own practice, and other times the root was applied to their expressions only by later authors. Others used the root to define allegorical practices in a technical sense. In Italy, a similar situation existed. Additionally, in Italy we observed terms other than *allegoria* being used to indicate the interpretive practice of allegory: *inverso, immutatio,* and *permutatio*. In Palestine, we observed that the authors of the sectarian texts of the Dead Sea Scrolls used similar interpretive practices both with פשר (cf. Pesher Habakkuk) and without it (cf. Damascus Document). This variety of practice also existed in Paul's letters, as Paul did not use terminology except in Gal 4:24.

Because of the ways in which ancient allegorists did and did not use terminology, it is dangerous to explain Paul's practice by means of ἀλληγορ- for the following reasons. First, it is unclear how well Paul understood the term and the different explanations of it. It could be that Paul had only a basic understanding of the term or that he used it only because he thought it might impress his audience. Second, one could ask if Paul truly understood what it meant, why did he use it only in Gal

---

73. This also was recognized in 1919 (Kennedy, *Philo's Contribution to Religion*, 41). I have found no one else who makes this argument.

4:24 when he demonstrably allegorizes elsewhere? Thus, although it is indeed possible to distinguish ancient interpretive practices from each other by terminology, this criterion amounts to nothing more than an organizational tool when analyzing Paul's practice alongside the interpretive practices of other allegorists.

3.3. Geographical Location

Regarding geographical location, the analysis demonstrates that similar interpretive practices are found in various geographical locations. These practices are similar regarding their source and allegorical entities, their variety of terminology, and their hermeneutical purposes. The chief example is "The Quarrel of the Body and the Head" found in Egypt, found later in Italy, and also found in Paul's own writings. There are, however, other important allegorical expressions. In Egypt, "The Blinding of Truth" personifies abstract source entities similar to Vergil and Ovid in Italy. In Italy, the allegorical expression of concrete entities into abstract entities (cf. Horace and Lucretius) is similar to what we observed in Alexandria (i.e., Pseudo-Aristeas, Aristobulus, and Philo) and in Josephus. Last, we observed the allegorical expression of objects by the *Dorshe Reshumot* and *Dorshe Hamurot*, which is similar to the practice in the Egyptian Book of the Dead. For Paul, we observed similar practices both within and outside Palestine. On the one hand, we observed Paul allegorizing the Torah as an object similarly to the *Dorshe Reshumot*'s allegorical expression of the Torah as an object. On the other hand, we observed him allegorizing objects into abstract entities similarly to the Ramesseum Dramatic Papyrus in Egypt and to Plato's "Allegory of the Cave" in Greece. The most significant example, noted above, is that Paul allegorized characters into abstract entities (i.e., as covenants) in Gal 4:24 no differently than Philo allegorized characters within the patriarchal narrative (i.e., as the human soul's progression to wisdom). For all these reasons, it is clear that practices used by allegorists in one location also were used by allegorists in other locations. Therefore, the criterion of geographical location—no differently than the criterion of terminology—amounts to nothing more than an organizational tool when employed for an analysis of Paul's practice within the ancient interpretive practice of allegory.

3.4. Next Steps

In this chapter, I demonstrated how facticity, terminology, and geographical location are not suitable criteria for selecting comparative examples because they do not distinguish one ancient allegorical practice from another in terms of their similarities and differences: facticity did not influence ancient allegorical practices, and both terminology and geographical location are only modern organizational tools. Therefore, comparative examples chosen by these criteria do not situate an analysis of Paul's interpretive practice appropriately within the ancient interpretive practice of allegory and therefore do not enable us to better understand Paul's interpretive practice by comparative analysis.

The use of these three criteria and the resultant comparative examples have birthed two interpretive schemata that prior scholarship has used to examine Paul's practice: (1) Hellenistic, Alexandrian, and Palestinian allegory, and (2) typology. In the next chapter, I examine these schemata and demonstrate how they misrepresent both Paul's practice and the ancient interpretive practice to which he belonged. Then, I proffer a different set of criteria for identifying comparative examples and my approach for attaining a more precise understanding of the interpretive practice behind Paul's use of ἀλληγορούμενα.

3

Evaluating the Interpretive Schemata Used by Prior Scholarship to Examine Paul's Interpretive Practice of Allegory, and My Approach

THIS CHAPTER EXAMINES THE interpretive schemata that prior scholarship has used to explain Paul's interpretive practice alongside comparative examples. Prior scholarship has used two interpretive schemata: (1) Hellenistic, Alexandrian, and Palestinian allegory, and (2) typology. In this chapter, I examine these two interpretive schemata and argue that they do not accurately reflect the way in which the ancient interpretive practice of allegory—including Paul's practice—operated. This misrepresentation is the result of (1) the first schema being based on the criteria of facticity and geographical location and (2) the second schema being based on facticity and terminology. At the end of this chapter, I provide a different approach—including a different set of criteria for selecting comparative examples—that enables the selection of suitable comparative examples that situates the examination of Paul's interpretive practice appropriately within the ancient interpretive practice of allegory and consequently enables a more precise understanding of Paul's interpretive practice. This chapter is divided into three sections: Hellenistic, Alexandrian, and Palestinian allegory; typology; my approach and criteria.

1. HELLENISTIC, ALEXANDRIAN, AND PALESTINIAN ALLEGORY

In 1959, within his seminal work *Allegory and Event*, R. P. C. Hanson solidified the first interpretive schema. He divided ancient allegory into three traditions: Hellenistic, Alexandrian, and Palestinian.[1] Although Hanson did not provide a precise explanation for each tradition, what follows are definitions based on a close reading of his text:

- The Hellenistic tradition was the earliest allegorical tradition, which began with either Theagenes of Rhegium or Pherecydes of Syros in the sixth century BCE.[2] These writers as well as the Stoics of the fourth and third century BCE used allegory to defend Homer's description of the gods against accusations of sacrilege.[3] This tradition was entirely unhistorical, taking "no account of the historical situation, the original meaning, or the material allegorized"; it was arbitrary and required no history at all. It was the tradition from which the Alexandrian tradition was born.[4]

- The Alexandrian tradition developed out of the Hellenistic tradition, examples being found in the writings of Aristobulus, Josephus, Philo, and Pseudo-Aristeas.[5] It retained the unhistorical nature of the Hellenistic tradition, yet other characteristics were different because each writer was a Jew.[6] In this tradition, the hermeneutical assumptions about the allegorized text were very different.[7] As a result, a literal sense of the text was preserved, although it acted only as an "outer shell" for the deeper and more important allegorical meanings.[8]

- The Palestinian tradition was a part of Palestinian Judaism and developed independently of either the Hellenistic or Alexandrian

---

1. R. P. C. Hanson, *Allegory and Event*, 11–64. Hanson was not the first to use location as a schema for categorizing allegorical practices. As early as 1900, other scholars treated allegory similarly (e.g., Thackeray, *Relation*, 190–200). A more recent precursor was Pépin, *Mythe et Allégorie*, 221–31. Hanson, however, remains the most substantial attempt to present traditions and a developmental schema for each.
2. R. P. C. Hanson, *Allegory and Event*, 55.
3. R. P. C. Hanson, *Allegory and Event*, 56.
4. R. P. C. Hanson, *Allegory and Event*, 62.
5. R. P. C. Hanson, *Allegory and Event*, 41, 53–54, 62.
6. R. P. C. Hanson, *Allegory and Event*, 62.
7. R. P. C. Hanson, *Allegory and Event*, 63.
8. R. P. C. Hanson, *Allegory and Event*, 25.

tradition.[9] In contrast to the Alexandrian tradition, this tradition never challenged the validity of the literal sense in favor of the allegorical sense.[10] It was "full of typology, closely linked with historical events, unenterprising in its speculation and motivation by either Messianic eschatological expectation or a tense devotion to the Torah."[11]

These three traditions do not accurately reflect the ancient interpretive practice of allegory for the following reasons. First, Hanson's traditions are based on geographical location—more specifically, on *his* perception of whether allegorists in those geographical locations were concerned with facticity. As I demonstrated in chapter 2, facticity did not influence allegorical practice, and geographical location does not distinguish allegorical expressions in terms of their similarities and differences within the ancient interpretive practice of allegory.[12] Second, Hanson aligns his traditions with three approaches towards Judaism: non-Jews who used non-Jewish methods (i.e., Hellenistic), Jews who used Hellenistic methods influenced by Judaism (i.e., Alexandrian), and Jews who used Jewish methods not influenced by Hellenism (i.e., Palestinian). This Judeocentric approach is not reflected within the ancient practice because it assumes that the influence of "Judaism"—as he understands it—on allegorists can be categorized neatly and because it places restrictions on how Jews used the practice.[13] Last, Hanson's developmental schema for the traditions, outlined in this visual diagram, does not accurately reflect the way in which the ancient interpretive practice operated.[14]

9. R. P. C. Hanson, *Allegory and Event*, 35.
10. R. P. C. Hanson, *Allegory and Event*, 25.
11. R. P. C. Hanson, *Allegory and Event*, 63.

12. The difficulty of maintaining these distinctions is evident in Hanson's own writings. For example, he concedes concerning Josephus: "One conclusion which might be drawn from this interesting variation is that there were more schools of thought than Philo's to be encountered in the Alexandrian tradition" (*Allegory and Event*, 54).

13. Hanson's Judeocentric approach has implications for the role of Judaism in the diaspora. On the one hand, his definitions for the Alexandrian and Palestinian traditions intimate the argument that a Jew can use a *Jewish* method only in Palestine. On the other hand, they intimate that a Jew cannot use a *Hellenistic* method unless in the diaspora. This is problematic both because of how he uses geographical location and because he distinguishes between a *Jewish* allegorical practice in contrast to a *Hellenistic* one. Neither is an appropriate distinction.

14. This developmental schema also permeates scholarship on ancient allegory. For example, Dawson argues: "Jewish and Christian reliance on allegorical techniques was enabled, but not mandated, by the wider Hellenistic culture," and "from the works of

Hellenistic	→	Alexandrian	←	Palestinian
(earliest)		(originates from Hellenistic, influenced by Palestinian)		(develops independently, influences Alexandrian)

This proposed development is difficult to accept for two reasons. First, it overlooks important extant evidence in Egypt and Italy, much of which was discussed in chapter 2. Second, Hanson's development evaluates the evidence as if it represents *standardized* traditions within the ancient interpretive practice of allegory. However, as I demonstrated in chapter 2, sections 2.2.2.2 and 2.3.2, even those who sought to define the practice in a standardized way only were describing what they observed (e.g., the rhetorical handbooks of Greece and Italy). For all these reasons, this schema misrepresents both Paul's practice and the ancient interpretive practice to which it belonged. *Put simply, there are no Alexandrian, Hellenistic, or Palestinian traditions, because allegorical practices cannot be siloed as Jewish, Greek, or any combination of the two.* This is significant because although most scholars have abandoned Hanson's terms, chapter 2, sections 1.1 (i.e., facticity) and 1.3 (i.e., geographical location), already have demonstrated how the criteria upon which they are based remain very influential in scholarship on Gal 4:21–31. We must abandon not only Hanson's terms *but also their assumptions* because neither enables an analysis of Paul's practice that produces a more precise understanding of it.

2. TYPOLOGY

In chapter 1, section 2.2.1, we observed how some scholars have labeled Paul's interpretive practice as typology in contrast to or in addition to allegory. Again, I quote Woollcombe's definition.

> Typological exegesis is the search for linkages between events, persons or things *within the historical framework of revelation*, whereas allegorism is the search for a secondary and hidden meaning underlying the primary and obvious meaning of the narrative. This secondary sense of a narrative, discovered by

---

Aristeas, Aristobulus, and others like them, Philo learned that allegory might be used to systematically associate nonscriptural, Hellenistic meanings with scripture" (*Allegorical Readers*, 24, 73). It remains unclear how one can distinguish *enabling*, *mandating*, and *learning* within the ancient interpretive practice of allegory.

allegorism, does not necessarily have any connection at all with the historical framework of revelation.[15]

In addition to Woollcombe, seven other scholars mention typology explicitly when describing Paul's interpretive practice in Gal 4:21–31 (cf. ch. 2n1) and others describe this concern using different nomenclature.[16] This schema does not accurately reflect the ancient interpretive practice of allegory for the following reasons. First, the argument for a "historical framework," as well as the various other scholars' similar explanations, demonstrates this schema is based on the criterion of facticity. However, facticity is not related to allegorical practice in this way (cf. ch. 2). Second, the argument that the root τύπ- (e.g., Paul's use of τύποι in 1 Cor 10:6 and τυπικῶς in 10:11) indicates Paul used typology demonstrates this schema also is based on the criterion of terminology. Although I already have demonstrated that terminology cannot be used in this way, four additional pieces of evidence confirm my position as it relates specifically to the root τύπ-. First, I have found no ancient author before or roughly contemporary to Paul who uses the root τύπ- to indicate any concept similar to Woollcombe's definition of typology.[17] Second, I have found no ancient allegorist who uses the root τύπ- differently than ἀλληγορ- (cf. the discussion of Philo in ch. 5, sect. 4). Third, I have found one roughly contemporary allegorist (i.e., the author of the Epistle of Barnabas) who uses τύπ- in the exact way from which some scholars hope to rescue Paul. This allegorist uses τύπ- to strip the historical meaning out of a text (cf. ch. 6, sect. 4). Fourth, as noted in chapter 2, section 2.4.2.3, Paul's allegorical practice in 1 Cor 10:1–11 *actually* is found within 10:4 ("The rock was Christ") and not in 10:6 or 10:11. The preceding evidence indicates that the explanation of Paul's practice as typology is based on a malnourished interpretation of one Pauline pericope (1 Cor 10:1–11) without considering the broader interpretive context to which it and Gal 4:21–31 belong.

---

15. Woollcombe, "Biblical Origins," 40; emphasis original.

16 For example, Svendsen describes the difference as vertical (i.e., allegory) or horizontal connections (i.e., typology) (*Allegory Transformed*, 56). James Barr describes it as a "resultant" system in which the interpretation works out (e.g., philosophy, theology, mysticism, etc.) (*Old and New*, 108). The most interesting example is G. P. Hugenberger, who offers a visual diagram distinguishing allegory from typology, symbolism, and moralism ("Introductory Notes on Typology," 340). Within these examples, facticity remains the most influential factor for distinguishing allegory from typology.

17. As noted previously in ch. 1n64 it is not until John Chrysostom in the fourth century CE that we observe allegory and typology distinguished from one another (*Hom. Gal.* 4:24).

Although others have posited that the distinction between allegory and typology is a false one within Paul's milieu,[18] I am the first to demonstrate it by means of a thorough and systematic engagement with the ancient interpretive practice of allegory up to Paul's time.

Although typology does not reflect the ancient interpretive practice of allegory in Paul's milieu, the intense discussion surrounding it has borne fruit. First, it has reminded us that Paul used his interpretive practice at a time when a Jesus-centric understanding of the Jewish Scriptures was not fully formed but developing.[19] In other words, Paul is not simply using previously established ways to talk about Christ; rather, he is one of those who is creating ways—including allegorical ways—to talk about Christ.

Second, the discussion has highlighted that typology does not provide the historical primacy often sought after in arguments for typology (cf. ch. 2, sect. 1.1).

> Even when a reader does not explicitly reject the first meaning, but simply adds a second to it, the mere presence of the addition implicitly denies the independence or exclusivity of the first meaning.[20]

This is correct. No matter how someone attempts to explain Paul's practice, Paul still ultimately denies "the independence or exclusivity" of prior interpretations of Gen 16–21.

A third piece of fruit borne from discussions of typology is an engagement with the concept of *sensus literalis*.[21] Although not concerned with ancient allegory, this discussion informs the analysis of the ancient interpretive practice of allegory in two ways. First, it demonstrates that the pervasive concern for facticity is a result of the rise of historical criticism. Before the rise of historical criticism, only the literal details of the source text were important. In his 1975 seminal work, *The Eclipse*

---

18. Damgaard, "Hinsides typologisk," 116; Goppelt, *Typos*, 4; Hays, *Echoes of Scripture*, 116; Svendsen, *Allegory Transformed*, 57; Young, "Alexandrian and Antiochene Exegesis," 1:337; Young, "Typology," 33.

19. Barr notes that, "Thus the men of the New Testament were able to be creative in relation to the habits of their time, just as non-Christian interpreters could be; but in so doing they did not recover the Old Testament, as it had been, in any level or homogeneous way" (Barr, *Old and New*, 130). See also Perriman, "Typology in Paul," 201.

20. Dawson, *Allegorical Readers*, 9.

21. In the last quarter of the twentieth century, one group of scholars—those associated with "canonical criticism"—has fought for allegory in response to the rise of historical criticism.

of Biblical Narrative, Hans Frei argued that the rise of historical critical scholarship in the eighteenth and nineteenth century created a division between literal and figural readings.

> Literal and figural reading of the biblical narratives, once natural allies, not only came apart, but the successors looked with great unease at each other—historical criticism and biblical theology were different enterprises and made for decidedly strained company.[22]

Although Frei did not apply his sentiments to modern scholarship, others soon did. Building on the work of Frei, Brevard Childs argued that what was once the *sensus literalis*—a reading not influenced by facticity—now has become synonymous with the *sensus originalis*—a reading grounded in facticity.[23] As Frei states, "If it seemed clear that a biblical story was to be read literally, *it followed automatically that it referred to and described actual historical occurrences*."[24] Therefore, argued Childs, historical critics were concerned more with the "multiple layers below the text," rather than the "multiple layers of meanings above the text."[25] In a response to Childs,[26] James Barr advanced this discussion by highlighting how the historical critical movement *in actuality* was focused on the *sensus historicus*.[27] Conversely, Barr argued that what is most important for allegory is not facticity but the literal details of a source text:

> From the beginning allegory was built upon the literal details of the text. Emphasis upon literal detail, and the ultimate

---

22. Frei, *Eclipse of Biblical Narrative*, 8.
23. Childs, "Sensus Literalis of Scripture," 89.
24. Frei, *Eclipse of Biblical Narrative*, 2; emphasis added.
25. Childs, "Sensus Literalis of Scripture," 93.

26. Twelve years after Childs's article, James Barr wrote a response ("Literal, Allegorical," 9). Childs then responded in the following year ("Critical Reflections"), to which Barr then again responded six years later ("Allegory and Historicism").

27. Barr also argued that historical critical scholarship itself misunderstood the historical sense and what role it plays in interpretation: "The trouble is, I think, that there is no one thing that can be clearly defined as 'the historical sense': there are a number of different operations, according to the type of text being considered and other factors. It may mean that the text gives an accurate historical report; or it may mean that it gives an inadequate historical report, in which case a better historical account can be worked out; or it may mean that we get back to the sense intended by the original writer or tell the historical circumstances out of which the text originated; or it may mean that we lay all the emphasis on the earliest knowable form of the text. There isn't any one thing that is 'the historical sense'" (Barr, "Literal, Allegorical" 9).

> allegorical explanation, can easily go together and have often done so.[28]

This explanation aligns precisely with what we observed in chapters 1 and 2. For Paul and other ancient allegorists, it was the literal details of the text—that is, how the characters and events were described—that were essential for their interpretive practices and not whether the characters and events actually existed in history. Within their interpretive practices of allegory, Paul and other ancient allegorists simply were not influenced by facticity. Facticity operated in a different interpretive domain.

A final piece of fruit borne from discussions of typology is an engagement with the concept of *meaning*. Within the discussion of the *sensus literalis*, two rabbinic distinctions often are employed: *peshat* and *derash*. Once thought to be synonymous with literal and figural, it has been demonstrated that *peshat* is better understood not as a literal reading but as an authoritative teaching, one that can be "recognized by the public as obviously authoritative, since familiar and traditional."[29] Although these two terms appear first in rabbinic literature, what the distinction between *peshat* and *derash* demonstrates for our purposes is that a figural reading also can be "literal."

> Consequently, although the "literal sense" has often been thought of as an inherent quality of literary text that gives it a specific and invariant character (often, a "realistic" character), *the phrase is simply an honorific title given to a kind of meaning that is culturally expected and automatically recognized by readers*. It is the "normal," "commonsensical" meaning, *the product of a conventional, customary reading*. The "literal sense" thus stems from a community's generally unself-conscious decision to adopt and promote a certain kind of meaning, rather than from its recognition of a text's inherent and self-evident sense.[30]

Therefore, what is significant for Paul is not what meanings can be described as literal or even historical, but what can be described as *authoritative*. Of equal importance is the question "Authoritative for whom?" The answer is "Authoritative for Paul." *Paul allegorizes a story whose source meanings he considers authoritative.* This is one characteristic of Paul's practice that is significant for understanding it among the interpretive

---

28. Barr, "Literal, Allegorical" 9.
29. Loewe, "'Plain' Meaning," 1:181; emphasis original.
30. Dawson, *Allegorical Readers*, 7–8; emphasis added.

practices of Jews roughly contemporary to him (cf. the criterion of authorial assumptions discussed in sect. 3).

This section has demonstrated that the interpretive schema of typology does not reflect how the ancient interpretive practice of allegory operated up to Paul's time or how Paul's practice fits within it. For these reasons, we must abandon this second schema—as we did the first—if we hope to understand the interpretive practice behind Paul's use of ἀλληγορούμενα more precisely.

3. MY APPROACH AND CRITERIA

Chapter 2 and sections 1–2 of this chapter demonstrate that prior scholarship's criteria for selecting comparative examples and the resultant interpretive schemata used to examine Paul's practice comparatively are the reasons for the unresolved state of scholarship on the interpretive practice behind Paul's use of ἀλληγορούμενα. *The result of these criteria and schemata has been numerous explanations for Paul's practice, of which one is no more convincing than the others.* Unless appropriate criteria and an approach are used, any future analysis will only repeat what already has been done. We must select criteria that produce suitable comparative examples and use an approach that situates an analysis of Paul's interpretive practice appropriately within the ancient interpretive practice of allegory.

The approach that accomplishes these tasks is to determine if an ancient allegorist—not an interpretive practice—is a suitable comparative example with Paul by using a different set of criteria. The criteria I use to determine if an allegorist is suitable are the allegorist's (1) milieu, (2) assumptions as an author, (3) perception of the situation for which the interpretive practice is used, and (4) the hermeneutical purpose of the interpretive practice of allegory. My approach and criteria succeed where prior scholarship has not succeeded (cf. chs. 1–3) because they take into consideration that *different allegorical practices are the processes and products of different allegorists*. Accordingly, by evaluating an allegorist first, I evaluate characteristics (i.e., my four criteria) that *actually* situate allegorical practices within the ancient interpretive practice of allegory in terms of their similarities and differences (and not in terms of an uninfluential concern [i.e., facticity] or organizational tools [i.e., terminology and geographical location]). Using this approach, a comparative analysis of an allegorical practice with Paul's practice provides meaningful information only if Paul and the other allegorist are determined to be suitable comparative examples with each other. Put simply, establishing an allegorist as a suitable comparative example with Paul *is the means by which* his allegorical practices become meaningful for better understanding Paul's practices. Therefore, a suitable practice for comparison with Paul's practice must belong to an allegorist who shares the following characteristics with Paul:

- Milieu—The allegorist must be roughly contemporary to Paul and must share his milieu, which is demonstrated by the allegorist engaging similar theological concerns and using similar interpretive practices in addition to the ancient interpretive practice of allegory.

- Assumptions as an author—The allegorist must hold similar assumptions as Paul about the text, about the interpretive practice of allegory, and about his relationship to the audience. First, he must view the Jewish Scriptures as an authoritative source for making persuasive arguments. Second, he must view the ancient interpretive practice of allegory as a valid practice for making persuasive arguments. Last, he must express a belief that he and the audience have a strong connection, one that he believes increases his argument's persuasiveness.

- Perception of the situation for which the interpretive practice is used—The allegorist must share the same view as Paul of the situation for which the interpretive practice of allegory is used: a serious situation in need of immediate attention. This context is important because an allegory cannot be understood apart from it.[31] However, it is not the actual historical context of the audience—often unrecoverable—that is most important, but rather how the allegorist perceives the situation.

- Hermeneutical purpose of the interpretive practice of allegory— The allegorist must use his interpretive practice of allegory for the

---

31. MacQueen is correct when he claims that allegory "stands, not in isolation, but in meaningful context" (*Allegory*, 23). John Whitman elaborates, "Acts of interpretive allegory are transactions between fluctuating critical communities and formative texts. While these transactions regularly draw upon shared interpretive methods, they are situated in times and place, marked by tensions and polemics, that are specific to each historical community and its developing canon" (*Allegory*, 2).

same function as Paul: to teach his audience about their present and future circumstances.

The next three chapters analyze Paul's practice comparatively with the practices of three Jewish interpreters of Scripture who were roughly contemporary to Paul—three allegorists I found to be suitable in the process of examining many allegorists. I begin each chapter by demonstrating an interpreter is a suitable comparative example. Then, I examine the allegorical practice of the interpreter separately from Paul's practice. Next, I compare the interpreter's allegorical practice with Paul's practice. Last, I discuss the significance of the comparison for understanding Paul's practice more precisely.

4

Comparative Analysis 1
The Sectarian Texts of the Dead Sea Scrolls

SINCE THE DISCOVERY OF the Dead Sea Scrolls, prior scholarship has analyzed the sectarian texts as a source for contextualizing Paul and his writings within Second Temple Judaism.[1] Some of these examinations have called attention to the fact that the sectarian texts and Paul used similar interpretive practices.[2] As it regards allegorical practice, this also has been recognized.

> The suggestion has been made that Paul's use of Scripture is similar to that of the Qumran Sect. In my opinion this is obvious only in one place, namely, the allegory of the two covenants.[3]

Despite the recognition of similar interpretive practices,[4] prior scholarship has not yet engaged the sectarian texts' interpretive practice of

---

1. Readers of the Dead Sea Scrolls recognized this relevance soon after their discovery: "Everything that is important for Judaism in the last two or three centuries before Christ and in the first century A.D. is important also for Christianity. By enriching our understanding of Judaism in the period in which Christianity arose, the Dead Sea Scrolls have given us material for a better understanding of the New Testament and early Christianity" (Burrows, *More Light*, 14).

2. Bruce, *Epistle to the Galatians*, 218; Di Mattei, "Paul's Allegory," 116, 122; Donfried, "Paul the Jew," 2:725; Ellis, "Note on Pauline Hermeneutics," 130–31; Johnson, "Paul and the Manual," 160; Longenecker, *Galatians*, 206; Pastor, "Alegoría o Tipología," 118; Sanders, "Habakkuk in Qumran," 238; Schoeps, *Paul*, 233.

3. LaSor, *Dead Sea Scrolls*, 176.

4. For other scholars who recognize, but do not engage, an allegorical practice,

allegory for the purpose of better understanding Paul's practice. This engagement is the task of this chapter.

Before this engagement, two clarifications are necessary. First, when I use the term "sectarian texts," I am not arguing that a sectarian community at Qumran composed the texts. Rather, I use the term to classify texts generally accepted as reflecting sectarian views. Second, some prior scholarship has argued for a direct connection between Paul and the authors of the sectarian texts.[5] My analysis does not assume or argue for a direct connection. This chapter is divided into four sections: the authors of the sectarian texts as suitable comparative examples, the allegorical practice of the sectarian texts, Gal 4:22–25 and the sectarian texts, and contributions to our understanding of Paul's interpretive practice.

1. THE AUTHORS OF THE SECTARIAN TEXTS AS SUITABLE COMPARATIVE EXAMPLES

1.1 Texts Examined in Section 1 and the Rationale

The authors of the sectarian texts are established as suitable comparative examples when evaluating them against the four criteria I presented in chapter 3, section 3. For this exercise, I engage the Damascus Document, *Miqṣat Ma' aśê ha-Torah* (4QMMT), the Pesher Habakkuk, and the Rule of the Community. I have chosen these three texts as representative examples because they (1) indisputably reflect sectarian views, (2) are substantially extant, and (3) together provide data sufficient for evaluating each criterion.

---

see Brownlee, "Biblical Interpretation"; Dimant, "Pesharim, Qumran"; Finkel, "Pesher of Dreams"; Horgan, *Pesharim*, 244–45; Kister, "Common Heritage"; Nitzan, *Pesher Habakkuk*, 51–54. Despite broad recognition in the pesharim, there is a lack of acknowledgement of the interpretive practice of allegory within the sectarian texts more generally. For example, there is no article on allegory or allegoresis in *EDSS*. Additionally, a search for each term among the twenty-one thousand plus entries within the Orion Center for the Study of the Dead Sea Scrolls and Associated Literature yields few results (see http://orion.huji.ac.il).

5. Benoit, "Qumran and New Testament," 19; Donfried, "Paul the Jew," 2:730; Eskenazi, "Paul," 119.

1.2. Criterion 1: Milieu

The following two subsections analyze shared theological concerns and interpretive practices in order to demonstrate a shared milieu between the authors of the sectarian texts and Paul.

1.2.1. Shared Theological Concerns

Prior scholarship typically has analyzed Paul and the sectarian texts for the purpose of better comprehending Paul's theology and not his interpretive practices. These studies routinely begin by recognizing shared terminology and then examine each author's stated beliefs. Using this approach, prior scholarship has compared their views on the law,[6] covenant,[7] justification,[8] dualism,[9] temple,[10] truth,[11] and spirit and flesh.[12] In Galatians,[13] Paul expresses two theological concerns that are shared

---

6. Abegg, "Paul," 52–55; Bachmann, *Anti-Judaism in Galatians*, 19–31; Dunn, "4QMMT and Galatians"; Dunn, "Paul," 122–27; Eskenazi, "Paul"; Fitzmyer, "Paul," 2:607–9; Kuhn, "Bedeutung der Qumrantextes," 202–13; Kuhn, "Impact of Selected Qumran Texts," 3:171–80; Lincicum, "Paul and Temple Scroll."

7. H. Braun, "Qumran und Neue Testament," 231–32; Flusser, "Dead Sea Sect," 236–42; Kuhn, "Impact of Selected Qumran Texts," 3:165–66.

8. F. M. Braun, "Arrière-fond judaïque," 32–38; H. Braun, *Qumran und Neue Testament*, 2:166–72; Dunn, "Paul," 106–7; Fitzmyer, "Paul," 2:602–5; Grundmann, "Teacher of Righteousness"; Kuhn, "Bedeutung der Qumrantexte," 177–78; LaSor, *Dead Sea Scrolls*, 168–73.

9. H. Braun, *Qumran und Neue Testament*, 2:172–77; Dunn, "Paul," 110–11; Kuhn, "Impact of Selected Qumran Texts," 3:181–84.

10. Donfried, "Paul the Jew," 2:726–28; Dunn, "Paul," 113–14; Kuhn, "Bedeutung der Qumrantexte," 178–82; Kuhn, "Impact of Selected Qumran Texts," 3:161–62.

11. Murphy-O'Connor, "Truth."

12. W. D. Davies, "Paul"; LaSor, *Dead Sea Scrolls*, 173–76; Kuhn, "Impact of Selected Qumran Texts," 3:177–78.

13. The most substantial work on Galatians and the Dead Sea Scrolls is H. Braun, "Qumran und Neue Testament," later published in the first volume of H. Braun, *Qumran und Neue Testament*. In these works, Braun discusses parallels between the Dead Sea Scrolls and Gal 1:4, 17, 18; 2:4, 9, 16; 3:11, 23—4:1, 27, 28; 4:1–3, 6, 10, 19, 22–24, 26–27; 5:12–23; 6:1, 7, 16. He discusses two sections of Gal 4:21–31: vv. 22–24 and 26–27. On Gal 4:22–24, he comments that although the authors share the concept of two covenants, they do not employ them in the same way. On Gal 4:26–27, he points out that the description of Jerusalem as mother and the use of Isa 54:1 harken to the way in which the sectarians describe the birth of their community through the Teacher of Righteousness ("Qumran und Neue Testament," 232). The second most substantial work on this topic is Kuhn, "Impact of Selected Qumran Texts," as well as Kuhn's

with the authors of the sectarian texts: "works of the law" and "covenant." The first theological concern, works of the law (cf. Gal 2:16), is found in 4Q398 14–7 II, 2b–4a (4QMMT C, 26b–28a).[14]

> Yet we know that a person is justified not *by the works of the law* [ἐξ ἔργων νόμου] but through faith in Jesus Christ. And we have come to believe in Christ Jesus, so that we might be justified by faith in Christ, and not *by doing the works of the law* [ἐξ ἔργων νόμου], because no one will be justified *by the works of the law* [ἐξ ἔργων νόμου]. (Gal 2:16; emphasis added)

> We have (indeed) sent you some *precepts of the Torah* [התרוה מעשי מקצת] according to our decision, for your welfare and the welfare of your people. For we have seen (that) you have wisdom and knowledge of the Torah. (4Q398 14–7 II, 2b–4a [4QMMT C, 26b–28a]; emphasis added)[15]

It is well established that Paul and the sectarians do not define or employ this concept in the same way.[16] What must not be overlooked, however, is that they share this theological concern about the law.[17]

The second shared theological concern, covenant, is the most significant concern for our purposes because it is found in Paul's interpretive

---

shorter contribution written earlier: "Impact of the Qumran Scrolls." Unlike Braun's work, which engages the text in order, Kuhn organizes his work by topic.

14. For 4QMMT, I cite the composite text in addition to individual manuscripts. For the composite text, see Qimron and Strugnell, *Miqṣat Ma'aśe ha-Torah*, 43–63.

15. Translations of 4QMMT are taken from Qimron and Strugnell, *Miqṣat Ma'aśe ha-Torah*, 43–63.

16. For others who discuss this theological concern, see n6.

17. Having acknowledged this, there also is an inherent danger to overextend the implications of these shared concerns. For example, Abegg has said, "Some scholars have suggested that Paul misunderstood the Jewish teaching of his day or, at the very least, that he created a straw man to bolster his own teaching regarding faith versus law. In the past, this position was supported by the fact that the phrase 'works of the law' nowhere appears in the foundational books of rabbinic Judaism. MMT, however, provides the 'smoking gun' for which students have been searching for generations, not from the pages of rabbinic literature, but from the sectarian teachings of the Qumran" ("Paul," 55). In response, James Dunn softened Abegg's "smoking gun" claim into a more balanced position: "But the weight of the evidence does seem to suggest that MMT preserves vocabulary and manner of theologizing which left its mark on a wider spectrum of Jewish thought and practice" (Dunn, "4QMMT and Galatians," 153).

practice behind his use of ἀλληγορούμενα.[18] In the same way that Paul discusses two covenants in Gal 4:24, so do the sectarians.[19]

> Unless they take care to perform according to the exact (requirements of) the Torah during the time of evil . . . and to observe the Sabbath day in its exact detail, and the appointed times and the day of the fast as it was found by those who entered into the new covenant in the land of Damascus. (CD VI, 14, 18b–19)

> The traitors together with the Man of the Lie, for (they did) not . . . the Righteous Teacher from the mouth of God. And it concerns the trait[ors to] the new [covenant,] f[o]r they were not faithful to the covenant of God [. . .] his holy name. (1QpHab II, 1b–4)

Once again, prior scholarship has been quick to point out that the authors do not share the same theological views on covenant and consequently the conversation stops.[20] However, the fact they express different theological views does not justify ignoring the implications of both expressing this concern for interpreting Gal 4:21–31: Paul participates in a conversation that is taking place within his milieu.[21]

1.2.2. Shared Interpretive Practices

Paul and the authors of the sectarian texts share three other interpretive practices in addition to the interpretive practice of allegory. First, both authors interpret Gen 15:6 as the pattern for normative faith:

> Just as Abraham "believed God, and it was reckoned to him as righteousness," so, you see, those who believe are the descendants of Abraham. (Gal 3:6–7)

---

18. For others who discuss this theological concern, see n7.
19. For additional statements, see CD VIII, 21; XIX, 33–34; XX, 10–12.
20. For example, "In addition to the fundamental difference between the Christian and Sectarian concepts of the two covenants, there is a difference of degree. . . . The problem derives basically from the attempt to apply the concept of dualism and grace to the relations of the sect with the rest of Judaism and the notion of Israel's salvation in the future" (Flusser, "Dead Sea Sect," 240–42).
21. For scholars who acknowledge that Paul was engaged in similar conversations as the sectarians but not related to Gal 4:21–31, see Brown, "Dead Sea Scrolls," 2–3; Burrows, *More Light*, 132; Donfried, "Paul the Jew," 2:728; Fitzmyer, *Dead Sea Scrolls*, 30; Flusser, "Dead Sea Sect," 263; Johnson, "Paul and the Manual," 160; Lim, *Pesharim*, 85; Wood, "Pauline Studies," 310.

> And this will be counted as a virtuous deed of yours, since you will be doing what is righteous and good in His eyes, for your own welfare and for the welfare of Israel. (4Q398 14–17 II, 7–8 [4QMMT C, 31–32])

The sectarians interpret Gen 15:6 to support their interpretations of the law; put simply, how a covenanter should *act* (i.e., faithfulness to how they interpret covenantal requirements). Paul, on the other hand, interprets Gen 15:6 to emphasize how someone should *believe*. Their interpretive practices are similar despite this difference in interpretation.[22]

The second shared interpretive practice is the use of a list to catalog vices:[23]

> Now the works of the flesh are obvious: fornication, impurity, licentiousness, idolatry, sorcery, enmities, strife, jealousy, anger, quarrels, dissensions, factions, envy, drunkenness, carousing, and things like these. I am warning you, as I warned you before: those who do such things will not inherit the kingdom of God. (Gal 5:19–21)

> But concerning the Spirit of Deceit (these are the principles): greed and slackness in righteous activity, wickedness and falsehood, pride and haughtiness, atrocious disguise and falsehood, great hypocrisy, fury, great vileness, shameless zeal for abominable works in a spirit of fornication, filthy ways in unclean worship, a tongue of blasphemy, blindness of eyes and deafness of ear, stiffness of neck and hardness of heart, walking in all the ways of darkness, and evil craftiness. The visitation of all those who walk in it (will be) many afflictions. . . . And all their times for their generations (will be expended) in dreadful suffering and bitter misery in dark abysses until they are destroyed. (1QS IV, 9–14a)

Although the lists are not identical, their similar literary form and content reflect a shared practice for describing those actions that an author considered disreputable.

---

22. This interpretive practice also is shared by the other two comparative examples: Philo uses it in *Leg.* 3.228 among other places (cf. ch. 5n42), and the author of the Epistle of Barnabas uses it in Barn. 13.7. For other examples, see Jas 2:23 and 1 Macc 2:52.

23. This interpretive practice also is shared by the other two comparative examples: Philo uses it in *Sacr.* 32 and the author of the Epistle of Barnabas in Barn. 20.1. Vice lists were common throughout the ancient world (López, "Vice Lists").

Comparative Analysis 1

The third interpretive practice shared by Paul and the sectarian writers was interpreting the struggle they perceived within each community through a lens of dualism:

> So with us; while we were minors, we were enslaved to the elemental spirits of the world. . . . Now, however, that you have come to know God, or rather to be known by God, how can you turn back again to the weak and beggarly elemental spirits? How can you want to be enslaved by them again? (Gal 4:3, 9)

> And it is written that [you will stray] from the path (of the Torah) and that calamity will meet [you] . . . Consider all these things and ask Him that He strengthen your will and remove from you the plans of evil and the device of Belial so that you may rejoice at the end of time, finding that some of our practices are correct. And this will be counted as a virtuous deed of yours, since you will be doing what is righteous and good in His eyes, for your own welfare and for the welfare of Israel. (4Q397 14–21 I, 12b–13a; 4Q398 14–17 II, 5–8 [4QMMT C, 12b, 28b–32])

These shared interpretive practices, as well as shared theological concerns, indicate that these authors operated within the same milieu.

1.3. Criterion 2: Authorial Assumptions

Paul and the authors of the sectarian texts believed that the Jewish Scriptures were an authoritative source for making persuasive arguments. Additionally, each believed that the interpretive practice of allegory was valid for making persuasive arguments. In chapter 2, section 2.4.2.3, we observed various expressions of Paul's allegorical practice. Section 2 of this chapter demonstrates that the authors of the sectarian texts used their allegorical practice prolifically. Paul and the authors of the sectarian texts also shared a third authorial assumption: the feeling of a strong connection to their audiences and the hope that such a strong connection would work to their advantage:

> Friends, I beg you, become as I am, for I also have become as you are. You have done me no wrong. You know that it was because of a physical infirmity that I first announced the gospel to you; though my condition put you to the test, you did not scorn or despise me, but welcomed me as an angel of God, as Christ Jesus. What has become of the good will you felt? For I

> testify that, had it been possible, you would have torn out your eyes and given them to me. Have I now become your enemy by telling you the truth? (Gal 4:12–16)[24]

> And now, sons, hearken to me and I will uncover your eyes so you may see and understand the works of God and choose that which he wants and despise that which he hates: to walk perfect in all his ways and not to stray in the thoughts of a guilty inclination and licentious eyes. (CD II, 14–16a)

1.4. Criterion 3: Perception of the Situation for Which the Interpretive Practice Is Used

As discussed in chapter 3, section 3, it is not the historical context of the audience that is most important for demonstrating compatibility, but it is the situation as perceived by the allegorist.[25] Paul believes he is allegorizing for a tumultuous context that must be addressed. We find evidence of similar contexts within the Damascus Document and the Pesher Habakkuk. One context that the sectarian authors perceive, evident in both the Damascus Document and the Pesher Habakkuk, is similar to the context that Paul perceives in Gal 1:6: members are abandoning the teachings of (and perhaps membership in) the community.

> I am astonished that you are so quickly deserting the one who called you in the grace of Christ and are turning to a different gospel. (Gal 1:6)

> Thus all the men who entered the new covenant in the land of Damascus and returned and betrayed and departed from the well of living water will not be accounted among the council of the people. (CD XIX, 33b–35a)

> And it concerns the trait[ors to] the new [covenant,] f[o]r they were not faithful to the covenant of God [. . .] his holy name. (1QpHab II, 3b–4)

---

24. For similar sentiments, also see Gal 5:2–10 and 6:1–10.

25. Bernstein, speaking specifically on the pesharim, expresses this another way: "The pesharim tell us more about the author, his group, his opponents, and the history of their times than they do about the meaning of the biblical text" ("Dead Sea Scrolls," 81).

A second context, evident in the Pesher Habakkuk, describes an intense persecution carried out by the Man of the Lie upon the Teacher of Righteousness and members of the community.[26] This also is similar to the situation that Paul describes in Gal 4:29:

> But just as at that time the child who was born according to the flesh persecuted the child who was born according to the Spirit, so it is now also. (Gal 4:29)

> "On account of human bloodshed and violence (done to) the land, the town, and all its inhabitants." Its interpretation concerns the [Wi]cked Priest, whom—*because of the wrong done to the Righteous Teacher and the men of his counsel*—God gave into the hand of his enemies to humble him with disease for annihilation in bitterness of soul, beca[u]se he had acted wickedly against his chosen ones. (1QpHab IX, 8–12a; emphasis added)

> "Woe to him who gives his neighbors to drink, mixing in his poison, indeed, making (them drink) in order that he might look upon their feasts." (VACAT) *Its interpretation concerns the Wicked Priest, who pursued the Righteous Teacher—to swallow him up with his poisonous vexation—to his house of exile. And at the end of the feast, (during) the repose of the Day of Atonement, he appeared to them to swallow them up and to make them stumble on the fast day*, their restful sabbath. (1QpHab XI, 2b–8a; emphasis added)

These texts reveal that the authors of the sectarian texts used the interpretive practice of allegory to address a context (as they perceived it) that was similar the context Paul perceived in Galatia.[27]

1.5. Criterion 4: Hermeneutical Purpose of the Interpretive Practice of Allegory

In chapter 1, I demonstrated that Paul used his interpretive practice to instruct the Galatians about their present and future circumstances. In

---

26. 1QpHab X, 5b–13, also may confirm that the Man of the Lie had persecuted other members of the community in addition to the Teacher and his close companions.

27. Their shared urgency becomes all the more understandable when their eschatological perspectives are considered. For the discussion on how Paul's eschatology influenced Gal 4:21–31, see ch. 1, sects. 2.2.2.2 and 2.2.3. For a discussion of the sectarians' eschatological views on אחרית הימים, see Collins, *Apocalypticism*, 52–109; P. Davies, "Teacher of Righteousness"; Kosmala, "At End of Days"; Steudel, "אחרית הימים."

both the Damascus Document and the Pesher Habakkuk, the sectarians also used their interpretive practice of allegory for this purpose:

> As he said, "And I will expel your king's booth and the *kywn* of your images from my tent (to) Damascus." The books of the Torah are the "booth of the king," as he said, "I will raise up the fallen booth of David." The "king" is the assembly, and the "*kywn* of the images" are the books of the prophets whose words Israel despised. And the "star" is the interpreter of the Torah who came to Damascus, as it is written: "A star stepped forth out of Jacob and a staff arose out of Israel." The "staff" is the prince of all the congregation, and when he arises, "he will destroy all the sons of Seth." (CD VII, 14b–21a)

> "For there is yet a vision concerning the appointed time. It testifies to the period, and it will not deceive." Its interpretation is that the last period will be prolonged, and it will be greater than anything of which the prophets spoke, for the mysteries of God are awesome. "If it tarries, wait for it, for it will surely come and it will not be late." Its interpretation concerns the men of truth, those who observe the Torah, whose hands do not grow slack in the service of the truth, when the last period is drawn out for them, for all of God's periods will come according to their fixed order, as he decreed for them in the mysteries of his prudence. (1QpHab VII, 5b–14a)

Jutta Jokiranta describes the hermeneutical purpose of the sectarian texts' interpretive practice in a different yet informative way: propaganda.

> What could be more powerful in labeling outsiders than to use a shared tradition and to label the outsiders as the wicked of this shared tradition? This is "propaganda" by its very nature. The reader of the pesharim gains the impression *that the Scriptures were all about the community and its adversaries*—Scripture is dualistic in its sharp division between two groups, and the world is manifested as a place of struggle and dichotomy.[28]

Jokiranta describes only the practice found within the sectarian texts, but my analysis in chapter 1 supports a similar understanding for Gal 4:21–31: *It is as if Gen 16–21 was all about the Galatians and their adversaries*. Accordingly, Paul and the authors of the sectarian texts used their interpretive practices of allegory for the same hermeneutical purposes.

---

28. Jokiranta, "Pesharim," 24; emphasis added.

2. THE ALLEGORICAL PRACTICE OF THE SECTARIAN TEXTS

The authors of the sectarian texts used the interpretive practice of allegory in more than one way. Sometimes, the authors describe texts as having a secondary meaning and then explain what is meant (similar to Philo).[29] Other times, they allegorize the Jewish Scriptures implicitly.[30] In this section, I examine those allegorical expressions that share a similar structure with Paul's allegorical practice in Gal 4: those in which the sectarians provide (1) a Jewish Scripture to be allegorized, (2) an indication that it means something else (i.e., allegoresis is at work), and (3) an allegorical interpretation (i.e., an allegory).

2.1. Texts Examined in Section 2 and the Rationale

Below are the texts that I examine. I chose these texts because they generally are accepted as reflecting sectarian views. These texts include commentaries as well as legal, poetic, and eschatological texts.

- Continuous biblical commentaries (Pesharim)—Habakkuk Pesher (1QpHab), Hosea Pesher 1 (4Q166 = 4QpHos^a), Hosea Pesher 2 (4Q167 = 4QpHos^b), Isaiah Pesher 1 (3Q4 = 3QpIsa), Isaiah Pesher 2 (4Q162 = 4QpIsa^b), Isaiah Pesher 3 (4Q163 = 4QpIsa^c), Isaiah Pesher 4 (4Q161 = 4QpIsa^a), Isaiah Pesher 5 (4Q165 = 4QpIsa^e), Isaiah Pesher 6 (4Q164 = 4QpIsa^d), Micah Pesher 1 (1Q14 = 1QpMic), Micah Pesher 2 (4Q168 = 4QpMic), Nahum Pesher (4Q169 = 4QpNah), Psalm Pesher 1 (4Q171 = 4QpPs^a), Psalm Pesher 2 (1Q16 = 1QpPs), Psalm Pesher 3 (4Q173 = 4QpPs^b), Zephaniah Pesher 1 (4Q170 = 4QpZeph), Zephaniah Pesher 2 (1Q15 = 1QpZeph)

- Thematic commentaries[31]—Catena A (4Q177 = 4QCat^a), Commentary on Genesis A (4Q252 = 4QCommGen A), Commentary on Genesis B (4Q253 = 4QCommGen B), Commentary on Genesis C (4Q254 = 4QCommGen C), Commentary on Genesis D (4Q255 =

---

29. Cf. 1QM X, 5b–8a; and 4Q397 14–17 I (4QMMT C, 11b–16).

30. I discuss implicit allegorical expressions within the sectarian texts and its relationship to the genre of "rewritten Bible" at the conclusion of this project.

31. For the classification "thematic commentary," see Carmignac, "Document de Qumran," 360–62.

4QCommGen D), Florilegium: A Midrash on 2 Samuel and Psalms 1–2 (4Q174 = 4QFlor), and Melchizedek (11Q13 = 11QMelch)

- Legal texts—The Damascus Document (CD), *Miqṣat Maʿaśê ha-Torah* (4QMMT), the Rule of the Community (1QS), and the Temple Scroll (11QTemple)
- Poetic texts—Thanksgiving Hymns (4QHodayot)
- Eschatological texts—The Rule of the Congregation (1QSa) and the War Scroll (1QM)

2.2. The Interpretive Practice of Allegory within the Sectarian Texts

For heuristic purposes, I have organized the allegorical expressions below by indicator and have provided subsections for variations in the order of their frequency. Additionally, because of the vast number of expressions, I provide two occurrences and list only references for the remaining occurrences of the same type. The authors of the sectarian texts typically indicated their interpretive practice of allegory by using פשר, although sometimes no indicator was used.

2.2.1. *With* פשר *as Indicator*

In this section, expressions are further organized by the words that accompany פשר.

2.2.1.1. פשר על

Expression 1:

> "For now I am raising up the Chaldeans, that bitter [and ha]sty nation." (VACAT) Its interpretation concerns [פשר על] the Kittim, w[ho ar]e swift and strong in battle, so as to destroy many [...] in the dominion of the Kittim, and the wick[ed ones ...]t, and they will not be faithful to the statutes of [Go]d. (1QpHab II, 10b–15)

Expression 2:

> For this is what it says: "To take possession of dwelling places not their own. Fearful and terrible are they. From them goes

out their judgment and dignity." Its interpretation concerns [פשרו על] the Kittim, fear and dread of whom are upon all the nations. And by design all their plans are to do evil, and with cunning and deceit they shall deal with all the peoples. (1QpHab III, 2–6a)

Other occurrences:

- 1QpHab II, 5–10a; III, 6b–13a*[32]; IV, 3b–9a, 9b–12a*; V, 8b–12a; VI, 8b–12a; VII, 3–5a, 9–14a, 17—VIII, 3a; VIII, 3b–13a; IX, 3b–7A, 8–12a; XI, 2b–8a, 8b–15; XII, 14b—XIII, 4.
- 4QpIsa^d I, 3b–8
- 4QpNah 3–4 I, 6–8a; II 3–6, 7–10a*; III, 1b–5a, 5b–8a*; IV, 1b–4a, 4b–6a*
- 11QMelch II, 11b–15a
- 4QpPs^a 1–10 I, 25–II, 1a*; II, 1b–4a, 7–9a, 9b–12, 13–16a, 16b–20; III, 7–8a, 14–17a; IV, 7–10a, 13–15*, 16–17a

2.2.1.2. פשר אשר

Expression 1:

"They scoff, and princes are to them a laughing matter." (VACAT) Its interpretation is that [פשרו אשר] they mock great ones and they despise honored ones; kings and princes they mock, and they scoff at a great people. (1QpHab IV, 1–3a)

Expression 2:

For this is what it says: "(You are) too pure of eyes to look on evil." (VACAT) Its interpretation is that [פשרו אשר] they did not whore after their eyes in the time of wickedness. (1QpHab V, 6b–8a)

Other occurrences:

- 1QpHab VI, 2b–5a, 5b–8a; VII, 5b–8, 14b–16
- 4QCommGen A 5 IV, 3b–7
- 4QpHos^a II, 1–6*, 8–14a, 14b–17a

---

32. I have marked with an asterisk those occurrences in which an indicator is reconstructed partially. Fully reconstructed occurrences are omitted.

- 4QpIsa^a 8–10 III, 26b–29
- 4QpPs^a 1–10 III, 2b–5a*

2.2.1.3. פשר הדבר על

Expression 1:

> "Woe to the one who builds a city with blood and founds a town on iniquity. Are not these from Yahweh of Hosts? People toil for fire and nations grow weary for nothing." (VACAT) The interpretation of the passage concerns [פשר הדבר על] the Spouter of the Lie, who caused many to err. (1QpHab X, 5b–13)

Expression 2:

> "What profit does an idol bring, when its maker has hewed (it), a molten statue and an image of falsehood? For the maker relies on the things he makes, fashioning mute idols." The interpretation of the passage concerns [פשר הדבר על] all the idols of the nations, which they have made so that they may serve them and bow down before them, but they will not save them on the day of judgment. (1QpHab XII, 10b–14a)

Other occurrences:

- 1QpHab VIII, 13b—IX, 2a*; IX, 12b—X, 1a*; XI, 17—XII, 6a
- 4QCat^a 1–4, 14, 24, 31 I, 6; 7, 9–11, 20, 26 I, 9*
- 4QpIsa^c 6–7 II, 1–8a
- 4QpPs^a 1–10 III, 17b–19*

2.2.1.4. פשר הדבר

Expression 1:

> "[]" The interpretation of the passage [פשר הדבר] (with regard) to the latter days concerns the condemnation of the land before the sword and the famine. And it will happen in the time of the visitation of the land. (4QpIsa^b II, 1–2a)

Expression 2:

"For if your people, O I[srael,] were [as the sand of the sea, (only) a remnant would return.]" The interpretation of the passage [פשר הדבר] (with regard) to the latter [days . . .] they will walk among the peni[tents of Israe]l [. . .]. (4QpIsa^c 6–7 II, 14–16)

Other occurrences:

- 4QFlor 1–2, 21, I, 14–15a, 18–19*
- 4QpIsa^c 23 II, 3–13*

2.2.1.5. פשר הדבר אשר

Expression 1:

"For judgment you have set him up, and a rock as his reprove you have established. (You are) too pure of eyes to look on evil, and to gaze at tribulation you are not able." The interpretation of the passage is that [פשר הדבר אשר] God will not destroy his people by the hand of the nations but into the hand of his chosen god will give the judgment of all the nations. And by means of their rebuke, all the wicked ones of his people will be convicted (by those) who have kept his commandments in their distress. (1QpHab V, 1–6a)

Expression 2:

["(I shall) remove its hedge that it may be for grazing; (I shall) break d]own its wall that it may become a trampled (pasture), which [I shall make a waste. It will not be pruned, nor will it be weeded, and there will grow up thorns and thistl]es." The interpretation of the passage [פשר הדבר אשר] is that he abandoned them. (4QpIsa^b I, 1–3a)

Other occurrences:

- 1QpHab X, 14—XI, 2a*

2.2.1.6. פשר ONLY

Expression 1:

But during all those years, Belial will run unbridled amidst Israel, as God spoke through the hand of the prophet Isaiah, son of Amoz, saying, "Fear and a pit and a snare are upon you, O inhabitant(s) of the land." This refers [פשרו] to the three nets of Belial, of which Levi, the son of Jacob, said that he (Belial) entrapped Israel with them, making them seem as if they were three types of righteousness. (CD IV, 12b–17a)[33]

Expression 2:

It says, "[For if your people, O Israel, were as the sand on the sea, (only) a remnant would return,]" its interpretation [פשרו] (concerns) "the few" [of humanity . . .]. (4QpIsa^c 6–7 II, 17–18)

Other occurrences:

- 1QpHab X, 1b–5a; XII, 6b–10a
- 4QpNah 3–4 II, 1b–2; III, 8b–9, 10–11a*, 11b—IV, 1a
- 4QpPs^a 1–10 II, 4b–5a
- 11QMelch II, 15b–18a

2.2.2. Without פשר as Indicator

Expression 1:

"And its splendor will go down, and its multitude, and its tumultuous (crowd) exulting in it." These (are) [אלה הם] the men of mockery who are in Jerusalem. (4QpIsa^b II, 6b–7a)

Expression 2:

"For all this [his anger] did not turn back, [and his hand is still stretched out.]" This [היא] is the congregation of the men of mockery, who are in Jerusalem. (4QpIsa^b II, 9b–10)

Other Occurrences:

- 1QS VIII, 14–16a
- 4QCat^a 1–4, 14, 24, 31 I, 13; 7, 9–11, 20, 26 I, 1
- 4QFlor 1–2, 21 I, 1–3a, 3b–7a, 7b–9, 10–12a, 12b–13, 15b–16a, 16b–17
- 4QpIsa^a 8–10 III, 6–8*, 9, 10–11a, 11b–13*

33. This allegorical expression is significant because it is the only use of פשר in the Damascus Document. For an analysis of its implications for interpreting the Damascus Document, see Goldman, "Exegesis and Structure." Also, Goldman discusses it briefly in her unpublished dissertation: "Biblical Exegesis," 190–93.

- CD III, 20b–IV, 4a; VI, 2b–11a; VII, 14b–21a; VIII, 8b–12a; XIX, 7b–9; XIX, 20–24a

3. GALATIANS 4:22–25 AND THE SECTARIAN TEXTS

In the preceding section, we observed many allegorical expressions that the authors of the sectarian texts structured similarly to Paul's allegorical expression in Gal 4. Paul and the authors of the sectarian texts not only could structure their allegorical expressions similarly but also could use that structure in similar ways. Six expressions are useful for demonstrating these similarities: CD VIII, 8b–12a; 1QpHab II, 10b–13a; VII, 3–5a; X, 1b–5a; XI, 17—XII, 6a; XII, 6b–9a.

3.1. Introduction: Galatians 4:22–23; CD VIII, 8b–12a; 1QpHab VII, 3–5a

The authors of the sectarian texts began their interpretive practice by introducing the Jewish Scriptures to be allegorized.

> *And they arrogantly became unruly, walking in the way of the wicked ones, of whom God said: "The poison of serpents (is) their wine and the head of asps (is) cruel."* The "serpents" are the kings of the peoples and "their wine" is their ways, and "the head of the asps" is the head of the kings of Greece, who will come to do vengeance among them. (CD VIII, 8b–12a; emphasis added)

> *And when it says, "so that he can run who reads it,"* its interpretation concerns the Righteous Teacher, to whom God made known all the mysteries of the words of his servants the prophets. (1QpHab VII, 3–5a; emphasis added)

In Gal 4:22–23, Paul also presents the Jewish Scripture that he is about to allegorize.

> For it is written that Abraham had two sons, one by a slave woman and the other by a free woman. One, the child of the slave, was born according to the flesh; the other, the child of the free woman, was born through the promise. (Gal 4:22–23)

3.2. Indication: Galatians 4:24; 1QpHab II, 10b–13a

After introducing the Jewish Scriptures to be allegorized, the authors used פשר to indicate that they were about to allegorize.

> "For now I am raising up the Chaldeans, that bitter [and ha]sty nation." *Its interpretation concerns* [פשרו על] the Kittim, w[ho ar]e swift and strong in battle so as to destroy many. (1QpHab II, 10b–13a; emphasis added)

This allegorical expression, and the numerous other occurrences it represents, reveal that the sectarians could use פשר for the same purpose that Paul used ἀλληγορούμενα in Gal 4:24:

> "Here is an interpretive practice of allegory!" [ἅτινά ἐστιν ἀλληγορούμενα]: these women are two covenants. One woman, in fact, is Hagar, from Mount Sinai, bearing children for slavery. (Gal 4:24)

3.3. Allegorical Interpretation: Galatians 4:25, 1QpHab X, 1b–5a; XII, 6b–9a

After each indication, the authors of the sectarian texts provide their allegorical interpretation. Also, we observe multiple expressions in which the authors immediately follow their indicator with a personal pronoun no differently than Paul does in Gal 4:24.[34]

> "Here is an interpretive practice of allegory!": *these women* [αὗται] are two covenants. One woman, in fact, is Hagar, from Mount Sinai, bearing children for slavery. (Gal 4:24; emphasis added)

> And when it says "cutting off many peoples and (even) the threads of your own soul," its interpretation: *This* [הוא], is the house of judgment when God will give his judgment in the midst of many peoples, and from there he will bring him up for judgment, and in their midst he will condemn him as guilty and with a fire of brimstone he will punish him. (1QpHab X, 1b–5a)

> And when it says "on account of the bloodshed of the town and violence (done to) the land," its interpretation: *the town* [היא]

---

34. In addition to the two expressions cited here, see also 4QpPs^a 1–10 II, 4b–5; 4QpNah 3–4, II 1b–2; III, 8b–9, 10–11a, 11b—IV, 1a.

is Jerusalem, where the Wicked Priest committed abominable deeds and defiled God's sanctuary. (1QpHab XII, 6b–9a)

Even more profound is that the sectarians could use their interpretive practice to connect source and allegorical entities in the same way as Paul.

> ["For the violence to Lebanon will cover you and the assault of beasts] will destroy. On account of human bloodshed and violence (done to) the land, the town and all who inhabit it." The interpretation of the passage concerns the Wicked Priest—to pay him his due inasmuch as he dealt wickedly with the Poor Ones; for *"Lebanon" is the Council of the Community* [עצת היחד הלבנון הוא], and the "beasts" are the simple ones of Judah, those who observe the Torah—(he it is) whom God will condemn to complete destruction because he plotted to destroy completely the Poor Ones. (1QpHab XI, 17—XII, 6a; emphasis added)

Just as the sectarians allegorically connected a location to people (cf. Lebanon and the Council of the Community), so does Paul in Gal 4:25: "Now Hagar is Mount Sinai in Arabia."

4. CONTRIBUTIONS TO OUR UNDERSTANDING OF PAUL'S INTERPRETIVE PRACTICE

This chapter makes three contributions to our understanding of Paul's interpretive practice. First, it demonstrates that a group of Jewish allegorists roughly contemporary to Paul used a similar interpretive practice as Paul. To demonstrate this more clearly, it is possible to rewrite Gal 4:22–25 in sectarian form.[35]

> "Abraham had two sons, one by a slave woman and the other by a free woman." Its interpretation: these women are two covenants. One woman, in fact, is Hagar, from Mount Sinai, bearing children for slavery. Now Hagar is Mount Sinai in Arabia and corresponds to the present Jerusalem, for she is in slavery with her children. But the Jerusalem above is free, and she is our mother.

To state the obvious, if such a passage appeared in the sectarian texts, it would be perfectly at home. This is significant because it indicates that Paul's interpretive practice is attested elsewhere in Jewish literature of the

---

35. For Rom 10:6–7, also restructured into sectarian form, see Barrett, "Interpretation of Old Testament," 1:392; for Rom 1:17 and Gal 3:11, see Bruce, *Biblical Exegesis*, 82.

Second Temple period despite his use of a word embedded in Hellenistic culture (cf. ἀλληγορούμενα).³⁶

The second contribution is that the relationship between the source and allegorical meanings within the sectarian texts' interpretive practice informs our understanding of that relationship within Paul's practice. Within the sectarian texts, the new allegorical meanings affirm the replaced source meanings because the source meanings were future-oriented (i.e., prophetic). For this reason, it is possible to understand the sectarian texts as saying *yes* to their source meanings and then *and* for their allegorical meanings. This stands in stark contrast to the complex relationship between the source and allegorical meanings within Paul's practice. On the one hand, Paul himself affirms the source meanings (i.e., he does not reject Jews' membership in the covenant) and includes gentiles without the requirement of law-observance. In this way, it can be said that Paul rhetorically says *yes* to his source meanings and then *and* for his allegorical meanings (no different than the sectarian texts' *yes* and then *and*). On the other hand, Paul's allegorical meanings do not affirm the replaced source meanings *because of the way in which he reconfigured their prior interpretation*. For Paul, what he understood in Genesis (i.e., the children of Sarah are Jews who observe the law) now has a contrasting meaning in Galatia (i.e., the children of Sarah are gentiles who do not observe the law). In this way, it can be said that Paul functionally says *no* to his source meanings and then *but* for his allegorical meanings (in contrast to the sectarian texts' *yes* and then *and*). Accordingly, what Paul does functionally stands in tension with what he does rhetorically. *Therefore, we observe the authors of the sectarian texts as roughly contemporary allegorists with whom Paul is rhetorically similar yet functionally different.* The full significance of this contribution for our understanding of Paul's practice can be realized only after examining the functional and rhetorical relationship of Paul's practice with those relationships found in the practices of the other two comparative examples. Accordingly, I return to this discussion at the conclusion of this project.

The third contribution is that my analysis provides one reason why Paul had to exert so much hermeneutical effort within his interpretive practice: he allegorized source entities and meanings that do not explicitly point to the future. For example, Gen 21:10 describes a specific request (i.e., cast out Hagar and Ishmael) made by a specific person (i.e., Sarah)

---

36. This is yet another indication that Paul's use of the ἀλληγορούμενα does not signal he uses a practice that can be defined by terminology or geographical location.

at a specific point in time. In this way, it does not give any indication of referencing the future (although Paul chooses to interpret it this way). In contrast, the sectarians, with only four exceptions—4QFlor 1–2, 21 I, 3b–7a (Exod 15:17–18); CD VI, 2b–11a (Num 21:18);[37] VIII, 8b–12a (Deut 32:33); XIX, 7b–9 (Zech 13:7)—used their interpretive practice to allegorize source entities and meanings that point to their fulfillment in the future (i.e., those found in prophetic texts). Because Paul understood his source entities already to have significant meanings, the effort he needed to exert would mirror how far he distanced his allegorical meanings from the prior source meanings that he understood as authoritative. Accordingly, Paul's argument is what forced him to exert so much hermeneutical effort. From this perspective, we may have another piece of evidence that supports the theory that Paul chose to interpret Gen 16–21 not by his own free will but in response to his opponents' use of it.

---

37. Within CD VI, 2b–11a (cited in ch. 2, sect. 2.4.2.1), the sectarians used Isa 54:16 as a subordinate biblical lemma to support their allegorical interpretation of Num 21:18. We observe this practice in Paul (cf. Isa 54:1 in Gal 4:27) and in the other two comparative examples. I discuss the significance of the sectarians' use of subordinate biblical lemmata in the conclusion after the examination of the other two allegorists.

5

Comparative Analysis 2
The Works of Philo of Alexandria

PHILO IS OF GREAT interest to scholars because he was a prolific interpreter of Scripture whose extant corpus is large. For example, prior scholarship has compared Philo's interpretive practices with practices found in Luke,[1] John,[2] Hebrews,[3] and Paul's letters (cf. n7–11). Because of the abundance both of Philo's extant writings and of scholarship on them, it is necessary to outline the boundaries of this chapter. First, I engage only a selection of Philo's writings and a selection of his allegorical expressions—sections 1.1 and 2.1 explain which ones and the rationale for those decisions—because his practice is spread generously throughout his surviving works that fill over three thousand pages within twelve volumes of the Loeb

---

1. Borgen, *Philo, John, and Paul*, 273–85; Chadwick, "St. Paul and Philo," 288; Siegert, "Philo and New Testament," 191–95; Seland, *Establishment Violence*; Sterling, "Place of Philo," 45–47.

2. Borgen, *Bread from Heaven*; Borgen, *Philo, John, and Paul*, 75–206; Daniélou, *Philo of Alexandria*, 167–73; Hurtado, "Does Philo Help Explain," 77–78; Runia, *Philo*, 78–83; Runia, *Exegesis and Philosophy*, 9–10; Sandmel, "Philo Judaeus"; Sandmel, *Philo of Alexandria*, 154–59; Schenck, *Brief Guide to Philo*, 86–90; Siegert, "Philo and New Testament," 195–209; Sterling, "Place of Philo," 47–51.

3. Daniélou, *Philo of Alexandria*, 173–77; R. P. C. Hanson, *Allegory and Event*, 84–96; Hurtado, "Does Philo Help Explain," 78–79; Runia, *Philo*, 74–78; Sandmel, *Philo of Alexandria*, 160–61; Schenck, *Brief Guide to Philo*, 81–86; Siegert, "Philo and New Testament," 177–83; Sowers, "Hermeneutics"; Sterling, "Place of Philo," 43–45; Svendsen, *Allegory Transformed*, 55–249; Williamson, *Philo and the Epistle*.

Classical Library.[4] Second, before I analyze Philo's and Paul's allegorical practices together, I examine Philo's practice independently of Paul's in order to safeguard against misrepresenting either allegorist. Although I treat the other comparative examples in the same way (cf. chs. 4 and 6), this is especially important for Philo because there is a history of allowing the interpretation of Paul or Philo to affect the interpretation of the other one. We observe this happening as early as the fourth century, when Didymus the Blind attempted to harmonize Paul's and Philo's interpretations of Sarah and Hagar.[5] Last, I engage only scholarship on Philo that is most relevant for the goals of this chapter. This chapter does not, for example, contain an introduction to Philo, a survey of his writings, or an attempt to recover the origin of his allegorical practice.[6] As in the previous chapter, this chapter is divided into four sections: Philo as a suitable comparative example, the allegorical practice of Philo, Gal 4:22–27 and *Leg.* 1.63–76, and contributions to our understanding of Paul's interpretive practice.

1. PHILO AS A SUITABLE COMPARATIVE EXAMPLE

Philo as an interpreter generally is accepted as relevant for understanding Paul as an interpreter. Prior scholarship has examined Philo's and Paul's perspectives on issues found in Romans,[7] Corinthians,[8] Galatians,[9]

---

4. LCL 226–27, 247, 261, 275, 289, 320, 341, 363, 379–80, 401.

5. Through a lengthy analysis, Justin Rogers argues that "[Didymus's] result is something that neither Paul nor Philo would have recognized as their own" ("Philonic and Pauline," 77).

6. Introductions to Philo, surveys of his writings, and discussions of his predecessors (e.g., Aristobulus and Pseudo-Aristeas) can be found in most general works on Philo. Of special significance is Kenneth Schenck's *A Brief Guide to Philo*. In addition to his concise introduction, Schenck provides a useful summary of every extant Philonic composition and ends his guide with a topical index unparalleled in the literature I have engaged (98–127). Also useful are the indices in LCL 379.

7. Barclay, "Paul and Philo"; Chadwick, "St. Paul and Philo," 292–95; Hurtado, "Does Philo Help Explain," 75–76; McFarland, "Whose Abraham, Which Promise."

8. Daniélou, *Philo of Alexandria*, 163–67; Galloway, *Freedom in the Gospel*, 103–48, 199–240; Kovelman, "Jeremiah 9:22–23"; Schenck, *Brief Guide to Philo*, 76–79; Siegert, "Philo and New Testament," 190–91; Stegmann, "Christ, 'Man from Heaven'"; Sterling, "Place of Philo," 41–43; Wan, "Charismatic Exegesis."

9. Borgen, *Philo, John, and Paul*, 233–49; Borgen, "Some Hebrew and Pagan Features"; Chadwick, "St. Paul and Philo," 299; Daniélou, *Philo of Alexandria*, 163–67; Lucchesi, "Nouveau parallèle"; McNutt, "Philo of Alexandria"; Rogers, "Philonic and Pauline."

Philippians,[10] and Colossians.[11] Philo even has been called "the single most important first-century Jewish *writer* for understanding the Jewish religious setting of early Christianity."[12] Despite the numerous comparative analyses listed above, for reasons discussed in chapters 2 and 3,[13] I found only one scholar who has engaged Philo's and Paul's interpretive practices of allegory.[14] As it regards the ancient interpretive practice of allegory, it is time to move the conversation past these authors' distinct views and towards those similar ways in which they expressed them.

1.1 Texts Examined in Section 1 and the Rationale

In this section, I engage selections from *De congressu eruditionis gratia, De decalogo, De migratione Abrahami, De praemiis et poenis, De somniis, De virtutibus,* and *De vita Mosis*. I chose these texts because they provide sufficient data for the assessment and because the relevant passages reflect views that are consistent with those views expressed throughout his other writings.

1.2. Criterion 1: Milieu

The following two subsections analyze shared theological concerns and interpretive practices in order to demonstrate a shared milieu between Philo and Paul.

---

10. Chadwick, "St. Paul and Philo," 301; Daniélou, *Philo of Alexandria*, 163–67; Todd, *Apostle Paul*, 285–96.

11. Chadwick, "St. Paul and Philo," 301–2; Daniélou, *Philo of Alexandria*, 163–67; Sandmel, "Philo Judaeus," 21.2:41–42; Schenck, *Brief Guide to Philo*, 79–81.

12. Hurtado, "Does Philo Help Explain," 74; emphasis original.

13. In addition to those reasons, a few scholars also have dismissed Philo because his allegorical expressions of Sarah and Hagar may be influenced by the Platonic interpretation of Penelope and her suitors (as introduced in Plutarch, *Lib. ed.* 7d). For examples, see Amir, "Transference of Greek Allegories," 15–18; and Colson, "Philo on Education."

14. Recently (2017), Jason Zurawski has proposed that the proper way for reading Paul's allegory is as a response to the allegorical interpretation of Hagar as paideia: "Nowhere else does Paul make such an unequivocal reference to his allegorical interpretation of scripture, and, in so doing, he attempts to alert his audience to the allegorical understanding of the narrative of which they were already aware, namely, an exegetical tradition similar to Philo's, the only allegorical interpretation of Hagar and Sarah we know of at this time" ("Mosaic Torah," 301).

1.2.1. Shared Theological Concerns

Prior scholarship has devoted much attention to Paul and Philo's shared theological concerns. What follows is a list of those shared concerns, including references both to the source material and to relevant discussions in scholarship.

- Adam[15]
- Charity[16]
- Christology and Logos[17]
- Circumcision[18]
- Conviction[19]
- Covetousness[20]
- Desire or lust[21]
- Foods corresponding to spiritual maturity[22]
- Future rejuvenation of the Jews[23]
- God brought being out of nonbeing[24]
- God dwelling in the body[25]
- God seen as if through a mirror[26]

---

15. 1 Cor 15:45–49; *Leg.* 1.31; *Opif.* 134; Daniélou, *Philo of Alexandria*, 166; Knox, *St Paul*, 133–35; Siegfried, *Philo von Alexandria*, 308.

16. 1 Cor 13; *Det.* 20–21; Chadwick, "St. Paul and Philo," 298.

17. Col 1:15–20; *Conf.* 146–47; *Her.* 188; Chadwick, "St. Paul and Philo," 302. 2 Cor 4:4; *Somn.* 1.239; Sandmel, *Philo of Alexandria*, 159.

18. Rom 2:25–29; *Migr.* 89–93; Barclay, "Paul and Philo"; Borgen, *Philo, John, and Paul*, 233–49.

19. Rom 5:13; *Deus* 134–35; Daniélou, *Philo of Alexandria*, 166.

20. 1 Cor 5:11; *Ios.* 144; Chadwick, "St. Paul and Philo," 297.

21. Rom 7:8; *Decal.* 142; Chadwick, "St. Paul and Philo," 295.

22. 1 Cor 3:2–3; 10:3; *Agr.* 9; *Congr.* 19; *Migr.* 29; Chadwick, "St. Paul and Philo," 297; Daniélou, *Philo of Alexandria*, 164.

23. Rom 11:11–24; *Mos.* 2.43–44; Hurtado, "Does Philo Help Explain," 75–77.

24. 1 Cor 1:26–31; *Leg.* 3.10; *Fug.* 46; Chadwick, "St. Paul and Philo," 296.

25. 2 Cor 6:16–17; *Somn.* 2.248; Knox, *St Paul*, 132.

26. 1 Cor 13:12; 2 Cor 3:18; *Decal.* 105; *Migr.* 190; Chadwick, "St. Paul and Philo," 298; Daniélou, *Philo of Alexandria*, 165.

- Greco-Roman religion[27]
- High priest[28]
- Knowledge of God[29]
- Man's depravity[30]
- πνευματικὸς and ψυχικός[31]
- Responsibility and guilt[32]
- σάρξ and πνεῦμα[33]
- Self-confident men[34]
- The world is passing away[35]
- Tribulations on the righteous man[36]
- Two as one flesh[37]

The primary contribution of these assessments to this project is they demonstrate that Paul and Philo both lived in and contributed to conversations in the same milieu. Henry Chadwick has said famously: "The numerous analogies in detail with St. Paul's letters show the extent to which both men fished from the same pool."[38] Larry Hurtado extended this analogy in order to clarify in which way these authors fished:

> If Paul and Philo are to be imagined as fishing from a common pool, then, to pursue Chadwick's analogy, they were clearly using different bait and equipment, were fishing from widely different points on the shore, and were aiming for very different catches.[39]

27. Rom 1:23; *Mos.* 2.171; Daniélou, *Philo of Alexandria*, 165.
28. Rom 8:34; *Gig.* 52, *Migr.* 102; Siegert, "Philo and New Testament," 186.
29. Rom 1–2; *Leg.* 3.97; *Somn.* 1.203; Chadwick, "St. Paul and Philo," 292.
30. Rom 7:24; *Her.* 270; *Leg.* 3.211; Siegert, "Philo and New Testament," 186.
31. 1 Cor 15:46; *Her.* 55; *Spec.* 4.122–24; Chadwick, "St. Paul and Philo," 297.
32. Rom 5:13; *Deus* 134; Siegert, "Philo and New Testament," 187.
33. Rom 7:5; *Gig.* 29; Daniélou, *Philo of Alexandria*, 164. Rom 8:5; *Gig.* 7; *Her.* 12; Knox, *St Paul*, 131.
34. 1 Cor 10:12; *Leg.* 3.164; Chadwick, "St. Paul and Philo," 297.
35. 1 Cor 7:31; *Cher.* 119, *Spec.* 1.295; Chadwick, "St. Paul and Philo," 297.
36. 2 Cor 6:4; *Det.* 34; Daniélou, *Philo of Alexandria*, 165.
37. 1 Cor 6:16; *Leg.* 2.49; Knox, *St Paul*, 131.
38. Chadwick, "St. Paul and Philo," 291–92.
39. Hurtado, "Does Philo Help Explain," 77.

Although Chadwick's observation is a consensus (and one I affirm), positions such as Hurtado's have led to the same approach I noted when examining the authors of the sectarian texts of the Dead Sea Scrolls: because theological views are different, some conversations do not consider the implications of these authors expressing a similar concern. As stated in chapter 4, the fact that the comparative examples express different theological views does not justify ignoring the implications of shared concerns. In this case, shared concerns demonstrate a shared milieu.

In addition to demonstrating a shared milieu, two of the shared theological concerns (listed above) demonstrate the usefulness of comparing these authors' interpretive practice of allegory. First is the shared theological concern of Adam. The relevant passages from Paul and Philo are as follows:

> Thus it is written, "The first man, Adam, became a living being"; the last Adam became a life-giving spirit. But it is not the spiritual that is first, but the physical, and then the spiritual. The first man was from the earth, a man of dust; the second man is from heaven. As was the man of dust, so are those who are of the dust; and as is the man of heaven, so are those who are of heaven. Just as we have borne the image of the man of dust, we will also bear the image of the man of heaven. (1 Cor 15:45–49)

> XII. "And God formed the man by taking clay from the earth, and breathed into his face a breath of life, and the man became a living soul" (Gen. ii. 7). There are two types of men; the one a heavenly man, the other an earthly. The heavenly man, being made after the image of God, is altogether without part or lot in corruptible and terrestrial substance; but the earthly one was compacted out of the matter scattered here and there, which Moses calls "clay." For this reason he says that the heavenly man was not moulded, but was stamped with the image of God. (*Leg.* 1.31 [Colson and Whitaker])

The significance of this shared theological concern for our purposes is not the use of Adam, but it is the distinction between a physical and spiritual Adam. Both Paul and Philo believed it was necessary to apply some interpretive practice to Adam by which two different meanings could be established. Additionally, this is one place where both authors engage with interpretations (i.e., Adam as spiritual or physical) that have no precedent in the Jewish Scriptures.[40] This shared need to apply dual

---

40. Daniélou, *Philo of Alexandria*, 166.

meanings to Adam, an interpretation not grounded in the Jewish Scriptures, is one piece of evidence that demonstrates—in contrast to Hurtado and others—that both authors were fishing closer together, were using more similar bait and equipment, and were aiming for closer catches than much prior scholarship has acknowledged.

The second theological concern that demonstrates the usefulness of this analysis is circumcision. The relevant passages from Paul and Philo are as follows:

> For a person is not a Jew who is one outwardly, nor is true circumcision something external and physical. Rather, a person is a Jew who is one inwardly, and *real circumcision is a matter of the heart—it is spiritual and not literal.* Such a person receives praise not from others but from God. (Rom 2:28–29; emphasis added)

> (Scripture) first makes it clearly apparent and demonstrable that in reality the sojourner is one who circumcises not his uncircumcision but his desires and sensual pleasures and the other passions of the soul. (*QE* 2.2 [Marcus])

> It is true that receiving circumcision does indeed portray the excision of pleasure and all passions, and the putting away of the impious conceit, under which the mind supposed that it was capable of begetting by its own power: *but let us not on this account repeal the law laid down for circumcising.* (*Migr.* 92 [Colson and Whitaker]; emphasis added)

Based on these interpretations of circumcision, one scholar has argued that Paul's opponents understood circumcision as Philo understood it (cf. *Migr.* 92): the allegorical interpretation of circumcision did not invalidate the literal command. Therefore, one reason why Paul allegorized the patriarchal narrative was to correct this misunderstanding.[41] Although it is not possible to prove this position (because we do not have any writings from Paul's opponents), it reveals an important characteristic of theological concerns: they can be closely connected to the interpretive practice

---

41. Borgen, *Philo, John, and Paul*, 236; for Borgen's full reconstruction of the situation in Galatia, see 236–37, 248–49. Philo's statements on Adam (*Leg.* 1.31; *Opif.* 134) also have been used to reconstruct a potential situation in Corinth. See Horsley, "Pneumatikos vs. Psychikos"; Pearson, *Pneumatikos-Psychikos Terminology*; Schenck, *Brief Guide to Philo*, 76–79; Sellin, *Streit um die Auferstehung*, 90–175; Siegert, "Philo and New Testament," 190–91; Sterling, "Place of Philo," 41–43; Sterling, "Wisdom among the Perfect."

by which they are communicated. In our specific situation, both authors used the ancient interpretive practice of allegory to cement a distinction between a source meaning (i.e., physical circumcision) and its allegorical meaning (i.e., spiritual circumcision). This second theological concern, as well as the first, demonstrate how significant the interpretive practice of allegory was to both interpreters of Scripture.

1.2.2. *Shared Interpretive Practices*

Paul and Philo share three other interpretive practices in addition to the interpretive practice of allegory. First, both authors use Gen 15:6 to define the pattern of normative faith. A selection of passages is as follows:[42]

> Just as Abraham "believed God, and it was reckoned to him as righteousness," so, you see, those who believe are the descendants of Abraham. (Gal 3:6–7)

> So then it is best to trust God and not our dim reasonings and insecure conjectures: "Abraham believed God and was held to be righteous" (Gen. xv. 6); and the precedence which Moses takes is testified to by the words he is "faithful in all My house" (Numb. xii. 7). But if we repose our trust in our own reasonings, we shall construct and build up the city of Mind that corrupts the truth: for "Sihon" means "corrupting." (*Leg.* 3.228 [Colson and Whitaker])

This shared interpretive practice is significant because it demonstrates how both Paul and Philo use Gen 15:6 as the "hermeneutical key" for their understanding of the patriarchal narrative:

> Abraham as an unfitting recipient does nothing to warrant the gift. Genesis 15:6 is the hermeneutical key for Paul's reading of Abraham's story, and the one act of Abraham that Paul ever emphasizes is Abraham's faith. . . . For Philo, virtue is the key that creates a proper relationship with God and makes one worthy to receive gifts from God.[43]

As with the authors of the sectarian texts of the Dead Sea Scrolls, we observe another Jewish interpreter of Scripture in the Second Temple

---

42. Paul also references Gen 15:6 in Rom 4:3, 9. For Philo, also see *Abr.* 262–74; *Deus* 4; *Her.* 90–95, 101; *Migr.* 44; *Mut.* 177, 186, 218; *Praem.* 27–30, 49–51; *Virt.* 215–16.

43. McFarland, "Whose Abraham, Which Promise," 119, 124.

period who uses Gen 15:6 as a paradigm for normative faith.[44] Unlike Paul, however, Philo uses Gen 15:6 to highlight the importance of virtue and wisdom.

The second shared interpretive practice is the use of a list to catalog vices:[45]

> Now the works of the flesh are obvious: fornication, impurity, licentiousness, idolatry, sorcery, enmities, strife, jealousy, anger, quarrels, dissensions, factions, envy, drunkenness, carousing, and things like these. I am warning you, as I warned you before: those who do such things will not inherit the kingdom of God. (Gal 5:19–21)

> Know then, my friend, that if you become a pleasure-lover you will be all these things: unscrupulous, impudent, cross-tempered, unsociable, intractable, lawless, troublesome, passionate, headstrong, coarse, impatient of rebuke, reckless, evil-planning, ill to live with, unjust, inequitable, unfriendly, irreconcilable, implacable, covetous, amenable to no law, without friend, without home, without city, seditious, disorderly, impious, unholy, wavering, unstable, excommunicate, profane, accursed, a buffoon, unblest, murder-stained, low-minded, rude, beast-like, slavish, cowardly, incontinent, unseemly, shame-working, shame-enduring, unblushing, immoderate, insatiable, braggart, conceited, stubborn, mean, envious, censorious, quarrelsome, slanderous, vainglorious, deceitful, cheating, aimless, ignorant, stupid, dissident, [faithless], disobedient, unruly, a swindler, dissembling, mischievous, mistrustful, ill-reputed, skulking, unapproachable, abandoned, evil-minded, inconsistent, prating, garrulous, a babbler, windy-worded, a flatterer, dull-minded, unconsidering, unforeseeing, improvident, negligent, unpreparing, tasteless, erring, tripping, utter failing, unregulated, unchampioned, lickerish, easily led, flaccid, pliable, full of cunning, double-minded, double-tongued, plot-hatching, treacherous, rascally, incorrigible, dependent, ever insecure, vagrant, agitated, a creature of impulse, an easy victim, frenzied, fickle, clinging to life, a glory-hunter, violent-tempered, ill-conditioned, sullen, disconsolate, quick to wrath, timorous, dilatory, dawdling, suspicious, faithless, stubborn, evil-thinking, a pessimist, lacrimose,

---

44. The author of the Epistle of Barnabas also shares this interpretive practice (cf. Barn. 13.7).

45. The author of the Epistle of Barnabas also shares this interpretive practice (cf. Barn. 20.1).

malicious, maniacal, deranged, unformed, mischief-plotting, filthy-lucre-loving, selfish, feud-loving, truckling to the mob, ill-managing, a mass of misery and misfortune without relief. (*Sacr.* 32 [Colson])

These lists reveal another Jewish interpreter of Scripture in the Second Temple period—in addition to the authors of the sectarian texts of the Dead Sea Scrolls—who uses a list to catalog vices.

The third shared interpretive practice is the use of athletic metaphors. A selection of passages is as follows:[46]

> I went up in response to a revelation. Then I laid before them (though only in a private meeting with the acknowledged leaders) the gospel that I proclaim among the Gentiles, in order to make sure that I was not running, or had not run, in vain. (Gal 2:2)

> Do you not know that in a race the runners all compete, but only one receives the prize? Run in such a way that you may win it. Athletes exercise self-control in all things; they do it to receive a perishable wreath, but we an imperishable one. So I do not run aimlessly, nor do I box as though beating the air; but I punish my body and enslave it, so that after proclaiming to others I myself should not be disqualified. (1 Cor 9:24–27)

> The other kind [of attack] we find in the case of an athlete in a boxing-match or pancratium for a crown of victory. As the blows fall upon him he brushes them off with either hand, or he turns his neck round this way and that and thus evades the blows, or often he rises on his tip-toes to his full height, or draws himself in and compels his adversary to lay about him in empty space, much as men do when practicing the movements. . . . Rather, let the tension of our minds be firm and braced, that so we may be strong to relieve and lighten the force and onset of the misfortunes which menace us. (*Cher.* 81–82 [Colson and Whitaker])

For Paul, he uses these metaphors to describe how to live a God-honoring life; for Philo, he uses them to describe how to live so that the soul finds virtue. This third shared interpretive practice, as well as the other shared

---

46. Paul also uses athletic metaphors in 1 Cor 15:32 and Phil 3:14. For Philo, also in *Fug.* 97; *Leg.* 2.108; 3.48; *Mut.* 81; *Praem.* 27.

practices and shared concerns, indicate that these two authors operated within the same milieu.[47]

1.3. Criterion 2: Authorial Assumptions

Both Paul and Philo are Jews who lived in the Second Temple Period and spent significant time in the diaspora. Similar to Paul, Philo is very explicit about certain aspects of his Jewish identity.[48] First, with Paul he shared the belief that the Jewish Scriptures were an authoritative source for making persuasive arguments: "The fact that the statement is made in a Bible verse guarantees its truth. Again and again a Bible verse is called to 'witness' for a claim."[49] Of special significance to Philo was the Torah, which he quotes thirteen times more often than he quotes other Jewish Scripture books.[50] Despite Philo's allegorical interpretations of the Torah, he still believed that Jews ought to distinguish themselves by their customs. In the famous passage *Migr.* 86–93 (part of which is cited above in section 1.2.1), Philo explains that Jews *never* should abandon observance of the Sabbath, festivals, and circumcision.[51] In stark contrast to Paul, however, Philo also believed that this applied to gentile proselytes.

47. Arkady Kovelman has argued for another shared interpretive practice: "The use of Jer 9:22–23 to reject the "'external' and 'carnal' goods in favor of 'understanding' and 'knowledge of God,'" and "explain the character of 'knowledge' and the way to 'understand and know'" ("Jeremiah 9:22–23," 175). I have excluded it from this section because (1) the allusions to Jeremiah that he cites are not clear in either Paul or Philo, and (2) I have found no additional evidence to support his position. Additionally, no other scholar offers evidence in favor of this position.

48. Three contrasting understandings of Philo's identity have developed into common views. Sze-Kar Wan explains them well ("Allegorical Interpretation," 156n8). A summary of his explanation is as follows: First, Philo was a *philosopher* who exchanged his Judaism for Hellenism (represented by John Drummon, David Winston, and Harry Wolfson). Second, Philo was a *mystic* who belonged to some cultic form of Judaism influenced heavily by Hellenism (represented by Emile Brehier, E. R. Goodenough, and Joseph Pascher). Third, Philo was an *exegete* of Scripture whose strongest loyalty was to the Jewish Scriptures (represented by Irmgard Christiansen, Valentin Nikiprowezky, and Carl Siegfried).

49. Amir, "Authority and Interpretation," 432. Regarding Philo, the more appropriate term for Amir's "Bible" is "Scripture," as it is anachronistic to speak of a completely closed canon at the time of Philo.

50. For a complete list of references, see Allenbach et al., *Philon d'Alexandrie*, 27–91. For discussions, see Amir, "Authority and Interpretation," 422; Kamesar, "Biblical Interpretation in Philo," 72. See also the extensive "scriptural index" in LCL 379.

51. Martha Himmelfarb has pointed out insightfully that this may explain why Philo does not consistently allegorize a person who performs a Jewish ritual (e.g., Philo,

> [Moses] having laid down laws for members of the same nation, he holds that the incomers too should be accorded every favour and consideration as their due, because abandoning their kinsfolk by blood, their country, their customs and the temples and images of their gods, and the tributes and honours paid to them, they have taken the journey to a better home, from idle fables to the clear vision of truth and the worship of the one and truly existing God. (*Virt.* 102 [Colson])

Second, Philo not only viewed the Jewish Scriptures as authoritative but also believed that the interpretive practice of allegory was valid for making persuasive arguments. Philo's extensive use of this ancient interpretive practice leaves no doubt to the value he placed upon it; the amount is unparalleled in the extant writings from the Second Temple Period. Last, it is clear that Philo shared with Paul the belief that he had a strong connection to his audience. This is evident not only by the innumerable places where he addresses Jews directly but also by his decision to lead a delegation to Emperor Gaius for the sake of procuring help amidst persecution.[52] For all these reasons, it is best to understand Philo as a Jew who "had a 'conservative streak' that valued his Jewish heritage even more than Greek Philosophy."[53]

The enormous collection of Philo's writings allows us to make three additional observations that demonstrate Philo's compatibility with Paul. First, in the same way that some prior scholarship has explained Paul's interpretive practice by means of the rabbis, so does prior scholarship attempt to explain Philo's practice. For example, "the only difference between the rabbis and Philo is that they did not try to guess what the hidden meaning of that law was. This is the conception of Scripture with which Philo started."[54] Although I demonstrated such comparisons are not helpful for understanding the ancient interpretive practice of allegory

---

Spec. 1.84–97), in contrast to his consistent allegorical expressions of named persons within the biblical narrative (*Kingdom of Priests*, 149).

52. Philo devoted an entire treatise to the Jewish persecutions under Gaius and describes the events of his expedition (cf. *Legat.* 166–83, 349–73).

53. Schenck, *Brief Guide to Philo*, 33.

54. Wolfson, *Philo*, 137–38. For discussions of Philo's conception of Scripture, see Borgen, *Bread from Heaven*, 1–27; Cohen, *Philo Judaeus*, 33–71; Hamerton-Kelly, "Some Techniques of Composition"; R. P. C. Hanson, *Allegory and Event*, 46; Wolfson, *Philo*, 134–38. For a summary of explanations from the late nineteenth and early twentieth century, see Mack, "Philo Judaeus."

(cf. chs. 2 and 3), they nevertheless emphasize the extent to which Paul and Philo's practices are similar.

Second, Greek philosophy influenced how Philo interpreted the Jewish Scriptures. In his writings, prior scholarship has found references to over forty-five philosophers.[55] However, although Philo regularly draws upon Greek philosophy, he rejects outright some Hellenistic religious beliefs:

> For some have deified the four elements, earth, water, air and fire, others the sun, moon, planets and fixed stars, others again the heaven by itself, others the whole world. But the highest and the most august, the Begetter, the Ruler of the great World-city, the Commander-in-Chief of the invincible host, the Pilot who ever steers all things in safety, *Him they have hidden from sight by the misleading titles assigned to the objects of worship mentioned above.* Different people give them different names: some call the earth Korē or Demeter or Pluto, and the sea Poseidon, and *invent* marine deities subordinate to him and great companies of attendants, male and female. (*Decal.* 53–54 [Colson]; emphasis added)[56]

In Romans, we observe that Paul rejects pagan religious beliefs in a similar way and for similar reasons as Philo:

> For the wrath of God is revealed from heaven against all ungodliness and wickedness of those who by their wickedness suppress the truth.... Claiming to be wise, they became fools; and they exchanged the glory of the immortal God for images

---

55. Wolfson provides an extensive summary: "Of pre-Socratic philosophers, Philo mentions the Pythagoreans, Parmenides, Zeno, Heraclitus, Empedocles, Democritus, Anaxogaras, Philolaus, the Sophists, and the individual Sophist Protagoras. Then he also mentions Socrates; the Cynic school, naming especially 'Aristippus and Diogenes' as following the teachings of that school; Plato; Aristotle. Of post-Aristotelian philosophy he mentions the various school or their leaders: the Stoic in general and individual Stoics, such as Zeno, Cleanthes, Chrysippus, Diogenes the Babylonian, Boethus the Sidonian, and Panaetius; Epicurus; the Peripatetic philosophy in general and individual Peripatetics, such as Theophrastus and Critolaus; the Sceptics in general; the Academicians in general; and finally the Neopythagorean Ocellus. Without mentioning names, he quotes, or draws upon, Anaximander, Anaximenes, the Pythagorean Epicharmus, the Atomist Anaxarchus, the Sophist Prodicus, the Stoics Aristo of Chios and Posidonius of Apamea, the Peripatetic Aristoxenes, and the Sceptic Aenesidemus. Besides these philosophers, Philo also mentions Homer, Hesiod, Pindar, Solon, Hippocrates, Ion, Euripides, Sophocles, and Aeschylus" (Wolfson, *Philo*, 93). To this list, George Nickelsberg adds Menander ("Philo among Greeks," 57–58).

56. See also Philo, *Decal.* 66, 80.

resembling a mortal human being or birds or four-footed animals or reptiles. (Rom 1:18, 22-23)

Last, both Paul and Philo believed that their authorship was divinely sanctioned and inspired:[57]

> But when God, who had set me apart before I was born and called me through his grace, was pleased to reveal his Son to me, so that I might proclaim him among the Gentiles, I did not confer with any human being, nor did I go up to Jerusalem to those who were already apostles before me, but I went away at once into Arabia, and afterwards I returned to Damascus. (Gal 1:15-17)

> Not that we are competent of ourselves to claim anything as coming from us; our competence is from God, who has made us competent to be ministers of a new covenant, not of letter but of spirit; for the letter kills, but the Spirit gives life. (2 Cor 3:5-6)

> I feel no shame in recording my own experience, a thing I know from its having happened to me a thousand times. On some occasions, after making up my mind to follow the usual course of writing on philosophical tenets, and knowing definitely the substance of what I was to set down, I have found my understanding incapable of giving birth to a single idea, and have given it up without accomplishing anything, reviling my understanding for its self-conceit, and filled with amazement at the might of Him that is to Whom is due the opening and closing of the soul-wombs. On other occasions, I have approached my work empty and suddenly become full, the ideas falling in a shower from above and being sown invisibly, so that under the influence of the Divine possession I have been filled with corybantic frenzy and been unconscious of anything, place, persons present, myself, words spoken, lines written. For I obtained language, ideas, an enjoyment of light, keenest vision, pellucid distinctness of

---

57. One area of scholarship in need of greater attention is Philo's place in the discussion of "charismatic exegesis." This term, coined first by H. L. Ginsberg (as noted in Aune, "Charismatic Exegesis," 126) to describe the mode of interpretation found in the Habakkuk commentary, has come to mean any Second Temple Jewish interpretation that is (1) hidden, (2) explained only by an interpreter gifted with divine insight, (3) eschatological, and (4) thought to be fulfilled in the author's own time (Aune, *Prophecy in Early Christianity*, 339). Philo rarely has been discussed in this context because he rarely speaks of inspiration or eschatology. However, we (1) observe here that Philo speaks of inspiration and (2) observe below that he is concerned with eschatology. Accordingly, Philo is in need of the same treatment that both Paul and the Dead Sea Scrolls have received regarding "charismatic exegesis."

objects, such as might be received through the eyes as the result of clearest shewing. (*Migr.* 34–35 [Colson and Whitaker])

I hear once more the voice of the invisible spirit, the familiar secret tenant, saying, "Friend, it would seem that there is a matter great and precious of which thou knowest nothing, and this I will ungrudgingly shew thee, for many other well-timed lessons have I given thee." (*Somn.* 2.252 [Colson and Whitaker])

1.4. Criterion 3: Perception of the Situation for Which the Interpretive Practice Is Used

As discussed in chapter 3, section 3, it is the situation as perceived by the allegorist that is most important for demonstrating suitability. Just as Paul used his interpretive practice of allegory to respond to a situation that he believed was critical, so does Philo. Philo, in many places, responds to those who either (1) abandon the requirements of the Torah for its allegorical meaning or (2) deny the allegorical meaning for the sake of a literal interpretation.[58] Philo's relationship with his fellow exegetes is complex. This is demonstrated by his various evaluations of their interpretations, including acceptance and rejection of both literalists' and allegorists' interpretations.[59] Most famous is *Migr.* 89, in which Philo reprimanded some of his contemporary allegorists:

> There are some who, regarding laws in their literal sense in the light of symbols of matters belonging to the intellect, are over-punctilious about the latter, while treating the former with easy-going neglect. *Such men I for my part should blame for handling the matter in too easy and off-hand a manner: they ought to have given careful attention to both aims, to a more full and exact investigation of what is not seen and in what is seen to be stewards without reproach.* (*Migr.* 89 [Colson and Whitaker]; emphasis added)

---

58. One comprehensive work on Philo's interaction with other allegorists is Hay, "Philo's References." In it, Hay analyzes the various ways that Philo treats his contemporary allegorists. Additionally, he demonstrates the ways in which Philo uses others' interpretive practices of allegory for his own benefit. See also Hay, "References to Other Exegetes."

59. In total, Hay cataloged seventy-four direct references to other allegorists in Philo's compositions ("Philo's References," 42–44). Additionally, Hay examined "Questions and Answers on Genesis" and "Questions and Answers on Exodus" for references to both allegorists and literalists. In these two Philonic texts, he cataloged forty-seven different references and noted whether Philo accepts or rejects each interpretation ("References to Other Allegorists," 82–84).

The ways in which Philo interacted with the exegetes indicates that he believed their approach and outcomes were incorrect. This perspective parallels what Paul described in Gal 1:6–9:

> I am astonished that you are so quickly deserting the one who called you in the grace of Christ and are turning to a different gospel—not that there is another gospel, *but there are some who are confusing you* and want to pervert the gospel of Christ. But even if we or an angel from heaven should proclaim to you a gospel contrary to what we proclaimed to you, let that one be accursed! As we have said before, so now I repeat, if anyone proclaims to you a gospel contrary to what you received, let that one be accursed. (Gal 1:6–9; emphasis added)

These texts reveal that Philo used his interpretive practice of allegory to address a perceived situation that was similar to Paul's perceived situation: a critical situation in need of attention.

1.5. Criterion 4: Hermeneutical Purpose of the Interpretive Practice of Allegory

In chapter 1, I demonstrated that Paul uses his interpretive practice to instruct the Galatians about their present and future. Philo also uses his practice for these reasons. We already have acknowledged Philo's commitment to his fellow Jews (cf. sect. 1.3).[60] His concern for the future, however, often is overlooked in scholarship. Philo demonstrates a great concern for the future in *Praem.* 165–72 and *Mos.* 2.43–44; he even describes his eschatology in *Praem.* 91–97. The most relevant excerpts from these lengthy passages are as follows:

> When they have arrived, the cities which but now lay in ruins will be cities once more; the desolate land will be inhabited; the barren will change into fruitfulness; all the prosperity of their fathers and ancestors will seem a tiny fragment, so lavish will be the abundant riches in their possession, which flowing from the gracious bounties of God as from a perennial fountain will bring to each individually and to all in common a deep stream of wealth leaving no room for envy. (*Praem.* 168 [Colson])

---

60. This commitment is so evident in Philo's writings that some prior scholarship has argued he taught in a synagogue (e.g., Culpepper, *Johannine School*, 197–214) or managed his own school (e.g., Sterling, "School of Sacred Laws").

> But, if a fresh start should be made to brighter prospects, how great a change for the better might we expect to see! I believe that each nation would abandon its peculiar ways, and, throwing overboard their ancestral customs, turn to honouring our laws alone. For, when the brightness of their shining is accompanied by national prosperity, it will darken the light of the others as the risen sun darkens the stars. (*Mos.* 2.44 [Colson])

> Some, without even any pursuer save fear, will turn their backs and present admirable targets to their enemies so that it would be an easy matter for all to fall slaughtered to a man. For "there shall come forth a man," says the oracle, and leading his host to war he will subdue great and populous nations, because God has sent to his aid the reinforcement which befits the godly, and that is dauntless courage of soul and all-powerful strength of body, either of which strikes fear into the enemy and the two if united are quite irresistible. (*Praem.* 95 [Colson])

These texts, in addition to those already cited in this section, reveal that Paul and Philo intended for their interpretive practices to function similarly for their audience.

2. THE ALLEGORICAL PRACTICE OF PHILO

Philo's interpretive practice of allegory typically is divided into three categories based on how he constructs his allegorical expressions. The first category, "*Questions and Answers on Genesis* and *Questions and Answers on Exodus*," consists of two texts—as named in the category—that alternate between questions on a Scripture passage and Philo's explanations. In these texts, Philo uses his interpretive practice of allegory as the means by which he provides answers to questions. The second category, the "Exposition of the Law," contains twelve compositions focused on either important themes or figures. In these texts, he uses his allegorical practice as one way (of many) to describe certain themes or events in people's lives. The final category, the "Allegory of the Laws," is an allegorical commentary on the book of Genesis. In these compositions, Philo provides (1) a Jewish Scripture to be allegorized, (2) an indication that it means something else (i.e., allegoresis is at work), and (3) an allegorical interpretation (i.e., an allegory). Because this category contains the interpretive practice of allegory whose structure aligns with the structure of Paul's allegorical practice in Gal 4, I use allegorical expressions from this category for the analysis.

2.1. Texts Examined in Section 2 and the Rationale

As noted above, Philo's use of the ancient interpretive practice of allegory is prolific. It is so prolific that it has been quipped, "So skillful was his manipulation of the allegorical method of interpretation that Philo could surely have extracted a statement of Plato's theory of ideas from a railway table."[61] I examine the first three compositions in the category "Allegory of the Laws" (*Leg.* 1–3) because they share the same structure as Paul's interpretive practice. Although "Allegory of the Laws" contains twenty-one compositions, it is possible to limit the dataset because the structure remains consistent throughout the entirety of this category.

2.2. Philo's Interpretive Practice of Allegory

For heuristic purposes, I have organized this list of expressions by indicator. It is important to note that Philo uses Greek words as indicators that he also uses for other purposes—as do other Greek writers. In other words, allegorical indication is only one of the ways that Philo uses these Greek words. Additionally, despite Philo having used the Greek root ἀλληγορ- forty-five times in all his writings—including *Leg.* 1–3—Philo never once uses it in a structure similar to Paul in Gal 4 (and it is not listed below).[62] These two notes are significant because they affirm our understanding—discussed in chapter 2, section 3—of how terminology was and was not used within the ancient interpretive practice of allegory.

In the following list, I provide one occurrence and footnote references for the remaining occurrences of the same type.

2.2.1. ἀντί as Indicator

> "To this one shall be given the title 'woman'" (Gen. ii. 23), as much as to say [ἀντί], for this cause shall perception be called "woman" because out of man that sets it in motion "this one is taken." (*Leg.* 2.44 [Colson and Whitaker])

---

61. Williamson, *Philo of Alexandria*, 145.

62. In *Leg.* 1–3, Philo uses the root τυπ- seven times (*Leg.* 1.61–62, 79, 100; 3.16, 83, 183). I discuss Philo's use of τυπ- in sect. 4.

2.2.2. ἑρμηνεύω as Indicator[63]

> "For he set his face towards the mountain of Gilead" (Gen xxxi:21). The meaning of this name [ἑρμηνεύεται] is "migration of witness"; for God caused the soul to migrate from the passions that are represented by Laban, and bore witness to it how greatly to its advantage and benefit its removal was, and led it on away from the evil things that render the soul low and grovelling up to the height and greatness of virtue. (*Leg.* 3.19 [Colson and Whitaker])

2.2.3. καλέω as Indicator

> "The fourth river," he says, "is Euphrates" (Gen ii:14). "Euphrates" means [καλεῖται] "fruitfulness," and is a figurative name [συμβολικῶς] for the fourth virtue, justice, a virtue fruitful indeed and bringing gladness to the mind. (*Leg.* 1.72 [Colson and Whitaker])

2.2.4. ὁράω as Indicator

> Let us look [ἴδωμεν] too at the particular words used. "A river," it says "issues forth from Eden to water the garden" (Gen ii:10). "River" is generic virtue, goodness. This issues forth out of Eden, the wisdom of God, and this is the Reason of God; for after that has generic virtue been made. (*Leg.* 1.65 [Colson and Whitaker])

2.2.5. ἴσον ἐστί as Indicator[64]

> The words "and thou didst eat of the tree of which alone I commanded thee not to eat" are equivalent to [ἴσον ἐστί] "thou didst consent to wickedness, which it is thy duty to keep off with all thy might": because of this "cursed"—not "art thou" but "is the earth in thy works" (Gen. iii. 17). (*Leg.* 3.246 [Colson and Whitaker])

---

63. Also, Philo, *Leg.* 2.89; 3.225.
64. Also, Philo, *Leg.* 3.253.

2.2.6. σύμβολον as Indicator

> The words, "for Whose sake thou hast done this thing" (Gen. xxii. 16) are a token [σύμβολον] of piety; for it is pious to do all things for the sake of God only. (*Leg.* 3.209 [Colson and Whitaker])

2.2.7. συμβολικῶς as Indicator[65]

> "And the name of the second river is Geon; this encircles all the land of Ethiopia" (Gen ii:13). This river figuratively represents [συμβολικῶς] courage; for the word Geon is "breast" or "butting"; and each of these indicates courage; for it has its abode about men's breasts, where the heart also is, and it is fully equipped for self-defence; for it is the knowledge of things that we ought to endure and not to endure, and of things that fall under neither head. (*Leg.* 1.68 [Colson and Whitaker]).

2.2.8. τουτέστι as Indicator[66]

> "And all the grass of the field" he says, "before it sprang up" (Gen ii:5), that is to say [τουτέστι], before the particular objects of sense sprang up, there existed by the Maker's forethought the generic "sensibly-perceptible," and that it is that he again calls "all." (*Leg.* 1.24 [Colson and Whitaker])

3. GALATIANS 4:22–27 AND *LEGUM ALLEGORIAE* 1.63–76

Each of the allegorical expressions above is structured similarly to Paul's practice in Gal 4, and one expression also is helpful for examining how Paul and Philo used their interpretive practices of allegory in similar ways: *Leg.* 1.63–76. David Runia has provided a useful system for understanding Philo's interpretive practice of allegory. He organizes Philo's practice into a system of components.[67] A summary of Runia's categories and how I use them is as follows:

---

65. Also, Philo, *Leg.* 1.72.
66. Also, Philo, *Leg.* 2.38, 41, 77, 92; 3.15, 153–54, 157.
67. The term "subordinate biblical lemma" was introduced in ch. 1n122 For more information on the "main biblical lemma" and "mode of transition," see Runia, "Structure," 238–44. Within this article, Runia also applies his system to the entire text of *Virtues*.

MBL: Main biblical lemma
The subheadings I use below (i.e., "citation," "initial observation," and "detailed allegorical explanations") are a part of Runia's classifications within MBL.

SBL: Subordinate biblical lemma
The subheading I use below (i.e., "proof of doctrine") is a part of Runia's classifications within SBL.

MOT: Mode of transition
The modes of transition are verbal and thematic.

Verbal—When "a word or phrase in the main biblical lemma catches Philo's attention and prompts him to recall another biblical passage where that same word or phrase also occurs."[68]

Thematic—When "a theme or topic raised in the main biblical lemma causes Philo to think of another biblical text which contains the same theme or can be used to illustrate that theme."[69]

Runia's system is a useful heuristic tool for demonstrating the similarities between Philo's and Paul's practices.

The following rendering is my application of Runia's categories to *Leg.* 1.63–76.[70] The underlined and bolded words are referenced in the discussion below.

§63a, citation MBL, Gen 2:10–14

"A river goes forth from Eden to water the garden; thence it is separated into four heads; the name of the one is Pheison; this is that which encircles all the land of Evilat, there where the gold is; and the gold of that land is good; and there is the ruby and the emerald. And the name of the second river is Geon; this encompasses all the land of Aethiopia. And the third river is

---

68. Runia, "Structure," 239.

69. Runia, "Structure," 240. For clarity, Runia adds, "It should be noted, moreover, that the first type includes the method of the second type, but not vice versa, for clearly, if two biblical texts contain the same word or phrase, then in Philo's eyes there will also be a thematic connection between them" (240).

70. Runia also applied his system to *Gig.* ("Observations," 133–34). I have modeled my use of his system below after his analysis of *Gig*. I am thankful to Runia for his clear explanations and thorough applications of his system, both of which aided me in transferring this system over to *Leg.* 1.63–76 and to Gal 4:22–27.

Comparative Analysis 2

<u>Tigris; this is that whose course is in front of Assyria. And the fourth river is Euphrates</u>" (Gen. ii. 10–14).

§§63b–64, initial observation (rivers, virtues)

By these rivers his purpose is to indicate the particular virtues. These are four in number, prudence, self-mastery, courage, justice. The largest river, of which the four are effluxes, is generic virtue, which we have called "goodness." The four effluxes are the virtues of the same number. Generic virtue takes its start from Eden, the wisdom of God, which is full of joy, and brightness, and exultation, glorying and priding itself only upon God its Father; but the specific virtues, four in number, are derived from generic virtue, which like a river waters the perfect achievements of each of them with an abundant flow of noble doings.

§§65–76a, detailed allegorical explanations

Let us look too at the particular words used. <u>"A river," it says "issues forth from Eden to water the garden"</u> (Gen ii:10). "River" is generic virtue, goodness. This issues forth out of Eden, the wisdom of God, and this is the Reason of God; for after that has generic virtue been made. And generic virtue waters the garden, that is, it waters the particular virtues. "Heads" he takes not in the sense of locality but of sovereignty. For each of the virtues is in very deed a sovereign and a queen. "Is separated" is equivalent to "has boundaries to define it." Prudence, concerned with things to be done, sets boundaries round them; courage round things to be endured; self-mastery round things to be chosen; justice round things to be awarded. <u>"The name of the one is Pheison." This is that which encompasseth all the land of Evilat, there where the gold is; and the gold of that land is good; and there is the ruby and the emerald</u>" (Gen ii:11). One species of the four virtues is prudence, which he has called "Pheison," owing to its "sparing" and guarding the soul from deeds of wrong. [Philo then interprets the other three rivers allegorically and continues as follows.] . . .

But, though in travail, it never brings to the birth, for the soul of the worthless man has not by nature the power to bring forth any offspring. What it seems to produce turn out to be wretched abortions [ἐκτρώματα] and miscarriages.

§76b, citation SBL, proof of doctrine, Num 12:12

MOT thematic ἐκτρώματα → ἔκτρωμα

Devouring half of its flesh, an evil tantamount to the death of the soul (Num ii:12). Accordingly Aaron, the sacred word, begs of Moses, the beloved of God, to heal the change in Miriam, that her soul may not be in travail with evils; and so he says "Let her not become as one dead, as an abortion [ἔκτρωμα] coming forth from the womb of a mother; consuming half of her flesh" (Num. xii. 12).

My application of Runia's categories to *Leg* 1.63–72 enable us to examine Philo's and Paul's practice more closely in the following ways.

3.1. Introduction: Galatians 4:22–23 and Legum allegoriae 1.63a, 65

Within *Leg.* 1.63a, 65, 66,[71] we observe that Philo introduces the Jewish Scriptures to be allegorized—underlined above—as Paul does in Gal 4:22–23:

> For it is written that Abraham had two sons, one by a slave woman and the other by a free woman. One, the child of the slave, was born according to the flesh; the other, the child of the free woman, was born through the promise. (Gal 4:22–23)

3.2. Indication: Galatians 4:24 and Legum allegoriae 1.65

Section 2.2 revealed how Philo used different indicators for his allegorical expression. In this pericope, we observe the terms ὁράω (cf. *Leg.* 1.65 bolded above), συμβολικῶς (cf. *Leg.* 1.68 elided here but cited earlier in sect. 2.2.7), and καλέω (cf. *Leg.* 1.72 elided here but cited earlier in sect. 2.2.3) being used similarly as ἀλληγορούμενα in Gal 4:24.

> "Here is an interpretive practice of allegory!" [ἅτινά ἐστιν ἀλληγορούμενα]: these women are two covenants. One woman, in fact, is Hagar, from Mount Sinai, bearing children for slavery. (Gal 4:24)

---

71. For similar introductions to the other three rivers, see Philo, *Leg.* 1.68, 69, 72.

3.3. Allegorical Interpretation: Galatians 4:22-27 and *Legum allegoriae* 1.64-76

The similarities between Paul and Philo's allegorical interpretations are best revealed by applying Runia's system to Gal 4:22-27.

> Gal 4:22, citation MBL, Gen 16:15 and 21:2
>
> For it is written that Abraham had two sons, one by a slave woman and the other by a free woman.
>
> Gal 4:23, initial observation (slave, flesh, free, promise)
>
> One, the child of the slave, was born according to the flesh; the other, the child of the free woman, was born through the promise.
>
> Gal 4:24-26, detailed allegorical explanations
>
> "Here is an interpretive practice of allegory!": these women are two covenants. One woman, in fact, is Hagar, from Mount Sinai, bearing children for slavery. Now Hagar is Mount Sinai in Arabia and corresponds to the present Jerusalem, for she is in slavery with her children. But the Jerusalem above is free, and she is our mother [μήτηρ].
>
> Gal 4:27, citation SBL, proof of doctrine, Isa 54:1
>
> MOT thematic μήτηρ → στεῖρα ... τέκνα τῆς ἐρήμου μᾶλλον
>
> For it is written, "Rejoice, you childless one [στεῖρα], you who bear no children, burst into song and shout, you who endure no birthpangs; for the children of the desolate woman are more numerous [τέκνα τῆς ἐρήμου μᾶλλον] than the children of the one who is married."

Although Runia never intended for his system to be applied to Galatians, my application of it is fruitful in three ways. First, it demonstrates how similar both allegorists could organize their interpretive practice of allegory. Second, it highlights how each author also can use εἰμί after his allegorical indicator in order to begin the allegorical interpretation.

> *"Here is an interpretive practice of allegory!"*: these women *are* [εἰσιν] two covenants. One woman, in fact, is Hagar, from Mount Sinai, bearing children for slavery. (Gal 4:24; emphasis added)

> *Let us look too at the particular words used.* "A river," it says "issues forth from Eden to water the garden" (Gen ii:10). "River" *is* [ἐστιν] generic virtue, goodness. This issues forth out of Eden, the wisdom of God, and this is the Reason of God; for after that has generic virtue been made. (*Leg.* 1.65 [Colson and Whitaker]; emphasis added)

Third, it reveals how both Paul and Philo could use the thematic mode of transition to employ a subordinate biblical lemma for the purpose of supporting their interpretation of a main biblical lemma.

4. CONTRIBUTIONS TO OUR UNDERSTANDING OF PAUL'S INTERPRETIVE PRACTICE

This chapter makes five contributions to our understanding of Paul's interpretive practice. The first contribution is the same as the first contribution of the analysis on the sectarian texts of the Dead Sea Scrolls: another roughly contemporary Jewish interpreter of Scripture used an allegorical practice similar to Paul's practice.

The second contribution is that the relationship between the source and allegorical meanings within Philo's interpretive practice informs our understanding of that relationship within Paul's practice. In the second contribution of chapter 4, section 4, we observed one reason why Paul had to exert so much hermeneutical effort was the way in which he allegorically expressed source entities and meanings that do not point explicitly to the future. As Philo also allegorized non-future-oriented entities and meanings, the question is how the relationship of Philo's source and allegorical meanings relate to that relationship within Paul's practice. Philo, as does Paul, affirms the source meanings as he understands them. In this way, it can be said that Philo and Paul rhetorically say *yes* to their source meanings and then *and* for their allegorical meanings. Unlike Paul, however, Philo crafted allegorical meanings—as did the authors of the sectarian texts of the Dead Sea Scrolls—that also affirmed the replaced source meanings he held as authoritative. In addition to the expressions above, this can be observed in Philo's own allegorical expression of Sarah and Hagar.[72]

---

72. For similar allegorical expressions of Sarah in Philonic literature, see the index in LCL 379:413–14; for Hagar, see LCL 379:317–18.

> Sarah, virtue, bears, we shall find, the same relation to Hagar, education, as the mistress to the servant-maid, or the lawful wife to the concubine, and so naturally the mind which aspires to study and to gain knowledge, the mind we call Abraham, will have Sarah, virtue, for his wife, and Hagar, the whole range of school culture, for his concubine. (*Congr.* 23 [Colson and Whitaker])

In this allegorical expression, Philo crafted allegorical meanings (i.e., Sarah as "virtue" and Hagar as "education") that did not contrast with the source meanings as he understood them (i.e., Sarah as Abraham's wife and Hagar as Abraham's concubine). Accordingly, Philo functionally says *yes* to his source meanings and then *and* for his allegorical meanings (in contrast to Paul who functionally says *no* and then *but*). *Therefore, we now observe Philo as another roughly contemporary allegorist—alongside the authors of the sectarian texts of the Dead Sea Scrolls—with whom Paul is rhetorically similar yet functionally different.* As noted previously, I return to the discussion of these relationships' significance for understanding Paul's practice more precisely after the examination of the third allegorist.

The third contribution is that Philo's use of subordinate biblical lemmata informs our understanding of Paul's use of Isa 54:1 within his allegorical interpretation. Philo uses subordinate biblical lemmata so frequently that, "in unraveling the structure of Philo's allegorical treatises, we must pay close attention to both the primary exegesis and the secondary exegesis, and to both the main biblical lemma and the subordinate lemmata."[73] When subordinate biblical lemmata were of great significance to Philo's allegorical practice, he expounded them with (secondary) exegesis at great length; when of little significance, he only quoted the subordinate biblical lemmata and provided no exegesis. This is relevant for Paul's use of Isa 54:1. If we were to apply a similar methodology to Paul, it would indicate that 54:1 is a subordinate biblical lemma that Paul used only to support his allegorical interpretation (in contrast to those who argue for a greater purpose; cf. ch. 1, sect. 2.2.3). Although by no means conclusive, this interpretation certainly aligns with Paul's choice to switch his attention back to the children so abruptly in Gal 4:28. At the conclusion of this project, I return to this discussion of subordinate biblical lemmata.

The fourth contribution is that Philo's use of τύπ- affirms that typology is not a useful schema for better understanding Paul's interpretive

---

73. Runia, "Structure," 238.

practice of allegory (cf. ch. 3, sect. 2). Philo uses τύπ- eighty-six times in his writings. Only three occurrences (i.e., *Opif.* 157; *Cher.* 55; *Det.* 78) indicate a meaning other than an image, shape, or reference (cf. LSJ, s.v. "τύπος"). All three of these occurrences demonstrate no concern for facticity. Although Philo does not use τύπ- to strip away the historical significance of a text—as does the author of the Epistle of Barnabas discussed in chapter 6—one of these three occurrences clearly indicates that Philo views τύπ- and facticity as operating in different interpretive domains. In *Opif.* 157, Philo states that the type (τύπ-) conveys its allegorical meaning (ἀλληγορ-) by means of hidden thoughts (ὑπόνοι-, cf. ch. 2n39)—not by historical characters or events. In other words, Philo makes no distinction between his use of ἀλληγορ- and τυπ- in the way argued by those who view typology as a distinct practice concerned with facticity. Ultimately, Philo's use of τύπ- affirms that typology is not a suitable interpretive schema for better understanding Paul's practice within the ancient interpretive practice of allegory.

The fifth contribution is that the impact of Hellenistic philosophy on Philo's interpretive practice of allegory informs our understanding of the impact of Jesus on Paul's interpretive practice of allegory. As discussed earlier in this chapter, Philo uses his interpretive practice of allegory to bring the Jewish Scriptures to bear upon his Hellenistic reality. Similarly, Paul uses his practice to bring the Jewish Scriptures to bear upon his new reality as a believer in Christ. This distinction brings the agency for Paul's interpretive practice into greater focus. For Philo, Hellenistic philosophy enabled him to allegorize as he did. For Paul, it was not Hellenistic philosophy (cf. Rom 1:23; Gal 4:8–9; 1 Cor 12:2) but Jesus (cf. Gal 3:23–26). This is significant because it reveals that it was Paul's understanding of Jesus that enabled him to allegorize Gen 16–21 in the way that he did.

6

Comparative Analysis 3
The Epistle of Barnabas

PRIOR SCHOLARSHIP ALREADY HAS analyzed the Epistle of Barnabas alongside the Dead Sea Scrolls, Philo's writings, and Paul's letters. Interestingly, Paul is the only one of these three whose allegorical practices have not been analyzed alongside the practices found in the Epistle of Barnabas. The similarities between the others' allegorical practices have been widely recognized.[1] For example, "the Epistle of Barnabas adopts *in toto* the allegorical method of interpretation which had reached its zenith in the voluminous writings of Philo.... However, embedded in the writer's fanciful allegorisation is another method of interpretation which has been found at Qumran."[2] It is surprising that Paul's and the author's—from here on, Barnabas—allegorical practices have not been analyzed comparatively because discussions of Paul's letters and the Epistle of Barnabas are many (cf. sect. 1). After demonstrating Barnabas is a suitable comparative example, I complete this analysis. As in the previous two chapters, this chapter is divided into four sections: Barnabas as a suitable comparative example; the allegorical practice of Barnabas; Gal 4:22–27 and Barn. 8, 10, 13; contributions to our understanding of Paul's interpretive practice.

---

1. For scholarship that compares the *Epistle of Barnabas* and the Dead Sea Scrolls, see Barnard, "Barnabas and Dead Sea Scrolls," 46–48; Barnard, "Barnabas in Contemporary Setting," 27.1:196–203; Dacy, "Epistle to Barnabas," 140; Kraft, "Epistle of Barnabas," 288; Paget, *Epistle of Barnabas*, 194–200. For scholarship that compares the *Epistle of Barnabas* and Philo's writings, see the discussion below in sect. 1.3.

2. Barnard, "Barnabas and Dead Sea Scrolls," 46.

1. BARNABAS AS A SUITABLE COMPARATIVE EXAMPLE

Unlike the other two comparative examples, Barnabas writes after the Second Temple Period ended and believes Jesus is the Messiah. Therefore, it is necessary to examine (1) if Barnabas's practice is relevant for examining practices within a period of history immediately preceding his letter and (2) if Barnabas was influenced by Paul's writings. It is important to note that both my examinations focus on the interpretive practice of allegory and do not seek to answer if (nor do I claim that) the Epistle of Barnabas is relevant for understanding *every* area of study within Second Temple Judaism or within Paul's letters. Regarding the first examination, Barnabas's practice is relevant because sections 1.1–4 demonstrate he is a suitable comparative example. I provide the second examination here. Although Barnabas does not mention Paul's name, it still is possible that Paul's letters could have influenced Barnabas.[3] Over the past 150 years, scholarship has debated whether Paul's letters influenced Barnabas and, if so, in what ways. Various proposals are as follows (and listed alphabetically by each scholar's last name):

- Barnabas likely was aware of Paul's letters, but "their literary influence on him was negligible beyond the general consideration that he adopted the epistle as a literary medium for religious instruction."[4] If Barnabas was influenced by one of Paul's letters, most likely it was Romans.[5]

- Barnabas, in Barn. 4.6 (cited below), responds to a position that Paul represents in Rom 11:12: "Now if their stumbling means riches for the world, and if their defeat means riches for gentiles, how much more will their full inclusion mean!"[6]

- Barnabas had an in-depth knowledge of Pauline theology, although dependence upon his letters cannot be demonstrated.[7]

---

3. The absence of Pauline references in the Epistle of Barnabas is part of a larger discussion on the absence of Pauline references in apostolic writers. Various explanations have been proposed, of which the most common is that orthodox writers did not mention Paul because heretics also used Paul's name in support of their arguments (e.g., Marcion). For a summary of this discussion, see Paget, "Paul and the Epistle," 359–62.

4. Barnett, *Paul Becomes*, 204.
5. Barnett, *Paul Becomes*, 207.
6. Böhl, "Christentum, Judentum," 107.
7. Dassmann, *Stachel im Fleisch*, 223–25.

Comparative Analysis 3

- Barnabas is familiar with Romans and Ephesians.[8]
- Barnabas radicalizes some of Paul's theological views, such as when Barnabas describes the twelve apostles as ὑπὲρ πᾶσαν ἁμαρτίαν ἀνομωτέρους in Barn. 5.9.[9]
- Barnabas is familiar with Paul: "Tat er tiefere Blicke in die Gedankenwelt des Apostels." Familiarity with Romans and (perhaps) Ephesians can be observed.[10]
- Barnabas is familiar with Paul and some of Paul's doctrines became the "Oberbau" of Barnabas's basis for moralizing the Jewish law.[11]
- Barnabas gives no indication of a direct historical connection with Paul, but some interpretive traditions used by Barnabas possibly were familiar with Romans.[12]
- Paul does not directly influence Barnabas, except perhaps at Barn. 4.9 and 1 Cor 4:13 (both contain περίψημα).[13] Paul and Barnabas share numerous ideas and terminology,[14] which "laissent supposer une influence littéraire de la part de l'Apôtre."[15]
- Barnabas is connected to Paul's theology, and he goes beyond it (similar to radicalists such as Marcion).[16] Barnabas also mixes Paul's views on salvation with rabbinic and Hellenistic traditions.[17] Paul's spiritual interpretation of Scripture is the "Voraussetzung" for Barnabas's interpretive practice.[18]
- In general, Paul and Barnabas "apparently draw from a 'pool' of OT passages that were used in early Christian circles to demonstrate

---

8. Committee of the Oxford Society, *New Testament*, 4–5; Goodspeed, *New Solutions*, 41.
9. Hilgenfeld, "Abfassungszeit und Zeitrichtung," 123.
10. Leipold, *Geschichte des neutestamentlichen Kanons*, 2:189.
11. Lietzmann, *Geschichte der alten Kirche*, 230.
12. Lindemann, *Paulus im ältesten Christentum*, 280.
13. Massaux, *Influence de l'Évangile*, 88.
14. For Massaux's list of shared ideas, see *Influence de l'Évangile*, 88–89; for his list of shared terminology, see 89–90.
15. Massaux, *Influence de l'Évangile*, 93.
16. Meinhold, "Geschichte und Exegese," 257.
17. Meinhold, "Geschichte und Exegese," 293.
18. Meinhold, "Geschichte und Exegese," 295.

that God is free to elect whomever he wants."[19] However, Barn. 13.7 is dependent upon Rom 4.[20]

- Barnabas marks a "Wendepunkt" in Pauline theology. Accordingly, Barnabas bends Paul's views towards a strong anti-Jewish slant, also mixing them with doctrines developing later.[21] Barnabas shares the same gnostic Paulinism found in Colossians and Ephesians.[22]

- Barnabas shows both a "weithin Anschluß" and "Abgrenzung" with the Pauline tradition. Barnabas belongs to the same tradition as the writers of the Pastoral Epistles, but he follows "gegenteilige Tendenzen."[23]

- Paul and Barnabas use the same interpretive practice to transform characters in the Genesis narrative into representatives of the Christian and Jewish community.[24] Accordingly, both Paul and Barnabas use their practice to support a claim of supersessionism.[25]

This survey reveals that prior scholarship has proposed various explanations based on different levels of analysis. Some scholarship even has recognized similar interpretive practices. Nevertheless, no consensus has emerged. In recent scholarship, the most extensive engagement of Paul's writings and the Epistle of Barnabas is James Paget's "Paul and the Epistle of Barnabas."[26] Before he begins his analysis, he explains the methodological difficulties in pursuing answers to this specific question of influence.

> Are we simply looking for a few concepts that we take to be Pauline, or for a general outlook? If we are looking for concepts,

---

19. Menken, "Old Testament Quotations," 304. Menken's article also is an excellent survey of passages throughout the Epistle of Barnabas that potentially are dependent on other texts in the New Testament. He helpfully divides his analysis into three categories: (1) common Old Testament quotations with agreement in use, (2) common Old Testament quotations that Barnabas derived from the New Testament, and (3) common Old Testament quotations that possibly depend on the New Testament ("Old Testament Quotations," 296–318).

20. Menken, "Old Testament Quotations," 313.

21. Pfleiderer, *Paulinismus*, 393.

22. Pfleiderer, *Urchristentum*, 561. Pauline authorship of these two letters is now disputed.

23. Wengst, *Didache*, 117–18.

24. Windisch, *Barnabasbrief*, 354, 376.

25. Windisch, *Barnabasbrief*, 308.

26. Paget builds upon the work that he began earlier in his published dissertation: *Epistle of Barnabas*, 207–14.

what should these be, i.e., what concepts are exclusively Pauline? If we are looking for a general outlook, what does this outlook constitute? Is there a Pauline outlook? Should we rather proceed on the basis of similarities in wording between a given text and a verse we find in Paul? But even when we discern a similarity in wording, could this be nothing more than evidence of a piece of Paul which has been mediated by a source/tradition to the author we are examining, rather than evidence of a direct usage of Pauline epistles? Furthermore, we must entertain at least the possibility that while an individual may not himself quote Paul, or even make allusion to Pauline concepts, whatever these might be, and may in fact contradict certain Pauline tenets, again as we understand them, he may himself have reached whatever position he has reached by virtue of reading Paul. Here, of course, we are faced with the complex problem of development within Paulinism. What might a developed Paulinism have looked like, and how might those developing Paulinisms have used Paul?[27]

Despite this sobering list of questions, Paget examines numerous potential connections based on Paul and Barnabas's various perspectives, use of language, and other occasions for possible agreement or disagreement.[28] After the analysis, Paget concludes in this way:

> We showed how difficult it was to establish a Pauline influence, either positively (*Barnabas* can be seen as a development of Paul's theology), or negatively (*Barnabas* reacts against Paul). *We concluded by arguing that it is better to explain the origins of Barnabas's own theology by reference to a Jewish-Christian milieu.* If we are right, then *Barnabas* provides us with evidence (and perhaps very early evidence) of the way in which some Christians, apparently not influenced by Paul, sought to appropriate the Jewish covenant for themselves and in so doing, argued against the literal implementation of some Jewish prescriptions.[29]

---

27. Paget, "Paul and the Epistle," 363.

28. For the following discussions, see Paget, "Paul and the Epistle," 367–77: Jewish understandings of the law (Barnabas's general outlook and 2 Cor 3:12–6); one or two sets of laws (Barn. 2.6; Rom 3:31; 1 Cor 9:21; 2 Cor 3:7, 11, 13; Eph 2:15; Gal 2:6); phases of the covenant (Barn. 4.6; Rom 9; Gal 3:19); circumcision (Barn. 9; Rom 4:11); identity of the people of God (Barn. 13.7; Rom 4); individuals as temples (Barn. 4; 1 Cor 3–4); the sinful past of Jesus's disciples (Barn. 5.9; 1 Cor 15:8; Eph 3:8; 1 Tim 1:15).

29. Paget, "Paul and the Epistle," 381; emphasis added. See also Paget's shorter treatment in his dissertation four years earlier (*Epistle of Barnabas*, 207–14) and his conclusion there: "What is clear to me is that B. is not a conscious opponent of Paul; and that

Not only do the following analyses in sections 1.1–4 function to demonstrate Barnabas is a suitable comparative example but also they support Paget's position that "it is better to explain the origins of Barnabas's own theology by reference to a Jewish-Christian milieu."[30]

1.1. Criterion 1: Milieu

The following two subsections analyze shared theological concerns and interpretive practices in order to demonstrate a shared milieu between Paul and Barnabas.

1.1.1. Shared Theological Concerns

The first evidence of a similar milieu is that Paul and Barnabas shared many theological concerns. What follows is a list of those concerns, including references both to the source material and to relevant discussions in scholarship.[31]

- Believers are a temple of God[32]
- Believers as heirs of the covenant[33]
- Believers as πνευματικός[34]
- Circumcision[35]
- Covenant[36]

---

he could have arrived at his theological position without having been influenced by Paul or Pauline communities" (214).

30. Paget, "Paul and the Epistle," 381. Paget's analysis is thorough, which perhaps is why I have found no scholar who has challenged his conclusions. An earlier analysis, completed by Albert Barnett in 1941 (*Paul Becomes*, 203–7) affirms Paget's conclusion: "The present study finds no instances that require explanation in terms of literary indebtedness to Paul's letters on the part of Barnabas" (207).

31. I have limited the discussions to those topics found in the undisputed Pauline Epistles, although others can be found in the disputed epistles (e.g., see Wengst, *Didache*, 117–18).

32. 1 Cor 3:16–7; 6:19; Barn. 4.11; 16.1, 7; Massaux, *Influence de l'Évangile*, 88.

33. Gal 3:29; Barn. 13.1–3; Massaux, *Influence de l'Évangile*, 89.

34. Gal 6:1; 1 Cor 2:13, 15; 3:1; 14:37; Barn. 4.11; Barnett, *Paul Becomes*, 205; Committee of the Oxford Society, *New Testament*, 11–12.

35. Rom 2:29; 4:11; Barn. 9.1, 6; Paget, "Barnabas 9:4." Also, Barnett, *Paul Becomes*, 206.

36. Gal 4:24, Rom 11; 1 Cor 11:25; 2 Cor 3:6; Barn. 4.8, 14; Böhl, "Christentum,

- Importance of a new way of living[37]
- Judgment in heaven based on earthly actions[38]
- Lawless and evil age[39]
- Perseverance in faith[40]
- "The elder shall serve the younger" (Gen 25:23)[41]
- "Two ways"—paths of light and darkness[42]

These shared theological concerns, many of which also are found in the other two comparative examples,[43] demonstrate that discussions from the Second Temple period are still relevant for Barnabas. Two of the shared theological concerns listed above also demonstrate the usefulness of engaging these authors' interpretive practices of allegory. First is the shared theological concern of circumcision. Both authors allegorize circumcision as a condition of the heart:[44]

> Rather, a person is a Jew who is one inwardly, and real circumcision is a matter of the heart—it is spiritual and not literal. Such a person receives praise not from others but from God. (Rom 2:29) For he speaks again about the ears, indicating how he has circumcised our hearts. The Lord says in the prophet, "They obeyed me because of what they heard with their ears." ... And, "Circumcise your hearts," says the Lord. (Barn. 9.1)[45]

The assumptions underlying each allegorical expression also offer insight into their interpretive practices. For Paul, he intimates nothing negative in his allegorical expression here about the physical act of

---

Judentum," 107; Paget, "Paul and the Epistle," 371–72.

37. Gal 5:1; Rom 3; Barn. 2.6, 9; Massaux, *Influence de l'Évangile*, 88.
38. 2 Cor 5:10; Barn. 4.12; Barnett, *Paul Becomes*, 205–6.
39. Gal 1:4; Barn. 4.9; 18.2.
40. 1 Cor 9:27; Barn. 4.9.
41. Rom 9:12; Barn. 13.2, 5; Lindemann, *Paulus im ältesten Christentum*, 280; Menken, "Old Testament Quotations," 303–5.
42. Rom 2; 2 Cor 4:6; 1 Thess 5:5; Barn. 17–20. Although Paul does not present a "two ways" section in the same form as Barnabas, as the author of the Didache, or as the authors of the sectarian texts of the Dead Sea Scrolls, his writings indicate a belief in a similar duality. For more on the "Two Ways," see n48.
43. Cf. sect. 1.2.1 in chs. 4 and 5.
44. Cf. Deut 10:16: "Circumcise, then, the foreskin of your heart, and do not be stubborn any longer."
45. Unless stated otherwise, translations of the Epistle of Barnabas are from Ehrman, *Epistle of Barnabas*, 12–83.

circumcision. His next statement even emphasizes the importance of circumcision so that a reader does not interpret his previous comment negatively:

> Then what advantage has the Jew? Or what is the value of circumcision? Much, in every way. For in the first place the Jews were entrusted with the oracles of God. (Rom 3:1–2)

In contrast to Paul, Barnabas uses his interpretive practice to nullify the physical act of circumcision, even claiming soon after his allegorical expression that an evil angel handed over the commandment:

> But even the circumcision in which they trusted has been nullified. For he has said that circumcision is not a matter of the flesh. But they violated his law, because an evil angel instructed them. (Barn. 9.4)

Barnabas supports his allegorical interpretation of circumcision in three ways. First, he lists various Jewish Scriptures in Barn. 9.1–3 that he believes support it. Second, he argues that circumcision must be allegorical because "every Syrian and Arab and all the priests of idols are circumcised as well" (Barn. 9.6).[46] Last, Barnabas exegetes the cross from Gen 14:14 by means of gematria.[47] In summary, because he crafts allegorical meanings that contrast how the source meanings already were interpreted, it can be said that he functionally says *no* to his source meanings and then *but* for his allegorical meanings. This relationship between his source and allegorical meanings is significant and I return to it in sections 3–4 of this chapter.

The second shared theological concern is covenant. Both authors believe that Jesus changed who is included within the covenant. Paul used his interpretive practice of allegory in Gal 4 to claim gentiles who believe in Christ could belong to God's covenant without circumcision. In contrast, Barnabas claimed that Jesus enabled the covenant to be passed to believers from nonbelievers who had lost the covenant at Sinai.

---

46. No historical evidence supports this claim and typically it is argued that Barnabas was confused (perhaps expanding the rituals practiced by priests in his area of Alexandria to the broader Mediterranean world [Windisch, *Barnabasbrief*, 355]).

47. "The number eighteen [in Greek] consists of an Iota [J], 10, and an Eta [E], 8. There you have Jesus. And because the cross was about to have grace in the letter Tau [T], he next gives the three hundred, Tau. And so he shows Jesus by the first two letters, and the cross by the other" (Barn. 9.8).

> But when they turned back to idols they lost [the covenant]. For the Lord says this: "Moses, Moses, go down quickly, because your people, whom you led from the land of Egypt, has broken the law." Moses understood and cast the two tablets from his hands. And their covenant was smashed—that the covenant of his beloved, Jesus, might be sealed in our hearts, in the hope brought through faith in him. (Barn. 4.8)

This pericope also provides insight into how an author's view of the source meanings can influence whether or not he uses an allegorical practice. Here, Barnabas did not use his allegorical practice because he did not view the source meanings' prior interpretations as authoritative (i.e., for Barnabas, Jews had lost the covenant). In contrast, Paul used the interpretive practice of allegory in Gal 4 because he wanted *both* to affirm the source meanings as authoritative *and* to contrast them. The theological concerns of covenant and circumcision indicate a shared milieu not only because Paul and Barnabas share these concerns but also because both authors could address them by reconfiguring source meanings—Barnabas by rejecting and Paul by amending—based on their individual views of the source meanings.

1.1.2. Shared Interpretive Practices

Paul and Barnabas share three other interpretive practices in addition to the interpretive practice of allegory. First, both authors use Gen 15:6 to define the pattern for normative faith:

> Just as Abraham "believed God, and it was reckoned to him as righteousness," so, you see, those who believe are the descendants of Abraham. (Gal 3:6–7)

> And if this is also brought to mind through Abraham, we maintain that our knowledge is perfect. What then does he say to Abraham, when he alone believed and was appointed for righteousness? See, Abraham, I have made you a father of the nations who believe in God while uncircumcised. (Barn. 13.7)

Barnabas interprets Gen 15:6 so that God only was speaking about the uncircumcised. Although Paul does not interpret Gen 15:6 in the same way as Barnabas, he does explain in Gal 3 how such a pattern also can be applied to uncircumcised gentiles.

The second shared interpretive practice is using a list to catalog vices:

> Now the works of the flesh are obvious: fornication, impurity, licentiousness, idolatry, sorcery, enmities, strife, jealousy, anger, quarrels, dissensions, factions, envy, drunkenness, carousing, and things like these. I am warning you, as I warned you before: those who do such things will not inherit the kingdom of God. (Gal 5:19–21)

> For it is the path of eternal death which comes with punishment; on it are those things that destroy people's souls: idolatry, impertinence, glorification of power, hypocrisy, duplicity, adultery, murder, robbery, arrogance, transgression, deceit, malice, insolence, sorcery, magic, greed, irreverence towards God. (Barn. 20.1)[48]

The observation that all four authors share this interpretive practice—in addition to the use of Gen 15:6—is a strong indication of a shared milieu.

The third interpretive practice used by Paul and Barnabas, as well as by Philo (*Agr.* 9; *Congr.* 19; *Migr.* 29), is the expression of spiritual maturity by means of food:

> I fed you with milk, not solid food, for you were not ready for solid food. Even now you are still not ready, for you are still of the flesh. (1 Cor 3:2–3)

> Why then does he speak of milk and honey? Because the child is first nourished by honey and then milk. So also, when we are nourished by faith in the promise and then by the word, we will live as masters over the earth. (Barn. 6.17)

These shared interpretive practices, as well as shared theological concerns, indicate that these authors operated within the same milieu.

---

48. This list of vices is found in a section of the letter that discusses "two ways" of living (Barn. 18–20), which was a common theme in Jewish literature at this time (cf. 1QS III, 13—IV, 26; and Did. 1:1–6). For two recent analyses, see Rhodes, "Two Ways Tradition"; and Julien Smith, "Epistle of Barnabas." Most useful is Smith's chapter-by-chapter analysis in "Epistle of Barnabas," 472–84. In early scholarship on the Epistle of Barnabas, Barn. 18–20 was considered a separate unit, perhaps even written by a separate author. However, recent scholarship has argued otherwise and for the centrality of the "two ways" motif in the entire letter (e.g., Barnard, "Barnabas and Dead Sea Scrolls," 57–59; and Hvalvik, *Struggle*, 3–4, 101, 200–201).

1.2. Criterion 2: Authorial Assumptions[49]

The authorship of the Epistle of Barnabas is a difficult and complex subject.[50] First, there is disagreement over whether Barnabas was a Jew[51] or a gentile.[52] The positions already have been summarized well.

> Those [scholars] in favor of a Jewish origin argue their case on the basis of the Jewish character of the epistle. In this respect particular attention is paid to the presence in the epistle of rabbinic traditions (chs. 7 and 8), to the use and knowledge of Jewish exegetical methods, to an outlook shared with Jewish apocalypses, a future hope expressed in terms of Jewish idioms of the land (6:8–19) and temple (4:11; 6:15; 16:7f), to the *Two Ways* material, which it is claimed is of Palestinian origin, to the great concern of the epistle with the interpretation of the law, and to its obvious respect for the law, and in one instance, to the contention that the epistle reflects the concerns of a supposed Tannaitic catechism. These arguments can appear powerful, especially when we note that passages in Barn only appear to be thinly Christianized. Those who oppose a Jewish origin for the author point to the stridency of the epistle's anti-Judaism, the apparent lack of knowledge of rabbinic traditions, the likening of the Jerusalem temple to a pagan place of worship, and at 16:7 and possibly 14:5, the imputation to the

---

49. For many of the interpretive options discussed in criteria 2–4, two scholars already have completed substantial histories of research: Hvalvik, *Struggle*; and Paget, *Epistle of Barnabas*. Therefore, when those works are relevant, I reference each and provide additional information from more recent scholarship in order to update the conversation. It is important to note, however, that no significant study has been published on the Epistle of Barnabas since these two magisterial works except for Prostmeier, *Barnabasbrief*; and Rhodes, *Epistle of Barnabas*. Even Rhodes acknowledges the substantial contribution of both Hvalvik and Paget before stating he will "chart a somewhat different course" (*Epistle of Barnabas*, vi).

50. Clement of Alexandria was the first to claim that Barnabas, Paul's companion, wrote this letter (*Strom.* 2.6:31; 2.7:35; 2.20:116; 5.10:63). Most scholars now consider this unlikely. For one substantial attempt in the last century to affirm Clement's attribution, see Burger, "Énigme de Barnabas," 191–93.

51. For those scholars in favor of Jewish authorship, see the lists in Hvalvik, *Struggle*, 43n5; and Paget, *Epistle of Barnabas*, 7–8n23–28. Regarding rabbinic literature, recent scholarship has focused on influence rather than authorship. For example, see Tim Hegedus's analysis of Midrash in the Epistle of Barnabas ("Midrash and the Letter").

52. For those scholars in favor of gentile authorship, see the lists in Hvalvik, *Struggle*, 43n6; and Paget, *Epistle of Barnabas*, 8n29. Both authors (Hvalvik, *Struggle*, 44; and Paget, *Epistle of Barnabas*, 9) support a gentile authorship, although Paget later changed his position ("Epistle of Barnabas," 442). One scholar has gone so far as to reconstruct a gentile profile for the author (Rhodes, "Two Ways Tradition," 815).

author and his readers of a former state of unbelief (see the words: at 16:7 πρὸ τοῦ ἡμᾶς πιστεῦσαι τῷ θεῷ).[53]

Second, it is not possible to determine how much Barnabas wrote of his text and how much he reworked from prior sources within Judaism. Some scholars attribute little composition to Barnabas,[54] while others attribute much.[55] Third, despite some scholars' attempts to soften the claim that Barnabas was anti-Jewish,[56] others uphold this traditional interpretation.[57]

Regarding the first and second debate, I affirm that Barnabas was a Jew and that the letter reflects his perspectives for the following reasons. First, the arguments against a Jewish authorship rely on a reader's assumptions (e.g., how a reader believes Barnabas would have described the temple and his previous life) and what Barnabas does not do (e.g., he does not demonstrate knowledge of some rabbinic traditions). In contrast, what Barnabas does (i.e., the concerns he discusses and how he chooses to discuss them) supports a Jewish authorship. Second, although Barnabas undoubtedly used some sources from previous traditions within Judaism—an argument often used in favor of a gentile authorship—both his organization and interaction with the material still supports a Jewish perspective.[58] Regarding the third debate, the position

---

53. Paget, *Epistle of Barnabas*, 7–8.

54. For scholars who attribute little composition to Barnabas, see Kraft, "Epistle of Barnabas"; Prigent, *Testimonia*; Wengst, *Tradition und Theologie* and *Didache*; Windisch, *Barnabasbrief*.

55. For scholars who attribute much composition to Barnabas, see the discussions in Hvalvik, *Struggle*, 323; and Paget, *Epistle of Barnabas*, 71.

56. Only in the last half of the twentieth century did scholarship begin to question this traditional interpretation, primarily based on the argument that Barnabas's sources appear Jewish. The most famous declaration is by Robert Kraft in his review of Prigent's *Testomonia*: "One would do well to dismiss [anti-Jewish] altogether from descriptions of the Epistle" (Kraft, Review of *Testimonia*, 405). James Rhodes's *Epistle of Barnabas* is the most recent monograph to address this issue. Although his argument focuses on salvation history, it speaks directly to Barnabas's views of Judaism. Rhodes concludes that to classify Barnabas as "nothing more than an anti-Jewish hack" is unfair (205). He argues that Barnabas understood the Jewish covenant as valid even after Sinai (despite Barn. 4.8) and that Barnabas's comments were "rhetorical hyperbole" (17). To support his position, he points to Barnabas's allegorical expression of many rituals established after Sinai (7) and Barnabas's interaction with Deuteronomic traditions (88–174).

57. Barnard, "Barnabas and Contemporary Setting," 27.1:203; Hegedus, "Midrash and the Letter," 21; Horbury, *Jews and Christians*, 130; Hvalvik, *Struggle*, 134; Paget, "Barnabas 9:4," 248; Paget, *Epistle of Barnabas*, 51.

58. For a discussion on how redaction criticism also demonstrates this, see Hvalvik, *Struggle*, 16; and Paget, "Barnabas and the Outsiders," 192–202.

for anti-Judaism must be qualified. Although Barnabas does not agree with the prior interpretations of the Jewish Scriptures as he understands them,[59] he still views the Scriptures as authoritative. Two characteristics of Barnabas support this interpretation. First, he praises the way in which Moses gave the law. Consequently, he also praises the law:

> Because the one who is upright both walks in this world and waits for the holy age. Do you see how well Moses has given the Law? (Barn. 10.11)

Second, Barnabas not only interprets the Jewish Scriptures but also uses them as *the* evidence for his arguments. This stands in stark contrast to numerous contemporary authors whose arguments were Jesus-centric and who avoided the Jewish Scriptures.[60] Barnabas placed so great an importance on the Jewish Scriptures that it has been said, "Almost more than any of the other Apostolic Fathers, with the possible exception of *1 Clement, Barnabas* attributes ultimate importance to this body of texts."[61] For these reasons, I affirm that Barnabas was a Jew. It is significant to point out that even Paget, who once was a strong proponent of a gentile authorship, later changed his position and viewed Barnabas as a Jew who is participating in an inter-Jewish dialogue.[62]

Barnabas's respect for the Jewish Scriptures and his choice to use them as evidence for his argument demonstrate that he shared the first authorial assumption with Paul: the Jewish Scriptures are an authority for making persuasive arguments. The second authorial assumption—whether the interpretive practice of allegory is valid for making persuasive arguments—is cemented by the numerous instances of Barnabas's allegorical practice. The final authorial assumption is whether Barnabas displayed a strong connection to his audience, a connection that he hoped would increase the persuasiveness of his arguments. Barnabas expressed strong personal feelings towards his audience no differently than Paul did:

> And so I share your joy all the more within myself, hoping to be saved; for truly I see that, in your midst, the Spirit has been

---

59. His discussions of these prior interpretations often include polemical statements against the Jews. For examples, see Barn. 2.9; 4.2, 6–8; 8.7; 9.4; 10.9; 13.6–7; 16.1–2.

60. Lowy, "Confutation of Judaism," 6:312–13. For similar observations, see Barnard, "Barnabas in Contemporary Setting," 27.1:190; Paget, "Paul and the Epistle," 379; Rhodes, "Two Ways Tradition," 810.

61. Paget, "Epistle of Barnabas," 445.

62. Paget, "Epistle of Barnabas," 442.

poured out upon you from the abundance of the Lord's fountain—*so amazed have I been by the sight of your face, which I have so desired*. And so, since I have been persuaded about this and realize that I who have spoken to you know many things (since the Lord has traveled along with me in the path of righteousness), *I have also felt fully compelled to love you more than my own soul.* . . . But I will show a few matters to you, *not as a teacher but as one of your own*; these will gladden your hearts in the present circumstances. (Barn. 1.3–4, 8; emphasis added)

And so you should understand. And yet again, I am asking you this as one who is from among you and who loves each and every one of you more than my own soul. (Barn. 4.6)

For the one who has placed the implanted gift of his covenant in us knew these things. No one has learned a more reliable lesson from me. But I know that you are worthy. (Barn. 9.9)

1.3. Criterion 3: Perception of the Situation for Which the Interpretive Practice Is Used

Uncertainty surrounds the historical context of Barnabas in three ways. First, it is unclear when he wrote the letter.[63] Prior scholarship has proposed dates in the reigns of Vespasian (69–79 CE),[64] Domitian (81–96 CE),[65] Nerva (96–98 CE),[66] and Hadrian (117–38 CE).[67] The various dates are a result of attempts to place Barnabas within the emperor's reign most suitable

---

63. Barn. 16 indicates that the temple is destroyed. Accordingly, the letter's *terminus post quem* is 70 CE. Most consider the *terminus ad quem* to be around 130 CE, although the exact date is Clement's reference to the letter in 190 CE.

64. For scholars who support a date in the reign of Vespasian, see the lists in Hvalvik, *Struggle*, 27n3; and Paget, *Epistle of Barnabas*, 14–15n63–65. In an interesting twist, Hvalvik argues that Vespasian is the best candidate based upon Barn. 4.3–5 (*Struggle*, 32), yet dismisses Barn. 4.3–5 as having "no bearing on the dating of *Barnabas*" (26).

65. For scholars who support a date in the reign of Domitian, see the list in Hvalvik, *Struggle*, 27n4.

66. For scholars who support a date in the reign of Nerva, see the lists in Hvalvik, *Struggle*, 27n5; and Paget, "Paul and the Epistle," 364n20. Although rarely supported by modern scholars, two recent proponents are Horbury, *Jews and Christians*, 133; and Paget, *Epistle of Barnabas*, 28.

67. For scholars who support a date in the reign of Hadrian, see the lists in Gunther, "Epistle of Barnabas," 146; Hvalvik, *Struggle*, 27n6; Paget, *Epistle of Barnabas*, 24n116–17. Barnard, "Barnabas and Dead Sea Scrolls," 45—not found in those lists—also holds this position.

Comparative Analysis 3   145

to hypothetical circumstances conjectured from two cryptic passages: Barn. 4.3–5.[68] and 16.3–4.[69] Still, some assert these passages provide no definitive evidence for dating Barnabas and therefore his date cannot be recovered.[70] Regarding the date, no proposed date is so far removed from Paul that they do not share similar theological concerns and interpretive practices—demonstrated above. The second uncertainty is the location from which Barnabas wrote. Prior scholarship typically favors Alexandria,[71] although Syria-Palestine and Asia Minor have been proposed.[72] Even if Barnabas wrote from Alexandria,[73] it is important to remember that geographical loca-

68. In Barn. 4.3–5, the author applies a prophecy in Dan 7 to his own historical context. The prophecy describes "ten horns" and one "small horn" that rises up from them. Prior scholarship has interpreted Barn. 4.3–5 in various ways (as summarized in Hvalvik, *Struggle*, 25–34), all of which attempt to identify the "small horn" as an emperor in the late first or early second century. A few of these interpretations also are discussed in Paget, *Epistle of Barnabas*, 9–17.

69. In Barn. 16.3–4, the author describes both the destruction and a rebuilding of a temple. Most assume this describes a growing hope for a physical temple to be rebuilt, although some have argued either for a spiritual interpretation or that the rebuilt temple is a reference to Hadrian's temple to Jupiter Capitolinus (see the summaries in Hvalvik, *Struggle*, 18–25; Paget, *Epistle of Barnabas*, 19–22; Rhodes, *Epistle of Barnabas*, 33–87). If Barnabas describes a hope for a physical temple—the consensus—then the question becomes under which emperor's reign are the conditions most suitable for this hope.

70. See the list in Hvalvik, *Struggle*, 17n3. Hvalvik affirms this position (25).

71. Hvalvik summarizes the evidence he uses to support an Alexandrian provenance as follows:
   1) The exegetical methods, in particular the use of allegory, show the epistle's closeness to the Alexandrian tradition.
   2) The influence from Philo indicates Alexandrian origin.
   3) The Epistle of Barnabas is known first and mainly by the theologians of Alexandria.
   4) The Epistle of Barnabas is found in Codex Sinaiticus—representing Alexandrian tradition with regard to canonicity. The same holds true also for the Clermont List, where it is found at the end of the Catholic epistles, between Jude and Revelation.
   5) The statement in 9:6 concerning the circumcision of Egyptian priests has been interpreted as a sign of Egyptian origin.
For comprehensive lists of scholars who support an Alexandrian provenance, see Hvalvik, *Struggle*, 35n3; and Paget, *Epistle of Barnabas*, 30n142. Since the mid 90s, no major arguments have been presented against an Alexandrian provenance that are not engaged already by Hvalvik or Paget.

72. For scholars who support a provenance in Syria-Palestine, see the list in Hvalvik, *Struggle*, 35n4. For scholars who propose Asia Minor, see Hvalvik, *Struggle*, 36n5. On this issue, Hvalvik and Paget differ: Paget argues against a Syrian Provenance (*Epistle of Barnabas*, 33–34) while Hvalvik argues that the indicators of provenance in Syria-Palestine are "at least as strong as those pointing to Alexandria" (*Struggle*, 40).

73. The evidence for an Alexandrian provenance is not absolute. For various difficulties with this position, see the discussions in Hvalvik, *Struggle*, 33–42; and Paget,

tion is not useful for distinguishing ancient interpretive practices of allegory. In other words, Barnabas's interpretive practice should not be considered simply a subset or outgrowth of Alexandria—specifically, of Philo's practices.[74] The third uncertainty is whether Barnabas wrote a nonthreatening intellectual exercise rooted in the Jewish Scriptures[75] or a response to real struggles.[76] Regarding this debate, the internal evidence does not indicate an argument "völlig akademisch,"[77] but a real struggle between the slowly emerging groups that would become Christianity and Judaism.[78]

> And so you should understand. And yet again, I am asking you this as one who is from among you and who loves each and every one of you more than my own soul: watch yourselves now and do not become like some people by piling up your sins, saying that the covenant is both theirs and ours. For it is ours. (Barn. 4.6–7)

Polemical passages such as Barn. 4.6–7, as well as the central role of the Jewish Scriptures in his interpretive practices, affirm that Barnabas is addressing a dire situation, one that—as Barnabas perceived it—was just as critical as the one Paul perceived in Galatia.

1.4. Criterion 4: Hermeneutical Purpose of the Interpretive Practice of Allegory

In chapter 1, I demonstrated that Paul uses his interpretive practice to instruct the Galatians about their present and future. Barnabas also uses his interpretive practice for this purpose. As discussed in criterion 3, Barnabas addresses a contemporary struggle. Some scholars have been quick

---

Epistle of Barnabas, 30–42. Paget, unlike Hvalvik, still attempts to argue for an Alexandrian provenance despite these difficulties (Paget, *Epistle of Barnabas*, 30).

74. For those who agree that there should be no connection made between Barnabas's and Philo's practices, see Hvalvik, *Struggle*, 36; Paget, *Epistle of Barnabas*, 32; A. Williams, "Date of the Epistle," 340. See also José Pablo Martín's analysis of Barnabas, Philo, Aristobulus, and Pseudo-Aristeas. Martín concludes that although many parallels exist, "non ci autorizzano da soli a concludere che Barnaba sia un document alessandrino" (Martín, "Interpretazione allegorica," 182).

75. For scholars who propose Barnabas wrote only an intellectual exercise, see the discussions in Hvalvik, *Struggle*, 93–94; and Paget, *Epistle of Barnabas*, 52–53. See also Rhodes, "Two Ways Tradition," 813.

76. For a discussion of this struggle within the Epistle of Barnabas, see sect. 1.4.

77. Dibelius, *Geschichte der urchristlichen Literatur*, 130.

78. Hvalvik, *Struggle*, 57–212. Also useful is his subsequent section, "Judaism as a Challenge to the Early Church," which supports this interpretation (213–319).

to reconstruct the details of this struggle,[79] including one reconstruction that mirrors the Galatian conflict: Judaizers. In fact, in the *editio princeps*, the audience of the Epistle of Barnabas is described as *galaticarentur*: "to become like the Galatians."[80]

> Cum Iudaei quidam ad fidem Christi conversi *galaticarentur* (ut cum Tertulliano loquar) hoc est, legem Mosaicam una cum evangelio retinendam esse putarent, idque multis Christianis persuaderent, sanctus Barnabas, sive quis alius, sanctum Paulum imitatus eorum doctrinam hac epistola convellere conatur, docetque multis scripturae locis, ac figuris legem Moysi iam abrogatam esse, eique evangelium successisse.[81]

The seriousness of the present struggle is demonstrated not only by Barnabas's general approach of reinterpreting the Jewish Scriptures by means of his allegorical practice but also by those passages in which he explicitly rejects Jewish interpretation (Barn. 9.4; 10.9; 16.1–2). His desire to instruct his audience about this present struggle is demonstrated by those passages in which he encourages his audience (cf. Barn. 1.3–4, 8; 4.6; 9.9). Barnabas also was concerned about the future of his audience, about which he also allegorized.

> Pay attention, children, to what it means that "he finished in six days." This means that in six thousand years the Lord will complete all things. For with him a day represents a thousand years. He himself testifies that I am right, when he says, "See, a day of the Lord will be like a thousand years." And so, children, all things will be completed in six days—that is to say, in six thousand years. (Barn. 15.4)

These pericopes demonstrate that Paul and Barnabas used their interpretive practices for similar hermeneutical purposes.

---

79. For scholars who argue that the community contemplates adopting law observance, see the list in Paget, *Epistle of Barnabas*, 52n267. Paget agrees ("Barnabas and the Outsiders," 192). For scholars who argue for converting to Judaism, see the lists in Hvalvik, *Struggle*, 9n21; and Paget, *Epistle of Barnabas*, 52n268. Both Hvalvik (*Struggle*, 134–36, 164) and Rhodes (*Epistle of Barnabas*, 205) agree.

80. This is my definition for "galaticarentur." Frederick Leverett defines this term as "to mix Jewish and Christian customs" (*New and Copious Lexicon*, "Galata, Galaticus, Galaticor," 353). *Galaticor*, a deponent, was used first by Tertullian in *Jejun*. 14 to describe behavior that he believed was similar to the Galatians' behavior.

81. Ménard, *Sancti Barnabae Apostoli*, 79; emphasis added.

2. THE ALLEGORICAL PRACTICE OF BARNABAS

As with the other comparative examples, Barnabas uses the interpretive practice of allegory in more than one way. He describes texts as allegorical,[82] occasionally uses the Greek root τύπ-,[83] and uses gematria (cf. n47). As in prior chapters, I examine allegorical expressions that share a similar structure with Paul's allegorical practice in Gal 4: those in which Barnabas provides (1) a Jewish Scripture to be allegorized, (2) an indication that it means something else (i.e., allegoresis is at work), and (3) an allegorical interpretation (i.e., an allegory).

2.1. Barnabas's Interpretive Practice of Allegory

For heuristic purposes, I have organized this list of allegorical expressions by indicator.

2.1.1. λέγω/λαλέω as Indicator

> Understand how he speaks [λέγει] to you simply. The calf is Jesus; the sinful men who make the offering are those who offered him up for slaughter. They are no longer men and the glory of sinners is no more. (Barn. 8.2)

> So, then, the commandment of God is not a matter of avoiding food; but Moses spoke [ἐλάλησεν] in the Spirit. (Barn. 10.2)

> Notice how he describes the water and the cross in the same place. He means [λέγει] this: how fortunate are those who went down into the water hoping in the cross, for he indicates [λέγει] the reward will come "in its season." (Barn. 11.8)

> What does he say then? "And a river was flowing from the right side, and beautiful trees were rising up from it. Whoever eats from them will live forever." This means [λέγει] that we descend into the water full of sins and filth, but come up out of it bearing

---

82. Barnabas describes texts as speaking allegorically to his audience's situation (Barn. 2.9; 6.13), to his opponents' situation (3.1), and to the entire nation of Israel (5.2). Also, he describes prophets as speaking in parables of the Lord (e.g., 6.10).

83. I discuss Barnabas's use of τύπ- in sect. 4.

the fruit of reverential fear in our heart and having the hope of Jesus in our spirits. (Barn. 11.10–11)

Pay attention, children, to what it means that "he finished in six days." This means [λέγει] that in six thousand years the Lord will complete all things. For with him a day represents a thousand years. He himself testifies that I am right, when he says, "See, a day of the Lord will be like a thousand years." (Barn. 15.4)

2.1.2. φημί, τουτέστιν as Indicator[84]

This is why he spoke about the pig: "Do not cling," he says [φησίν], "to such people, who are like pigs." That is to say [τουτέστιν],[85] when they live in luxury, they forget the Lord, but when they are in need, they remember the Lord. (Barn. 10.3)

2.1.3. αἰσθάνομαι as Indicator

You ought to perceive who Isaac represents and who Rebecca [αἰσθάνεσθαι ὀφείλετε, τίς ὁ Ἰσαὰκ καὶ τις ἡ Ῥεβέκκα (ἐστιν)], and whom he means when he shows that this people is greater than that one. (Barn. 13.3)

3. GALATIANS 4:22–27 AND EPISTLE OF BARNABAS 8, 10, 13

Three expressions from the preceding list are useful for evaluating how Barnabas and Paul used their interpretive practices of allegory in similar ways: Barn. 8, 10, and 13.

3.1. Introduction: Galatians 4:22–23 and Epistle of Barnabas 8.1; 10.1–2a; 13.1–2, 4–5

Barnabas begins his interpretive practice by introducing the Jewish Scriptures to be allegorized.

---

84. For five similar expressions that use φημί and τοιοῦτος, see Barn. 10.4–11 (discussed below in sect. 3.3).

85. Philo uses τουτέστιν in a similar way (cf. ch. 5, sect. 2.2.8).

Barn. 8.1	Barn. 10.1–2a	Barn. 13.1–2, 4–5
And what do you suppose is the type[86] found in his command to Israel, that men who are full of sin should offer up a heifer, and after slaughtering it burn it, and that children should then take the ashes and cast them into vessels, and then tie scarlet wool around a piece of wood (see again the type[86] of the cross and the scarlet wool!), along with the hyssop, and that the children should thus sprinkle the people one by one, that they might be purified from their sins?	And when Moses said, "Do not eat the pig, or the eagle, or the hawk, or the crow, or any fish without scales," he received three firm teachings in his understanding. Moreover, he said to them in the book of Deuteronomy, "I will establish a covenant with this people in my righteous demands."	Now let us see whether it is this people or the first one that receives the inheritance, and whether the covenant is for us or them. Hear what the Scripture says concerning the people, "Isaac prayed for Rebecca his wife, because she was infertile. And then she conceived." Then, "Rebecca went to inquire of the Lord, and the Lord said to her, 'There are two nations in your womb and two peoples in your belly, and one people will dominate the other and the greater will serve the lesser.'" ... In another prophecy Jacob speaks more plainly to Joseph his son, when he says, "See, the Lord has not kept me from your presence. Bring your sons to me that I may bless them." He brought Ephraim and Manasseh, wanting him to bless Manasseh since he was the elder. So Joseph brought him to the right hand of his father Jacob. But Jacob saw in the Spirit a type[89] of the people who was to come later. And what does it say? "Jacob crossed his hands and placed his right hand on the head of Ephraim, the second and younger, and blessed him. And Joseph said to Jacob, 'Switch your right hand onto Manasseh's head, because he is my firstborn son.' Jacob said to Joseph, 'I know, my child, I know. But the greater will serve the lesser, and it is this one who will be blessed.'"

In all these expressions, Barnabas introduces the Jewish Scriptures to be allegorized by means of summaries (Num 19:1–22 in Barn. 8.1; Lev 11:7–15 and Deut 14:8–14 in Barn. 10.1–2a; Gen 25:21–23 in Barn. 13.2; Gen 48 in Barn. 13.4–5) as Paul does in Gal 4:22–23:

> For it is written that Abraham had two sons, one by a slave woman and the other by a free woman. One, the child of the slave, was born according to the flesh; the other, the child of the free woman, was born through the promise. (Gal 4:22–23)

Additionally, we observe that Paul and Barnabas can both precede their introductions with a question and use ἀκούω in the same way:

---

86. I discuss Barnabas's use of τύπος in sect. 4.

Tell me, you who desire to be subject to the law, will you not listen [ἀκούετε] to the law? (Gal 4:21)

Now let us see whether it is this people or the first one that receives the inheritance, and whether the covenant is for us or them. Hear [ἀκούσατε] what the Scripture says concerning the people. (Barn. 13.1–2)

3.2. Indication: Galatians 4:24 and Epistle of Barnabas 8.2a; 10:2b; 13.3

After Barnabas's introductions of the Jewish Scriptures, he indicates that those source texts are being allegorized.

Barn. 8.2a	Barn. 10.2b	Barn. 13.3
Understand how he speaks [λέγει] to you simply.	So, then, the commandment of God is not a matter of avoiding food; but Moses spoke [ἐλάλησεν] in the Spirit. [Barnabas later reinforces this interpretation in Barn. 10.9: "But they received his words according to the desires of their own flesh, as if he were actually speaking about food."]	You ought to perceive [αἰσθάνεσθαι] who Isaac represents and who Rebecca, and whom he means when he shows that this people is greater than that one.

In a similar way as Paul indicated his allegorical expression in Gal 4:24 (cf. ἀλληγορούμενα), so can Barnabas indicate his allegorical expression (cf. λέγω in Barn. 8.2a; λαλέω in Barn. 10.2b; αἰσθάνομαι in Barn. 13.3).

3.3. Allegorical Interpretation: Galatians 4:25-27 and Epistle of Barnabas 8.2b-3; 10.3-11; and 13.6

After each indication of an allegorical expression, Barnabas provides his allegorical interpretation.

Barn. 8.2b-3	Barn. 10.3-11	Barn. 13.6
The calf is Jesus; the sinful men who make the offering are those who offered him up for slaughter. Then they are no longer men and the glory of sinners is no more. The children who sprinkle are those who proclaimed to us the forgiveness of sins and the purification of our hearts. To them he has given the authority to preach the gospel. There are twelve of them as a witness to the tribes, for there were twelve tribes in Israel.	This is why he spoke about the pig: "Do not cling," he says, "to such people, who are like pigs." That is to say, when they live in luxury, they forget the Lord, but when they are in need, they remember the Lord. This is just like the pig: when it is eating, it does not know its master, but when hungry, it cries out until it gets its food, and then is silent again. [In Barn. 10.4-8 and 11, Barnabas provides five more allegorical interpretations that follow the same pattern—introduction, indicator, interpretation—as Barn. 10.1-3] "And do not eat the eagle, the hawk, the kite, or the crow." "You must not," he says, "cling to such people or be like them, people who do not know how to procure food for themselves through toil and sweat, but by their lawless behavior seize food that belongs to others. And they are always on the watch, strolling about with ostensible innocence, but looking to see what they can plunder because of their greed." For these are the only birds that do not procure their own food, but sit by idly, waiting to see how they might devour the flesh procured by others, being pestilent in their evil.	You see about whom he has decreed, that this people will be first, and the heir of the covenant.

All three expressions demonstrate how Paul and Barnabas could allegorize similarly. First, we observe that Barnabas can employ εἰμί immediately following his allegorical indicator in Barn. 8.2–3 as Paul does in Gal 4:24:

> "Here is an interpretive practice of allegory!"; these women *are* [εἰσιν] two covenants. One woman, in fact, is Hagar, from Mount Sinai, bearing children for slavery. (Gal 4:24; emphasis added)

> Understand how he speaks to you simply. The calf *is* [ἐστίν] Jesus; the sinful men who make the offering are those who offered him up for slaughter. Then they are no longer men and the glory of sinners is no more. The children who sprinkle *are* [elided εἰσιν] those who proclaimed to us the forgiveness of sins and the purification of our hearts. To them he has given the authority to preach the gospel. There are twelve of them as a witness to the tribes, for there were twelve tribes in Israel. (Barn. 8.2–3; emphasis added)

Second, Barnabas supports his allegory with a subordinate biblical lemma (cf. Ps 1:1) in Barn. 10.10 as Paul does in Gal 4:27 (cf. Isa 54:1):

> For it is written, "Rejoice, you childless one, you who bear no children, burst into song and shout, you who endure no birth-pangs; for the children of the desolate woman are more numerous than the children of the one who is married." (Gal 4:27)

> And David received the knowledge of the same three firm teachings and spoke in a similar way: "How fortunate is the man who does not proceed in the counsel of the impious like the fish who proceed in darkness in the depths and does not stand in the path of sinners like those who appear to fear God but sin like the pig and does not sit in the seat of the pestilent like the birds who sit waiting for something to seize." Here you have a perfect lesson about food. (Barn. 10.10)[87]

Finally, Barnabas uses his allegorical practice to transpose contemporary figures onto characters within his source text in Barn. 13.6 as Paul does in Gal 4:25:

> Now Hagar is Mount Sinai in Arabia and corresponds to the present Jerusalem, for she is in slavery with her children. (Gal 4:25)

---

87. Here, Barnabas makes implicit changes to Ps 1:1, a practice that we also observe Paul doing in Gal 4:30 (cf. Gen 21:10). This similarity is discussed in sect. 4 of the conclusion.

> You see about whom he has decreed, that this people will be first, and the heir of the covenant. (Barn. 13.6)

These three expressions demonstrate not only that Paul and Barnabas could use their interpretive practices of allegory to reinterpret source meanings for their contemporary situations but also that each could use subordinate biblical lemmata to support their allegorical interpretations.

4. CONTRIBUTIONS TO OUR UNDERSTANDING OF PAUL'S INTERPRETIVE PRACTICE

This chapter makes three contributions to our understanding of Paul's interpretive practice. The first contribution is the same as the first contribution in the other comparative analyses: Jewish interpreters of Scripture roughly contemporary to Paul used interpretive practices of allegory similar to Paul's practice.

The second contribution is that the relationship between the source and allegorical meanings within Barnabas's interpretive practice informs our understanding of that relationship within Paul's practice. I already have demonstrated that Barnabas viewed the Scriptures as authoritative (cf. sect. 1.2). What Barnabas did not view as authoritative, however, were the (prior) source meanings as he understood them. We observe this implicitly throughout the letter as well as explicitly. Two examples are as follows:

> But even the circumcision in which they trusted has been nullified. For [the Lord] said that circumcision is not a matter of the flesh. But they violated the law, because an evil angel instructed them. (Barn. 9.4)

> But they received his words according to the desires of their own flesh, as if he were actually speaking about food. (Barn. 10.9)

For Barnabas, the Jewish Scriptures had no significance apart from their allegorical meanings. Put another way, the allegorical meanings replaced the prior meanings. Barnabas's view of allegorical meanings *as* the source meanings not only is demonstrated on a thematic level but also on a linguistic level.[88] In Barn. 11.10–11, Barnabas uses the same Greek term to introduce a Jewish Scripture *and* to indicate its allegorical interpretation:

---

88. To my knowledge, I am the first to draw attention to this characteristic of Barnabas's interpretive practice of allegory.

> What does he say [λέγει] then? "And a river was flowing from the right side, and beautiful trees were rising up from it. Whoever eats from them will live forever." This means [λέγει] that we descend into the water full of sins and filth, but come up out of it bearing the fruit of reverential fear in our heart and having the hope of Jesus in our spirits. (Barn. 11.10–11)

Barnabas's interpretive practice of allegory reveals that he is rhetorically different than yet functionally similar to Paul. He is rhetorically different because Barnabas did not view the source meanings as authoritative (i.e., he did not share Paul's view regarding Jews as members of God's covenant). Accordingly, Barnabas rhetorically says *no* to his source meanings and then *but* for his allegorical meanings (in contrast to Paul who rhetorically said *yes* and then *and*). Barnabas is functionally similar to Paul because he crafts allegorical meanings that contrast the prior interpretations of the replaced source meanings. Barn. 13.1, 5–6 demonstrates this similarity:

> Now let us see whether it is this people or the first one that receives the inheritance, and whether the covenant is for us or them. . . . He brought Ephraim and Manasseh, wanting him to bless Manasseh since he was the elder. So Joseph brought him to the right hand of his father Jacob. But Jacob saw in the Spirit a type of the people who was to come later. And what does it say? "Jacob crossed his hands and placed his right hand on the head of Ephraim, the second and younger, and blessed him." And Joseph said to Jacob, "Switch your right hand onto Manasseh's head, because he is my firstborn son." Jacob said to Joseph, "I know, my child, I know. But the greater will serve the lesser, and it is this one who will be blessed." You see about whom he has decreed, that this people will be first, and the heir of the covenant. (Barn. 13.1, 5–6)

In this allegorical expression, Barnabas crafts allegorical meanings (i.e., Ephraim as believers in Christ) that contrast their source meanings (i.e., Ephraim as Jews who do not believe in Jesus) no differently than Paul crafted allegorical meanings (i.e., gentiles who do not observe the law are the children of Sarah) that contrast their source meanings (i.e., Jews who observe the law are the children of Sarah). Accordingly, both Paul and Barnabas functionally say *no* to their source meanings and then *but* for their allegorical meanings. By setting both interpretive practices alongside each other, we now observe an allegorist roughly contemporary to Paul with whom Paul is functionally similar yet rhetorically different (in contrast to Paul's relationship with Philo and the authors of the sectarian texts of the Dead Sea Scrolls in which he was rhetorically similar yet functionally different). In the next chapter, I discuss the significance of this relationship and the other comparative examples' relationships for understanding Paul's practice more precisely.

The third contribution is that Barnabas's use of τυπ- affirms typology is not a useful schema for better understanding Paul's interpretive practice of allegory (cf. ch. 3, sect. 2). Because Barnabas used the Greek root τυπ-, it has been argued that Barnabas used typology (as some have argued for Paul).[89] One argument for this position divides Barnabas's uses of τυπ- into three categories: types of "Christ," of "the cross," and of "the new people (the Christians)."[90] It argues that "as far as historicity is concerned, it must be stressed that *Barnabas* recognizes the 'types' as historical persons and events."[91] In response to this position, there are two reasons why Barnabas's use of τυπ- does not indicate he is using typology. First, like Paul, Barnabas's use of τυπ- (cf. Barn. 6.11; 7.3, 7, 10–11; 8.1; 12.2, 5–6, 10; 13.5; 19.7) demonstrates no concern for facticity.[92] Barnabas used τυπ- when allegorizing both concrete source entities (e.g., persons and events; cf. Barn. 12.2–10) and abstract source entities (e.g., rituals; cf. Barn. 7–8). In both situations, there is no observable concern for facticity. Second, Barnabas also used τυπ- to strip the historical meaning out of a text. For example, in Barn. 7–8, it is the types revealed by the sacrificial rites that are most important. Another example is Barn. 12. In this text, the Spirit tells Moses to make types of the cross and of Jesus. Moses's actions have no meaning apart from their type. Barnabas's use of τυπ- to strip a text of its historical meaning is significant because *this is the purpose from which some attempt to rescue Paul* when they argue that his uses of τυπ- in Corinthians indicate his practice in Galatians is typology. Ultimately, Barnabas's use of τυπ- affirms typology is not a suitable interpretive schema for better understanding his or Paul's practice within the ancient interpretive practice of allegory.[93]

---

89. R. P. C. Hanson, *Allegory and Event*, 99; Hegedus, "Midrash and the Letter," 25; Hvalvik, *Struggle*, 114–19; O'Hagan, "Early Christian Exegesis," 36.

90. Hvalvik, *Struggle*, 115.

91. Hvalvik, *Struggle*, 117.

92. Even Hvalvik acknowledges, "What is peculiar is that they have no other meaning than being 'types' of Christ and his cross" (*Struggle*, 117).

93. Leonard Goppelt, who has written the most extensive treatment on Christian typology, also agrees there is no typology in the Epistle of Barnabas (*Typos*, 203–4).

7

Conclusion

IN THIS CHAPTER, I bring together the contributions of previous chapters and coalesce those ways in which they have provided a more precise understanding of the interpretive practice behind Paul's use of ἀλληγορούμενα. Then, I demonstrate how this understanding of Paul's practice contributes to the state of scholarship on other interpretive issues in Gal 4:21–31. Last, I discuss three opportunities for future research that my contributions reveal including the implications of my contributions for conversations within Pauline scholarship. This chapter is divided into four sections: a short review of prior criteria, prior interpretive schemata, and my approach; a more precise understanding of the interpretive practice behind Paul's use of ἀλληγορούμενα; its significance for other interpretive issues in Gal 4:21–31; opportunities for future research.

1. A SHORT REVIEW OF PRIOR CRITERIA, PRIOR INTERPRETIVE SCHEMATA, AND MY APPROACH

In chapter 2, I demonstrated the three criteria that prior scholarship on Gal 4:21–31 has used for selecting comparative examples—facticity, terminology, and geographical location—cannot situate an analysis of Paul's practice appropriately within the ancient interpretive practice of allegory because they do not distinguish one practice from another in terms of their similarities and differences: (1) a concern for facticity did not influence the ancient interpretive practice of allegory and (2) terminology and geographical location function only as organizational tools. In chapter 3, I demonstrated the interpretive schemata that prior scholarship on Gal 4:21–31 has used for the purpose of examining Paul's practice—Hellenistic, Alexandrian, and Palestinian allegory; typology—do not enable a better understanding of Paul's interpretive practice because they do not reflect how the ancient interpretive practice of allegory operated up to the time of Paul. Also in chapter 3, I presented a different approach within the methodology of comparative analysis that employed different criteria. My approach establishes allegorists as suitable comparative examples (in contrast to looking for similar practices) and then examines their interpretive practices. This approach enables a better understanding of Paul's practice because it takes into consideration the characteristics of allegorical practices that appropriately situate them within the ancient interpretive practice of allegory. In chapters 4–6, I examined comparatively the allegorical practice of Paul alongside the allegorical practices of three other interpreters by (1) demonstrating each interpreter was a suitable comparative example with Paul, (2) examining the allegorical practice of the interpreter separately from Paul's practice, (3) comparing the interpreter's allegorical practice with Paul's practice, and then (4) discussing the significance of the comparison for understanding Paul's practice more precisely.

2. A MORE PRECISE UNDERSTANDING OF THE INTERPRETIVE PRACTICE BEHIND PAUL'S USE OF ΑΛΛΗΓΟΡΟΥΜΕΝΑ

This project provides a more precise understanding of the interpretive practice behind Paul's use of ἀλληγορούμενα in four ways. *First, this project defines Paul's interpretive work.* Paul understood Gen 16–21 to have prior meanings that he believed to be authoritative (i.e., the children of Sarah are Jews who observe the law). However, these prior meanings did not include uncircumcised gentiles (i.e., the Galatians) whom he believed through Christ now should be included. Therefore, Paul needed to change these prior meanings without completely denying or replacing them. The ancient interpretive practice of allegory enabled him to do this by means of its source entities and meanings alongside their corresponding allegorical entities and meanings.

Second, this project explains how Paul used his allegorical practice to accomplish his interpretive work: he used it on two levels (i.e., rhetorical and functional) that stood in a contrasting relationship. Paul both affirmed the source meanings (as he understood them to be authoritative) and included gentiles without the requirement of law observance. In this way, Paul rhetorically said *yes* to his source meanings and then *and* for his allegorical meanings. However, Paul also crafted allegorical meanings (i.e., the children of Sarah are gentiles who do not observe the law) that contrasted the source meanings (i.e., the children of Sarah are Jews who observe the law), so he functionally said *no* to his source meanings and then *but* for his allegorical meanings. Accordingly, what Paul did rhetorically stands in tension with what he did functionally. This tension between rhetoric and function is how Paul used his allegorical practice to accomplish his interpretive work.

The third contribution of this project is it reveals that Paul's practice is a part of his own repertoire as an interpreter of Scripture. There are many places where Paul used the ancient interpretive practice of allegory (cf. ch. 2, sect. 2.4.2.3), even if those allegorical expressions do not contain the same tension between rhetoric and function found in Gal 4. I have demonstrated that although Paul used the root ἀλληγορ- only in Gal 4:24, it is not appropriate (1) to use this term to limit his allegorical practice to this one pericope or (2) to claim it is not an allegorical practice by referencing other pericopes where Paul uses either τύπ- or no term at all. Therefore, Paul's allegorical practice in Gal 4 should not be understood as a Pauline aberration. In other words, it is not a proverbial exception to Paul's methods of interpretation. This is significant because much scholarship seeks to explain away Paul's practice by arguing it is atypical for him or the result of his circumstances. For example, we find statements such as, this practice is "more forced and artificial than is usual for Paul,"[1] and "since the kind of OT exegesis found in this passage is by no means generally characteristic of Paul, the natural inference is that there was a special reason for its use here."[2] It is unfortunate that prior scholarship has spent so much effort attempting to explain away Paul's practice.[3]

---

1. Barclay, *Obeying the Truth*, 53.
2. Fung, *Epistle to the Galatians*, 219.
3. It is my view that these attempts to explain away Paul's practice are the result of hermeneutical concerns—perhaps theologically driven—among some interpreters. Accordingly, it may be that what these scholars define as the Pauline practice behind his use of ἀλληγορούμενα is what corresponds to their own hermeneutical standards.

The final contribution of this project is it reveals Paul's practice is a part of his repertoire as a Jewish interpreter of Scripture in the Second Temple period. This does not mean that what he does is Jewish—we rejected such ways of categorization in chapters 2 and 3—but rather he is interpreting texts in the same way as other Jews of his milieu. The comparative analyses of chapters 4–6 demonstrate this contribution in two ways. First, Paul and his roughly contemporary allegorists are able to structure their interpretive practices of allegory similarly. Each provides (1) a Jewish Scripture to be allegorized, (2) an indication that it means something else (i.e., allegoresis is at work), and (3) an allegorical interpretation (i.e., an allegory). Second, Paul's interpretive work is rhetorically and functionally similar to his contemporaries'. Because the authors of the sectarian texts of the Dead Sea Scrolls affirmed the source meanings they held as authoritative and their allegorical meanings were not contrasting, it can be said that Paul was rhetorically similar to yet functionally different from them. The same can be said for Philo. In contrast, because the author of the Epistle of Barnabas did not affirm the source meanings (i.e., the allegorical meanings replaced the source meanings) and his allegorical meanings were contrasting, it can be said that Paul was functionally similar to but rhetorically different from the author of the Epistle of Barnabas. In summary, Paul shares (1) what he does rhetorically with the authors of the sectarian texts and Philo and (2) what he does functionally with the author of the Epistle of Barnabas. These relationships are important because they demonstrate Paul interpreted similarly to other Jewish interpreters of Scripture within his milieu. This is significant because much scholarship seeks to explain Paul's practice by other contexts. For example, we have observed (1) the heavy use of Greek or rabbinic sources to explain Paul's practice—in particular, the projection of Greek interpretative practices and the retrojection of rabbinic interpretive practices onto Paul—and (2) the argument that Paul is using a practice not found until later (i.e., typology). It is unfortunate that prior scholarship has either overlooked or dismissed Paul's closest contemporaries when attempting to explain his interpretive practice of allegory. This approach prevented us from better understanding Paul within a Jewish context.

3. ITS SIGNIFICANCE FOR OTHER INTERPRETIVE ISSUES IN GALATIANS 4:21–31

This more precise understanding of Paul's practice also informs our understanding of other interpretive issues within Gal 4:21–31. This section is divided into four subsections: the function of 4:21–31 in the letter, the translation of ἀλληγορούμενα, the function of Isa 54:1, and why Paul interpreted Gen 16–21.

3.1. The Function of Galatians 4:21–31 in the Letter

As discussed in chapter 1, section 1.4, scholarship has debated whether Paul intended for this pericope to stand as a strong argument or as a supplemental addition. Scholars who hold the second position often use the interpretive practice behind Paul's use of ἀλληγορούμενα as evidence. They argue that Paul understood or employed the interpretive practice of allegory as an inferior method of interpretation. Nine scholars from 1535 to 1998 make this claim when discussing Gal 4:21–31.[4] Below are four examples.

> Allegories do not provide solid proofs in theology; but, like pictures, they adorn and illustrate a subject. *For if Paul had not proved the righteousness of faith against the righteousness of works by more substantial arguments, he would not have accomplished anything with this allegory.* But because he already fortified his case with more solid arguments—based on experience, on the case of Abraham, on the evidence of Scripture, and on analogy—*now, at the end of the argument, he adds an allegory as a kind of ornament.* (1535)[5]

> Allegorical and incorrect exegesis could never create an idea. They only illustrate one which has been suggested in other ways. (1900 [1988, 1993])[6]

---

4. These scholars are listed in chronological order. I include dates to demonstrate this view's pervasiveness. Those who demonstrate this concern are as follows: Luther, "Lectures on Galatians, 1535," 26:435–36 (1535); Thackeray, *Relation*, 202 (1900); Blackwelder and Stamm, "Epistle to the Galatians," 540 (1953); R. P. C. Hanson, *Allegory and Event*, 83 (1959); Lincoln, *Paradise*, 13 (1981); Fung, *Epistle to the Galatians*, 219 (1988); Hansen, *Abraham in Galatians*, 214–15 (1989); Perriman, "Rhetorical Strategy," 42 (1993); Vouga, *An die Galater*, 114 (1998).

5. Luther, "Lectures on Galatians, 1535," 26:435–36; emphasis added.

6. Thackeray, *Relation*, 202. For nearly identical statements, see Fung, *Epistle to the Galatians*, 219; and Perriman, "Rhetorical Strategy," 42.

> The wonder is that Paul has so little allegory. *His restraint is explained partly by his training as a Pharisee.... [Paul's] argument however, is never strengthened by allegorical symbolism and typology, for these are convincing only to those who by imagination can find them so.... His gospel does not rest on the quicksands of allegory, a specious method of interpreting scripture.* (1953)[7]

> Zum einen ist die Allegorese die logische Konsequenz der Neu-Definitionen von Gal 3,6–29; sie ergibt sich nicht als Evidenz aus der Schrift, sondern sie ergibt sich aus der Schrift, wie sie von der Gottesoffenbarung in Christus her auszulegen ist. *Gal 4,21—5,1 ist deshalb nicht als exegetische Beweisführung, sondern vielmehr als Zusammenfassung der theologischen Grundthese von Gal 1,10-12 und der daraus folgenden Argumentation zu verstehen.* (1998)[8]

In addition to these nine scholars, this denigratory view of allegorical practices remains a foundational assumption for many current positions that interpret Paul's allegorical practice as typology (cf. the discussion of typology in ch. 1, sect. 2.2.1, and ch. 3, sect. 2). These positions are a misunderstanding of Paul's practice because *this project demonstrates there is no evidence to support any claim that Paul viewed his allegorical practice here (or elsewhere) as an inferior method of interpretation.* Accordingly, the practice itself is not evidence that Paul intended this pericope to be less important than or as secondary to any other pericope in the letter.

3.2. The Translation of ἀλληγορούμενα

In chapter 1, section 2.2.1, I discussed how prior translations of ἅτινά ἐστιν ἀλληγορούμενα can be categorized into two categories: those that use the term "allegory" and its cognates and those that do not. Furthermore, those in the first category can be subdivided into those who translate it as a product and those who translate it as a process. I have demonstrated this is an oversimplification of Paul's interpretive practice. Based on my interpretive work in this project, I propose the translation "Here is an interpretive practice of allegory!" for three reasons. First, to describe Paul's practice only as a process or product does not reflect the interrelationship between the two. My translation reflects that Paul both responds and produces

---

7. Blackwelder and Stamm, "Epistle to the Galatians," 540; emphasis added.
8. Vouga, *An die Galater*, 114; emphasis added.

simultaneously. Second, this new translation can mitigate against translator bias—as noted previously, translators often have translated in ways reflecting assumptions that misrepresent Paul's practice and the broader ancient interpretive practice of allegory. My translation requires its meaning to be defined by what is taking place in its surrounding context. Last, this new translation can mitigate against reader bias. Readers are less likely to assume they know what Paul is doing if they do not read terms such as "allegory" or "typology." What also would be helpful is for publishers to accompany my translation with an explanatory note when possible. For all these reasons, "Here is an interpretive practice of allegory!" both accurately represents Paul's practice and provides the best opportunity for that practice to be communicated appropriately to readers of Galatians.

3.3. The Function of Isaiah 54:1

In chapter 1, section 2.2.3, we discussed two interpretations of Isa 54:1 in Gal 4:27. The first interpretation is that it provides one last proof to support Paul's allegorical interpretation. The second interpretation is that Isa 54:1 was more influential or perhaps even the hermeneutical key by which to understand all of Gal 4:21–31. With the comparative analyses completed, it is possible to better understand Paul's use of Isa 54:1 in two ways. First, all four roughly contemporary interpreters of Scripture could use secondary biblical lemmata in their allegorical practice. Accordingly, we again see Paul using Scripture in a way that was common among other allegorists within his milieu. Second, when secondary biblical lemmata are used by Paul's contemporaries, the presence or lack of secondary exegesis supports the first interpretation (i.e., its influence should be limited). In fact, it only was Philo who provided secondary exegesis for some (and not all) subordinate biblical lemmata. Additionally, he provided it only for those lemmata that greatly influenced his arguments. In most places, he simply cited it in the same way as Paul and the other two interpreters. If we apply this methodology to Paul, the practices of the comparative examples strongly indicate that because Paul did not provide secondary exegesis for his subordinate biblical lemma (i.e., Isa 54:1), then he used the lemma only as a final proof to support his allegorical interpretation. *Therefore, as is the majority position, Gal 4:21–31 should not be interpreted through Isa 54:1, but rather Isa 54:1 should be interpreted within Gal 4:21–31.*

3.4. Why Paul Interpreted Genesis 16–21

In chapter 1, section 2.3.2, we discussed the theory that Paul used the characters and events of Gen 16–21 within his interpretive practice because his opponents had used them previously in Galatia. The summary of changes between Gen 16–21 and Gal 4:21–31 found in that section helped to illuminate how much hermeneutical effort Paul had to exert in order to use Genesis for his purposes. This project has clarified why Paul had to exert so much hermeneutical effort: Paul was rhetorically affirming the source meanings but functionally contrasting them. Consequently, it is my view that Paul's interpretive practice provides additional evidence to support the position that Paul interpreted Gen 16–21 because his opponents already had interpreted it differently.

4. OPPORTUNITIES FOR FUTURE RESEARCH

This project provides at least three significant opportunities for future research. The first opportunity is the relationship of Gal 4:30 to the genre of "rewritten Bible." In Gal 4:30, Paul updates Sarah's command to Abraham found in Gen 21:10 for the situation he has perceived in Galatia.

> So she said to Abraham, "Cast out this slave woman with her son; for the son of this slave woman shall not inherit along with my son Isaac." (Gen 21:10)

> But what does the scripture say? "Drive out the slave and her child; for the child of the slave will not share the inheritance with the child *of the free woman*." (Gal 4:30; emphasis added)

This implicit textual change is very similar to a technique described as "rewritten Bible."[9] Rewritten Bible now typically is understood as a text that (1) rewrites a large portion of Scripture and (2) follows the arrangement of its source text.[10] In other words, a rewritten Bible text must be a "comprehensive or broad scope rewriting of narrative and/

---

9. The earliest explanation of this term (I found) is in Vermes, *Scripture and Tradition*, 95. Vermes describes it as inserting haggadic development into a biblical narrative "in order to anticipate questions, and to solve problems in advance."

10. Vermes's category was later refined by Philip Alexander, whose two characteristics became the basic framework for future conversations (Alexander, "Retelling the Old Testament," 116–18). For a reevaluation of these characteristics, see Campbell, "Rewritten Bible," 53.

or legal material woven into the fabric *implicitly*."[11] Although Paul's interpretive practice in Gal 4:30 does not rewrite a large portion of a scriptural text, the practice is similar. Additionally, a resurgence of discussion surrounding rewritten Bible in the last decade has brought attention to the way in which an ancient author could use rewritten Bible within the ancient interpretive practice of allegory.[12] This project affirms that the discussion of rewritten Bible may be significant for the ancient interpretive practice of allegory in Paul's time because, in closely reading the comparative examples, I discovered that the other three interpreters also made implicit textual changes to the Jewish Scriptures in a way similar to Paul.

Paul in Gal 4:30:

> So she said to Abraham, "Cast out this slave woman with her son; for the son of this slave woman shall not inherit along with my son Isaac." (Gen 21:10)

> *But what does the scripture say?* "Drive out the slave and her child; for the child of the slave will not share the inheritance with the child *of the free woman.*" (Gal 4:30; emphasis added)

The authors of the sectarian texts in 11QTemple L, 4b–6:

> Whoever in the open field touches one who has been killed by a sword, or who has died naturally, or a human bone, or a grave, shall be unclean seven days. (Num 19:16)

> And any man who touches in an open field the bone of a dead person—whether stabbed (by) a sword or (naturally) dead—or the blood of a dead person, or a grave, *then he shall be purified according to the statue of this precept.* (11QTemple L, 4b–6; emphasis added)

---

11. Bernstein, "Rewritten Bible," 195; emphasis added. For a similar definition, see Crawford, *Rewriting Scripture*, 12.

12. See pt. 2 ("Redefining Rewritten Bible") and pt. 3 ("Inner Biblical Rewritings" and "Early Jewish Rewritings") of Zsengellér, *"Rewritten Bible,"* 11–292. After engaging this topic directly in his contribution to that volume, Stephen Fraade concludes: "Thus, as important and useful as the distinction between 'rewritten Bible' and '(allegorical) commentary' is, we should not allow that distinction to conceal the ways in which they are intersecting partners in the multifaceted dynamics of ancient scriptural interpretation" ("Between Rewritten Bible," 231).

Philo in Mos. 1.290:

> A man will come out from his offspring, and he will rule many nations, and his kingdom will be exalted beyond Gog, and his kingdom will be made larger. God guided him out of Egypt. (Num 24:7–8 LXX, my translation)

> There shall come forth from you one day a man and he shall rule over many nations, and his kingdom *spreading every day* shall be exalted *on high*. This people, throughout its journey from Egypt, has had God as its guide, *Who leads the multitude in a single column*. (*Mos.* 1.290 [Colson]; emphasis added)

The author of the Epistle of Barnabas in Barn. 10.10:

> Happy are those who do not follow the advice of the wicked, or take the path that sinners tread, or sit in the seat of scoffers. (Ps 1:1)

> And David received the knowledge of the same three firm teachings and spoke in a similar way: "How fortunate is the man who does not proceed in the counsel of the impious *like the fish who proceed in darkness in the depths* and does not stand in the path of sinners *like those who appear to fear God but sin like the pig* and does not sit in the seat of the pestilent *like the birds who sit waiting for something to seize*." Here you have a perfect lesson about food. (Barn. 10.10; emphasis added)

In the same way I have examined the interpretive practice behind Paul's use of ἀλληγορούμενα, this technique of implicit reinterpretation could be examined in order to determine its significance for both Paul and the other interpreters.

Second and third opportunities for future research are to examine how Paul's allegorical practice can inform other areas of research within Pauline studies. The second opportunity is to investigate how Paul's practice is relevant for interpreting other pericopes within Galatians. For example, by comparing Paul's interpretive practice in Gal 4:21–31 with his practice in 3:6–9, there is potential to better understand how and why Paul only discusses one set of Abrahamic descendants in 3:6–9 instead of two as in 4:21–31. The third opportunity is to investigate how Paul's allegorical practice can inform the interpretation of pericopes within his other letters. For example, by comparing Paul's interpretive practice in

4:21–31 with his practice in Rom 4, there is the potential to better understand—and therefore, better interpret—each pericope. By situating the contributions of this project within those two areas of research, they can make additional contributions to broader questions about Paul's perspectives and about him as an interpreter of Scripture. This is especially true for questions about those contexts into which we place Paul as an interpreter, and my contributions are particularly helpful for those who seek to understand him within a Jewish context.

Bibliography

PRIMARY SOURCES

Ambrosiaster. "Commentary on Galatians." In *Commentaries on Galatians-Philemon*, translated by Gerald L. Bray, 1–34. Ancient Christian Texts. Downers Grove, IL: IVP Academic, 2009.

Aquinas, Thomas. *Commentary on Saint Paul's Epistle to the Galatians* [*Super Epistolam B. Pauli ad Galatas Lectura*]. Translated by F. R. Larcher. Albany: Magi, 1966.

Aristotle. *Art of Rhetoric* [*Rhetorica*]. Translated by J. H. Freese. LCL 193. Cambridge: Harvard University Press, 1926.

Artemidorus. *Artemidorus' Oneirocritica: Text, Translation, and Commentary.* Translated by Daniel Harris-McCoy. Oxford: Oxford University Press, 2012.

Athenaeus. *The Deipnosophists: or, Banquet of the Learned of Athenaeus* [*Deipnosophistae*]. Translated by C. D. Yonge. 3 vols. Bohn Classical Library. London: Bohn, 1853–54.

Augustine. *Augustine's "Commentary on Galatians": Introduction, Text, Translation, and Notes* [*Expositio in epistulam ad Galatas*]. Translated by Eric Plumer. Oxford Early Christian Studies. New York: Oxford, 2003.

Calvin, John. *Commentaries on the Epistles of Paul to the Galatians and Ephesians.* Translated by William Pringle. Grand Rapids: Baker, 2003.

Chrysostom, John. "Commentary on Galatians" [*Homiliae in epistulam ad Galatas commentaries*]. In *NPNF*[1], edited by Philip Schaff, 13:8–95. Repr., Peabody, MA: Hendrickson, 1994.

Cicero. *On the Orator* [*De oratore*]. In *On the Orator: Book 3. On Fate. Stoic Paradoxes. Divisions of Oratory,* translated by E. W. Sutton, 2–188. LCL 349. Cambridge: Harvard University Press, 1942.

———. *Orator.* In *Brutus. Orator,* translated by G. L. Hendrickson and H. M. Hubbell, 297–509. LCL 342. Cambridge: Harvard University Press, 1939.

[Cicero.] *Rhetorica ad Herennium.* Translated by Harry Caplan. LCL 403. Cambridge: Harvard University Press, 1954.

Demetrius. "On Style" [*De elocutione*]. In *Aristotle: "Poetics." Longinus: "On the Sublime." Demetrius: "On Style,"* translated by Doreen C. Innes, 309–522. LCL 199. Cambridge: Harvard University Press, 1995.

Ehrman, Bart D., trans. *Epistle of Barnabas*. In *Epistle of Barnabas. Papias and Quadratus. Epistle to Diognetus. The Shepherd of Hermas*, 3–85. Vol. 2 of *The Apostolic Fathers*. LCL 25. Cambridge: Harvard University Press, 2003.

Eusebius. "The Fragments" [*Praeparatio evangelica*]. In *Fragments from Hellenistic Jewish Authors*, translated by Carl R. Holladay, 3:128–97. Texts and Translations: Pseudepigrapha 13. Atlanta: Scholars, 1995.

Heraclitus. *Heraclitus: "Homeric Problems"* [*Quaestiones Homericae*]. Edited and translated by David Konstan and D. A. Russell. Writings from the Greco-Roman World 14. Atlanta: SBL, 2005.

Hermogenes. *Hermogenes' "On Types of Style."* Translated by Cecil Wooten. Chapel Hill: University of North Carolina Press, 1987.

Horace. *Satires. Epistles. The Art of Poetry*. Translated by H. Fairclough. LCL 194. Cambridge: Harvard University Press, 1926.

Jerome. "Commentary on Galatians, Book 2" [*Commentariorum in Epistulam ad Galatas libri II*]. In *St. Jerome's Commentaries on Galatians, Titus, and Philemon*, translated by Thomas Scheck, 184–96. Notre Dame, IN: University of Notre Dame Press, 2010.

Josephus. *Jewish Antiquities*. Translated by H. St. J. Thackeray. 9 vols. LCL. Cambridge: Harvard University Press, 1930–65.

Lucretius. *On the Nature of Things* [*De rerum natura*]. Translated by W. H. D. Rouse. LCL 181. Cambridge: Harvard University Press, 1924.

Luther, Martin. "Lectures on Galatians, 1519." In *Luther's Works*, edited by Helmut T. Lehman and Jaroslav Pelikan, 26:310–13. St. Louis: Concordia, 1964.

———. "Lectures on Galatians, 1535." In *Luther's Works*, edited by Helmut T. Lehman and Jaroslav Pelikan, 26:432–37. St. Louis: Concordia, 1964.

Ovid. *Metamorphoses*. Translated by Frank Miller. 2 vols. LCL. Cambridge: Harvard University Press, 1916.

Philo. *Allegorical Interpretation of Genesis 2 and 3* [*Legum allegoriae*]. In *On the Creation. Allegorical Interpretation of Genesis 2 and 3*, translated by F. H. Colson and G. H. Whitaker, 140–474. LCL 226. Cambridge: Harvard University Press, 1929.

———. "Moses 1 and 2" [*De vita Mosis*]. In *On Abraham. On Joseph. On Moses*, translated by F. H. Colson, 274–596. LCL 289. Cambridge: Harvard University Press, 1935.

———. "On Abel and the Sacrifices Offered by Him and by Cain" [*De sacrificiis Abelis et Caini*]. In *On the Cherubim. The Sacrifices of Abel and Cain. The Worse Attacks the Better. On the Posterity and Exile of Cain. On the Giants*, translated by F. H. Colson and G. H. Whitaker, 88–197. LCL 227. Cambridge: Harvard University Press, 1929.

———. "On Abraham" [*De Abrahamo*]. In *On Abraham. On Joseph. On Moses*, translated by F. H. Colson, 2–137. LCL 289. Cambridge: Harvard University Press, 1935.

———. "On Dreams" [*De somniis*]. In *On Flight and Finding. On the Change of Names. On Dreams*, translated by F. H. Colson and G. H. Whitaker, 285–580. LCL 275. Cambridge: Harvard University Press, 1934.

———. "On Flight and Finding" [*De fuga et inventione*]. In *On Flight and Finding. On the Change of Names. On Dreams*, translated by F. H. Colson and G. H. Whitaker, 3–127. LCL 275. Cambridge: Harvard University Press, 1934.

———. "On Husbandry" [*De agricultura*]. In *On the Unchangeableness of God. On Husbandry. Concerning Noah's Work As a Planter. On Drunkenness. On Sobriety*, translated by F. H. Colson and G. H. Whitaker, 104–206. LCL 247. Cambridge: Harvard University Press, 1930.

———. "On Joseph" [*De Iosepho*]. In *On Abraham. On Joseph. On Moses*, translated by F. H. Colson, 138–273. LCL 289. Cambridge: Harvard University Press, 1935.

———. "On Mating with the Preliminary Studies" [*De congressu eruditionis gratia*]. In *On the Confusion of Tongues. On the Migration of Abraham. Who Is the Heir of Divine Things? On Mating with the Preliminary Studies*, translated by F. H. Colson and G. H. Whitaker, 451–552. LCL 261. Cambridge: Harvard University Press, 1932.

———. "On Providence" [*De providentia*]. In *Every Good Man Is Free. On the Contemplative Life. On the Eternity of the World. Against Flaccus. Apology for the Jews. On Providence*, translated by F. H. Colson, 447–508. LCL 363. Cambridge: Harvard University Press, 1941.

———. "On Rewards and Punishments" [*De praemiis et poenis*]. In *On the Special Laws, Book 4. On the Virtues. On Rewards and Punishments*, translated by F. H. Colson, 309–424. LCL 341. Cambridge: Harvard University Press, 1939.

———. "On the Account of the World's Creation Given by Moses" [*De opificio mundi*]. In *On the Creation. Allegorical Interpretation of Genesis 2 and 3*, translated by F. H. Colson and G. H. Whitaker, 140–474. LCL 226. Cambridge: Harvard University Press, 1929.

———. "On the Change of Names" [*De mutatione nominum*]. In *On Flight and Finding. On the Change of Names. On Dreams*, translated by F. H. Colson and G. H. Whitaker, 128–284. LCL 275. Cambridge: Harvard University Press, 1934.

———. "On the Cherubim, the Flaming Sword, and Cain" [*De cherubim*]. In *On the Cherubim. The Sacrifices of Abel and Cain. The Worse Attacks the Better. On the Posterity and Exile of Cain. On the Giants*, translated by F. H. Colson and G. H. Whitaker, 3–87. LCL 227. Cambridge: Harvard University Press, 1929.

———. "On the Confusion of Tongues" [*De confusion linguarum*]. In *On the Confusion of Tongues. On the Migration of Abraham. Who Is the Heir of Divine Things? On Mating with the Preliminary Studies*, translated by F. H. Colson and G. H. Whitaker, 2–122. LCL 261. Cambridge: Harvard University Press, 1932.

———. "On the Decalogue" [*De decalogo*]. In *On the Decalogue. On the Special Laws, Books 1–3*, translated by F. H. Colson, 3–97. LCL 320. Cambridge: Harvard University Press, 1937.

———. "On the Embassy to Gaius (The First Part of the Treatise on Virtues)" [*Legatio ad Gaium*]. In *On the Embassy to Gaius. General Indexes*, translated by F. H. Colson, 2–188. LCL 379. Cambridge: Harvard University Press, 1962.

———. "On the Giants" [*De gigantibus*]. In *On the Cherubim. The Sacrifices of Abel and Cain. The Worse Attacks the Better. On the Posterity and Exile of Cain. On the Giants*, translated by F. H. Colson and G. H. Whitaker, 443–80. LCL 227. Cambridge: Harvard University Press, 1929.

———. "On the Migration of Abraham" [*De migration Abrahami*]. In *On the Confusion of Tongues. On the Migration of Abraham. Who Is the Heir of Divine Things? On Mating with the Preliminary Studies*, translated by F. H. Colson and G. H. Whitaker, 123–269. LCL 261. Cambridge: Harvard University Press, 1932.

———. "On the Posterity of Cain and His Exile" [*De posteritate Caini*]. In *On the Cherubim. The Sacrifices of Abel and Cain. The Worse Attacks the Better. On the Posterity and Exile of Cain. On the Giants*, translated by F. H. Colson and G. H. Whitaker, 323–442. LCL 227. Cambridge: Harvard University Press, 1929.

———. "On the Special Laws" [*De specialibus legibus*]. In *On the Decalogue. On the Special Laws, Books 1–3*, translated by F. H. Colson, 98–610. LCL 320. Cambridge: Harvard University Press, 1937.

———. "On the Special Laws 4" [*De specialibus legibus*]. *On the Special Laws, Book 4. On the Virtues. On Rewards and Punishments*, translated by F. H. Colson, 3–157. LCL 341. Cambridge: Harvard University Press, 1939.

———. "On the Unchangeableness of God" [*Quod Deus sit immutabilis*]. In *On the Unchangeableness of God. On Husbandry. Concerning Noah's Work As a Planter. On Drunkenness. On Sobriety*, translated by F. H. Colson and G. H. Whitaker, 3–103. LCL 247. Cambridge: Harvard University Press, 1930.

———. "On the Virtues" [*De virtutibus*]. *On the Special Laws, Book 4. On the Virtues. On Rewards and Punishments*, translated by F. H. Colson, 158–308. LCL 341. Cambridge: Harvard University Press, 1939.

———. *Questions and Answers on Genesis* [*Quaestiones et solutiones in Genesin*]. Translated by Ralph Marcus. LCL 380. Cambridge: Harvard University Press, 1953.

———. *Questions and Answers on Exodus* [*Quaestiones et solutiones in Exodum*]. Translated by Ralph Marcus. LCL 401. Cambridge: Harvard University Press, 1953.

———. "That the Worse Is Wont to Attack the Better" [*Quod deterius potiori insidiari soleat*]. In *On the Cherubim. The Sacrifices of Abel and Cain. The Worse Attacks the Better. On the Posterity and Exile of Cain. On the Giants*, translated by F. H. Colson and G. H. Whitaker, 198–322. LCL 227. Cambridge: Harvard University Press, 1929.

———. "Who Is the Heir of Divine Things" [*Quis rerum divinarum heres sit*]. In *On the Confusion of Tongues. On the Migration of Abraham. Who Is the Heir of Divine Things? On Mating with the Preliminary Studies*, translated by F. H. Colson and G. H. Whitaker, 270–450. LCL 261. Cambridge: Harvard University Press, 1932.

Photius of Constantinople. "Photius von Constantinople." In *Pauluskommentare aus der Griechischen Kirche: Aus Katenenhandschriften Gesammelt und Herausgegeben*, edited by Karl Staab, 470–661. Münster: Aschendorff, 1892.

Plato. *Republic*. Translated by Christopher Emlyn-Jones and William Preddy. 2 vols. LCL. Cambridge: Harvard University Press, 2013.

Plutarch. *Essay on the Life and Poetry of Homer*. Translated by J. J. Keaney and Robert Lamberton. Society for Classical Studies American Classical Studies. Atlanta: Scholars, 1996.

———. *Moralia*. Translated by Harold Cherniss et al. 15 vols. LCL. Cambridge: Harvard University Press, 1927–76.

Porphyry. "The Life of Pythagoras by Porphyry of Trye" [*De vita Pythagorae*]. In *The Pythagorean Sourcebook and Library: An Anthology of Ancient Writings Which Relate to Pythagoras and Pythagorean Philosophy*, edited by David Fideler, translated by Kenneth Guthrie, 123–36. Grand Rapids: Phanes, 1987.

———. *Porphyry's Homeric Questions on the "Iliad"* : *Text, Translation, Commentary* [*Quaestiones homericarum ad Odysseam pertinentium reliquiae*]. Translated by John A. MacPhail Jr. New York: de Gruyter, 2011.

Pseudo-Aristeas. "Letter of Aristeas." In *The Old Testament Pseudepigrapha*, edited by James H. Charlesworth, translated by R. J. H. Shutt, 12–34. New York: Doubleday, 1985.

Qimron, Elisha, and John Strugnell. *Miqṣat Ma'aśe Ha-Torah*. DJD 10. Oxford: Clarendon, 1994.

Quintilian. *Institutio Oratoria*. Translated by Donald Russell. 5 vols. LCL. Cambridge: Harvard University Press, 2002.

Severian of Gabala. "Severian von Gabala." In *Pauluskommentare aus der Griechischen Kirche: Aus Katenenhandschriften Gesammelt und Herausgegeben*, edited by Karl Staab, 213–351. Münster: Aschendorff, 1892.

Theodore of Mopsuestia. *Ad Galatas*. In *The Commentaries on the Minor Epistles of Paul*, translated by Rowan Greer, 108–33. WAW 26. Atlanta: SBL, 2010.

Tryphon. *Peri tropon*. In *Rhetores Graeci*, edited by Leonhard von Spengel, 191–256. Leipzig: Tübner, 1856.

Tryphon II. "Tryphon *De Tropis*." *CQ* 15 (1965) 230–48.

Vergil. *Eclogues. Georgics. Aeneid: Books 1–6*. Translated by H. Fairclough. LCL 63. Cambridge: Harvard University Press, 1916.

Victorinus, Marius. *Marius Victorinus' Commentary on Galatians* [*In epistolam Pauli ad Galatas libri duo*]. Translated by Stephen Cooper. Oxford Early Christian Studies. New York: Oxford, 2005.

SECONDARY SOURCES

Abegg, Martin. "Paul, 'Works of the Law,' and MMT." *BAR* 20 (1994) 52–61.

Alexander, Philip. "Retelling the Old Testament." In *It is Written: Scripture Citing Scripture; Essays in Honour of Barnabas Lindars*, edited by D. A. Carson and H. G. M. Williamson, 99–121. Cambridge: Cambridge University Press, 1988.

Allan, John. *The Epistle of Paul the Apostle to the Galatians: Christian Freedom*. Cambridge: Cambridge University Press, 1911.

Allenbach, Jean, et al. *Philon d'Alexandrie*. BiPa Supplement. Paris: CNRS, 1982.

Amir, Yehoshua. "Authority and Interpretation of Scripture in the Writings of Philo." In *Mikra: Text, Translation, Reading and Interpretation of the Hebrew Bible in Ancient Judaism and Early Christianity*, edited by Jan Mulder, 421–53. CRINT 2.1. Assen, Neth.: Van Gorcum, 1988.

———. "The Transference of Greek Allegories to Biblical Motifs in Philo." In *Nourished with Peace: Studies in Hellenistic Judaism in Memory of Samuel Sandmel*, edited by Frederick E. Greenspahn et al., 15–25. Scholars Press Homage Series. Chico, CA: Scholars, 1984.

Amoit, François. *Épitre aux Galates, Épitres aux Thessaloniciens*. Paris: Beauchesne et ses Fils, 1956.

Anderson, R. Dean, Jr. *Ancient Rhetorical Theory and Paul*. CBET 18. Kampen, Neth.: Kok Pharos, 1996.

———. *Glossary of Greek Rhetorical Terms Connected to Methods of Argumentation, Figures and Tropes from Anaximenes to Quintilian.* CBET 24. Leuven: Peeters, 2000.

Auerbach, Erich. "Figura." In *Scenes from the Drama of European Literature*, 11–76. Minneapolis: University of Minnesota Press, 1973.

Aune, David E. "Charismatic Exegesis in Early Judaism and Early Christianity." In *The Pseudepigrapha and Early Biblical Interpretation*, edited by James H. Charlesworth and Craig Evans, 126–50. JSOTSup. Sheffield: Sheffield University Press, 1993.

———. *Prophecy in Early Christianity and the Ancient Mediterranean World.* 1983. Reprint, Eugene, OR: Wipf & Stock, 2003.

Baasland, Ernst. "Persecution: A Neglected Feature in the Letter to the Galatians." *ST* 30 (1984) 135–50.

Bachmann, Michael. *Anti-Judaism in Galatians? Exegetical Studies on a Polemical Letter and on Paul's Theology.* Translated by Robert L. Brawley. Grand Rapids: Eerdmans, 2008.

Baker, David L. "Typology and the Christian Use of the Old Testament." *SJT* 29 (1976) 137–57.

Balla, Peter. "Paul's Use of Slavery Imagery in the Hagar Allegory." *IDS* 43 (2009) 119–34.

Baltzer, Klaus. *Deutero-Isaiah: A Commentary on Isaiah 40–55.* Translated by Margaret Kohl. Hermeneia. Minneapolis: Fortress, 2001.

Barclay, John, M. G. "Mirror-Reading a Polemical Letter: Galatians as a Test Case." *JSNT* 31 (1987) 73–93.

———. *Obeying the Truth: A Study of Paul's Ethics in Galatians.* Edinburgh: T. & T. Clark, 1988.

———. "Paul and Philo on Circumcision: Romans 2.25–9 in Social and Cultural Context." *NTS* 44 (1998) 536–56.

———. *Paul and the Gift.* Grand Rapids: Eerdmans, 2015.

Barclay, John M. G., and Benjamin G. White. "Posing the Questions." In *The New Testament in Comparison: Validity, Method, and Purpose in Comparing Traditions*, edited by John M. G. Barclay and Benjamin G. White, 1–7. LNTS 600. New York: T&T Clark, 2020.

———, eds. *The New Testament in Comparison: Validity, Method, and Purpose in Comparing Traditions.* LNTS 600. London: T. & T. Clark, 2020.

Barker, Patrick G. "Allegory and Typology in Galatians 4:21–31." *SVTQ* 38 (1994) 193–209.

Barnard, Leslie W. "The Epistle of Barnabas and the Dead Sea Scrolls: Some Observations." *SJT* 13 (1960) 45–59.

———. "The Epistle of Barnabas in Its Contemporary Setting." In *ANRW* II.27.1:159–207, edited by Hildegard Temporini and Wolfgang Haase. Berlin: de Gruyter, 1989.

Barnett, Albert E. *Paul Becomes: A Literary Influence.* Chicago: University of Chicago Press, 1941.

Barr, James. "Allegory and Historicism." *JSOT* 69 (1996) 105–20.

———. "The Literal, the Allegorical, and Modern Biblical Scholarship." *JSOT* 44 (1989) 3–17.

———. *Old and New in Interpretation: A Study of the Two Testaments.* New York: Harper & Row, 1966.

Bibliography

Barrett, C. K. "The Allegory of Abraham, Sarah, and Hagar in the Argument of Galatians." In *Essays on Paul*, 154–70. Philadelphia: Westminster, 1982.

———. *Freedom and Obligation: A Study of the Epistle to the Galatians*. Philadelphia: Westminster, 1985.

———. "The Interpretation of the Old Testament in the New." In *The Cambridge History of the Bible*, edited by P. R. Ackroyd and C. F. Evans, 1:377–411. Cambridge: Cambridge University Press, 1970.

Baur, F. C. *Paul the Apostle of Jesus Christ—His Life and Work, His Epistles and Doctrine*. 2 vols. Translated by Eduard Zeller. 1873–76. Peabody, MA: Hendrickson, 2003.

Benoit, Pierre. "Qumran and the New Testament." In *Paul and Qumran: Studies in New Testament Exegesis*, edited by Jerome Murphy-O'Connor, OP, 1–30. Melbourne: Priority, 1968.

Bernstein, Moshe J. "The Dead Sea Scrolls and Jewish Biblical Interpretation in Antiquity: A Multi-Generic Perspective." In *The Dead Sea Scrolls at 60*, edited by Lawrence Schiffmann and Shani Tzoref, 55–90. STDJ 89. Leiden: Brill, 2010.

———. "'Rewritten Bible': A Generic Category Which Has Outlived Its Usefulness?" *Text* 22 (2005) 169–96.

Betz, Hans D. *Galatians: A Commentary on Paul's Letter to the Churches in Galatia*. Hermeneia. Minneapolis: Fortress, 1979.

Blackwelder, Oscar F., and Raymond T. Stamm. "The Epistle to the Galatians." In *Corinthians, Galatians, Ephesians*, 429–593. IB 10. Nashville: Abingdon-Cokesbury, 1953.

Blenkinsopp, Joseph. *Isaiah 40–55*. AB 19A. New York: Doubleday, 2000.

Blessing, Kamila. "The Background of the Barren Woman Motif in Galatians 4:27." PhD diss., Duke University, 1996.

———. "Desolate Jerusalem and Barren Matriarch: Two Distinct Figures in the Pseudepigrapha." *JSP* 18 (1998) 47–69.

Blomberg, Craig L. *Interpreting the Parables*. Downers Grove, IL: IVP Academic, 1990.

Blomkvist, Vemund. *Euthalian Traditions: Text, Translation and Commentary*. TUGAL 170. Boston: De Gruyter, 2012.

Böhl, Franz de Liagre. "Christentum, Judentum und Altes Testament in ihrem gegenseitigen Verhältnis nach dem Brief des Barnabas." In *Schrift en Uitleg: Studies aangeboden aan W. H. Gispen*, 95–111. Kampen: Kok, 1970.

Bonnard, Pierre. *L'Épitre de Saint Paul aux Galates*. Neuchatel, Switz.: Delachaux & Niestlé, 1953.

Bonsirven, Joseph. "Exégèse allégorique chez les Rabbins tannaites." *RSR* 23 (1933) 513–41.

———. *Exégèse rabbinique et Exégèse Paulinienne*. Paris: Beauchesne, 1939.

Borgen, Peder. *Bread from Heaven: An Exegetical Study of the Concept of Manna in the Gospel of John and the Writings of Philo*. NovTSup 10. Leiden: Brill, 1965.

———. "Paul Preaches Circumcision and Pleases Men." In *Paul and Paulinism: Essays in Honour of C. K. Barrett*, edited by M. D. Hooker and S. G. Wilson, 37–46. London: SPCK, 1982.

———. *Philo, John, and Paul: New Perspectives on Judaism and Early Christianity*. BJS 131. Atlanta: Scholars, 1987.

———. *Philo of Alexandria: An Exegete for His Time*. NovTSup 86. Leiden: Brill, 1997.

———. "Some Hebrew and Pagan Features in Philo's and Paul's Interpretation of Hagar and Ishmael." In *The New Testament and Hellenistic Judaism*, edited by Peder Borgen and Soren Giversen, 151–64. Peabody, MA: Hendrickson, 1997.
Bouwman, Gijs. "Die Hagar- und Sara-Perikope (Gal 4,21–31). Exemplarische Interpretation zum Schrifbeweis bei Paulus." *ANRW* II.25.4:3135–55, edited by Hildegard Temporini and Wolfgang Haase. Berlin: de Gruyter, 1987.
Boyarin, Daniel. *A Radical Jew: Paul and the Politics of Identity*. Berkeley: University of California Press, 1994.
Brandenburger, Egon. *Fleisch und Geist: Paulus und die dualistische Weisheit*. WMANT 29. Neukirchen-Vluyn: Neukirchener, 1968.
Braun, F. M. "L'arrière-fond judaïque du quatrième Évangile et la Communauté de l'Alliance." *RB* 62 (1955) 5–44.
Braun, Herbert. *Qumran und das Neue Testament*. 2 vols. Tübingen: Mohr Siebeck, 1966.
———. "Qumran und das Neue Testament. Ein Bericht über 10 Jahre Forschung (1950–1959)." *TRu* 29 (1963) 97–234.
Bring, Ragnar. *Commentary on Galatians*. Philadelphia: Muhlenberg, 1961.
Brisson, Luc. *How the Philosophers Saved Myths: Allegorical Interpretation and Classical Mythology*. Chicago: Chicago University Press, 2004.
Broer, Ingo. "'Vertreibe die Magd und ihren Sohn!' Gal 4,21–31 im Horizont der Debatte über den Antijudaismus im Neuen Testament." In *Der bezwingende Vorsprung des Guten: Exegetische und theologische Werkstattberichte*, edited by Wolfgang Harnisch et al., 167–98. Münster: Lit, 1994.
Brooke, George J. *The Dead Sea Scrolls and the New Testament*. Minneapolis: Fortress, 2005.
———. "Genre Theory, Rewritten Bible and Pesher." *DSD* 17 (2010) 332–57.
Brown, Raymond. "The Dead Sea Scrolls and the New Testament." In *John and the Dead Sea Scrolls*, edited by James H. Charlesworth, 1–8. New York: Crossroad, 1990.
Brownlee, William. "Biblical Interpretation among the Sectaries of the Dead Sea Scrolls." *BA* 14 (1951) 54–76.
Bruce, F. F. "'Abraham Had Two Sons: A Study in Pauline Hermeneutics." In *New Testament Studies: Essays in Honor of Ray Summers in His 65th Year*, edited by Huber Drumwright and Curtis Vaughan, 71–84. Waco: Baylor University Press, 1975.
———. *Biblical Exegesis in the Qumran Texts*. Grand Rapids: Eerdmans, 1960.
———. *The Epistle to the Galatians*. NIGTC. Grand Rapids: Eerdmans, 1982.
Buckel, John. *Free to Love: Paul's Defense of Christian Liberty in Galatians*. Louvain Theological & Pastoral Monographs. Leuven: Peeters, 1993.
Burger, J. D. "L'Énigme de Barnabas." *MH* 3 (1946) 180–93.
Burrows, Millar. *More Light on the Dead Sea Scrolls: New Scrolls and New Interpretations*. New York: Viking, 1958.
Burton, Ernest. *A Critical and Exegetical Commentary on the Epistle to the Galatians*. ICC 35. Edinburgh: T. & T. Clark, 1921.
Buscemi, Alfio. *Lettera ai Galati: Commentario esegetico*. Jerusalem: Franciscan, 2004.
Byrne, Brendan, SJ. "Jerusalems Above and Below: A Critique of J. L. Martyn's Interpretation of the Hagar-Sarah Allegory in Gal 4:21–5.1." *NTS* 60 (2014) 215–31.
Callaway, Mary. "The Mistress and the Maid: Midrashic Traditions behind Gal 4,21–31." *Radical Religion* 2 (1975) 94–101.

———. *Sing, O Barren One: A Study in Comparative Midrash*. SBLDS 91. Atlanta: Scholars, 1986.
Campbell, Jonathan. "Rewritten Bible: A Terminological Reassessment." In *"Rewritten Bible" after Fifty Years: Texts, Terms, or Techniques? A Last Dialogue with Géza Vermes*, edited by József Zsengellér, 49–81. SJSJ 166. Leiden: Brill, 2014.
Caneday, Ardel. "Covenant Lineage Allegorically Prefigured: 'Which Things Are Written Allegorically.'" *Southern Baptist Journal of Theology* 14 (2010) 50–77.
Carlson, Stephen. "'For Sinai Is a Mountain in Arabia': A Note on the Text of Galatians 4,25." *ZNW* 105 (2014) 80–101.
Carmignac, Jean. "Le document de Qumran sur Melkisédeq." *RevQ* 7 (1970) 343–78.
Castelli, Elizabeth. "Allegories of Hagar: Reading Galatians 4:21–31 with Postmodern Feminist Eyes." In *New Literary Criticism and the New Testament*, edited by Elizabeth Struthers Malbon and Edgar V. McKnight, 228–50. JSNTSup 109. Sheffield: Sheffield Academic, 1994.
Chadwick, Henry. "St. Paul and Philo of Alexandria." *BJRL* 48 (1966) 286–307.
Charlesworth, James H., ed. *Old Testament Pseudepigrapha*. 2 vols. New York: Doubleday, 1983, 1985.
Childs, Brevard S. "Critical Reflections on James Barr's Understanding of the Literal and Allegorical." *JSOT* 46 (1990) 3–9.
———. *Isaiah*. OTL. Louisville: Westminster: John Knox, 2001.
———. "Sensus Literalis of Scripture: An Ancient and Modern Problem." In *Beiträge zur Alttestamentliche Theologie. Festschrift für Walther Zimmerli zum 70. Geburtstag*, edited by Herbert Donner et al., 80–93. Göttingen: Vandenhoeck Ruprecht, 1977.
Christiansen, Irmgard. *Die Technik der allegorischen Auslegungswissenschaft bei Philon von Alexandrien*. BGBH 7. Tübingen: Mohr Siebeck, 1969.
Cohen, Naomi G. *Philo Judaeus: His Universe of Discourse*. BEATAJ 24. New York: Lang, 1995.
Collins, John J. *Apocalypticism in the Dead Sea Scrolls*. Literature of the Dead Sea Scrolls. New York: Routledge, 1997.
Colson, F. H. "Philo on Education." *JTS* 18 (1917) 151–62.
Committee of the Oxford Society of Historical Theology, A. *The New Testament in the Apostolic Fathers*. Oxford: Clarendon, 1905.
Corsani, Bruno. "L'interpretazione tipologica della storia di Ager e Sara in Gal 4." *Parola Spirito e Vita* 24 (1991) 213–24.
Cosgrove, Charles. "The Law Has Given Sarah No Children." *NovT* 29 (1987) 219–35.
Cothenet, Édouard. "A l'arrière-plan de l'allégorie d'Agar et de Sara (Ga 4,21–31)." In *De la Tôrah au Messie: Études d'exégèse et d'herméneutique bibliques offertes à Henri Cazelles pour ses 25 années d'enseignement à l'Institut Catholique de Paris (Octobre 1979)*, edited by Maurice Carrez et al., 457–65. Paris: Desclée, 1981.
Crawford, Sidnie White. *Rewriting Scripture in Second Temple Times*. Grand Rapids: Eerdmans, 2008.
———. "The Rewritten Bible at Qumran." In *The Hebrew Bible and Qumran*, edited by James H. Charlesworth, 173–95. North Richland Hills, TX: Bibal, 1998.
———. *The Temple Scroll and Related Texts*. Companion to the Qumran Scrolls. Sheffield: Sheffield Academic, 2000.
Crossan, John D. "Parable and Example in the Teaching of Jesus." *Semeia* 1 (1974) 63–104.

Culpepper, R. Alan. *The Johannine School: An Evaluation of the Johannine-School Hypothesis Based on an Investigation of the Nature of Ancient Schools*. SBLDS 26. Atlanta: SBL, 2007.

Dacy, Marianne. "The Epistle to Barnabas and the Dead Sea Scrolls." In *The Dead Sea Scrolls: Fifty Years after Their Discovery; Proceedings of the Jerusalem Congress, July 20–25, 1997*, edited by Lawrence H. Schiffman, 139–47. Jerusalem: Israel Exploration Society, 2000.

Damgaard, Finn. "Hinsides typologisk og allegorisk fortolkning: En reokonstruktion af antikkens fortolkningsparadigme." *DTT* 66 (2003) 107–19.

Daniélou, Jean, SJ. *The Lord of History*. Translated by Nigel Abercrombie. London: Longmans, 1958.

———. *Philo of Alexandria*. Translated by James G. Colbert. Eugene, OR: Cascade Books, 2014.

Das, A. Andrew. *Galatians*. Concordia Commentary. St. Louis: Concordia, 2014.

Dassmann, Ernst. *Der Stachel im Fleisch: Paulus in der frühchristlichen Literatur bis Irenäus*. Münster: Aschendorff, 1979.

Daube, David. "Rabbinic Methods of Interpretation and Hellenistic Rhetoric." *HUCA* 22 (1949) 239–64.

Davies, James. *Paul among the Apocalypses? An Evaluation of the "Apocalyptic Paul" in the Context of Jewish and Christian Apocalyptic Literature*. Edited by Chris Keith. LNTS 562. New York: Bloomsbury, 2016.

Davies, Philip. "The Teacher of Righteousness at the End of Days." *RevQ* 13 (1988) 313–17.

Davies, W. D. "Paul and the Dead Sea Scrolls: Flesh and Spirit." In *The Scrolls and the New Testament*, edited by Krister Stendahl, 157–82. New York: Crossroad, 1992.

Davis, Anne. "Allegorically Speaking in Galatians 4:21–5:1." *BBR* 14 (2004) 161–74.

Dawson, David. *Allegorical Readers and Cultural Revision in Ancient Alexandria*. Berkeley: University of California, 1992.

De Boer, Martinus C. *Galatians: A Commentary*. NTL. Louisville: Westminster John Knox, 2011.

———. "Paul's Quotation of Isaiah 54.1 in Galatians 4.27." *NTS* 50 (2004) 370–89.

Demura, Miyako. "Origen and the Exegetical Tradition of the Sarah-Hagar Motif in Alexandria." In *Rediscovering Origen*, edited by Markus Vinzent, 73–81. StPatr 56. Leuven: Peeters, 2013.

DeSilva, David A. *The Letter to the Galatians*. NICNT. Grand Rapids: Eerdmans, 2018.

Dewolf, Lotan H. *Galatians: A Letter for Today*. Grand Rapids: Eerdmans, 1975.

DeYoung, James. "But As Then . . . So Even Now": Toward an Understanding of Paul's Allegory in Galatians 4.21–31." Paper presented at the Northwest Region of the Evangelical Theological Society, Tacoma, WA, Mar. 8, 1997.

Dibelius, Martin. *A Fresh Approach to the New Testament and Early Christian Literature*. International Library of Christian Knowledge. New York: Scribner, 1936.

———. *Geschichte der urchristlichen Literatur*. 2 vols. Sammlung Göschen. Berlin: de Gruyter, 1926.

Dimant, Devorah. "Pesharim, Qumran." *ABD* 5:244–51.

Di Mattei, Steven. "Paul's Allegory of the Two Covenants (Gal 4.21–31) in Light of First-Century Hellenistic Rhetoric and Jewish Hermeneutics." *NTS* 52 (2006) 102–22.

Dockery, David S. *Biblical Interpretation Then and Now: Contemporary Hermeneutics in Light of the Early Church*. Grand Rapids: Baker, 1992.

Dodds, E. R. "The Parmenides of Plato and the Origin of the Neoplatonic One." *CQ* 22 (1928) 129–42.
Donfried, Karl. "Paul the Jew and the Dead Sea Scrolls." In *The Dead Sea Scrolls in Context: Integrating the Dead Sea Scrolls in the Study of Ancient Text, Language, and Cultures*, edited by Armin Lange et al., 2:721–33. VTSup. Leiden: Brill, 2011.
Dunn, James D. G. "4QMMT and Galatians." *NTS* 43 (1997) 147–53.
———. *The Epistle to the Galatians*. BNTC. Peabody, MA: Hendrickson, 1993.
———. "Paul and the Dead Sea Scrolls." In *Caves of Enlightenment: Proceedings from the American Schools of Oriental Research. Dead Sea Scrolls Jubilees Symposium (1947–97)*, edited by James H. Charlesworth, 105–27. North Richland Hills: BIBAL, 1998.
Eastman, Susan. "'Cast Out the Slave Woman and Her Son': The Dynamics of Exclusion and Inclusion in Galatians 4.30." *JSNT* 28 (2006) 309–36.
Ebeling, Gerhard. *The Truth of the Gospel: An Exposition of Galatians*. Translated by David Green. Minneapolis: Fortress, 1985.
Echeverría, Raquel. "Una re-lectura de la alegoría de Agar y Sara en Gálatas 4:21–31." *Teología y Cultura* 13 (2016) 25–36.
Eckstein, Hans-Joachim. *Verheißung und Gesetz: Eine exegetische Untersuchung zu Galater 2,15–4,7*. WUNT 1/86. Tübingen: Mohr Siebeck, 1996.
Egger, John A. "A Most Troublesome Text: Galatians 4:21—5:1 in the History of Interpretation." PhD diss., University of St. Michael's College, 2015.
Ellicott, C. J. *Critical and Grammatical Commentary on St. Paul's Epistle to the Galatians*. London: Parker, 1854.
Elliott, Susan. "Choose Your Mother, Choose Your Master: Galatians 4:21–5:1 in the Shadow of the Anatolian Mother of the Gods." *JBL* 118 (1999) 661–83.
Ellis, Earle. "Note on Pauline Hermeneutics." *NTS* 2 (1955) 127–33.
———. *Paul's Use of the Old Testament*. 1957. Reprint, Eugene, OR: Wipf & Stock, 2003.
Emerson, Matthew. "Arbitrary Allegory, Typical Typology, or Intertextual Interpretation? Paul's Use of the Pentateuch in Galatians 4:21–31." *BTB* 43 (2013) 14–22.
Eskenazi, Tamara. "Paul and the Dead Sea Scrolls on the Law." *World Congress of Jewish Studies* 8 (1982) 119–24.
Fee, Gordon. "Who Are Abraham's True Children? The Role of Abraham in Pauline Argumentation." In *Perspectives on "Our Father Abraham": Essays in Honor of Marvin R. Wilson*, edited by Steven A. Hunt, 126–37. Grand Rapids: Eerdmans, 2010.
Feeny, D. C. *The Gods in Epic: Poets and Critics of the Classical Tradition*. Oxford: Oxford University Press, 1991.
Feldman, Asher. *The Parables and Similes of the Rabbis: Agricultural and Pastoral*. Cambridge: Cambridge University Press, 1924.
Fields, Weston. "Early and Medieval Jewish Interpretation of the Song of Songs." *GTJ* 1 (1980) 221–31.
Fitzmyer, Joseph A., SJ. *According to Paul: Studies in the Theology of the Apostle*. New York: Paulist, 1993.
———. *The Dead Sea Scrolls and Christian Origins*. Grand Rapids: Eerdmans, 2000.
———. "Paul and the Dead Sea Scrolls." In *The Dead Sea Scrolls after Fifty Years: A Comprehensive Assessment*, edited by Peter Flint and James C. Vanderkam, 2:599–621. Leiden: Brill, 1999.
Finkel, Asher. "The Pesher of Dreams and Scriptures." *RevQ* 4 (1963–64) 357–70.

Flusser, David. "The Dead Sea Sect and Pre-Pauline Christianity." In *Aspects of the Dead Sea Scrolls*, edited by Chaim Rabin et al., 215–66. Jerusalem: Magnes, 1965.

———. *Judaism of the Second Temple Period*. Translated by Azzan Yadin. 2 vols. Grand Rapids: Eerdmans, 2007.

Foulks, Francis. *The Acts of God: A Study of the Basis of Typology in the Old Testament*. London: Tyndale, 1958.

Fowl, Stephen E. "Who Can Read Abraham's Story? Allegory and Interpretive Power in Galatians." *JSNT* 55 (1994) 77–95.

Fraade, Steven. "Between Rewritten Bible and Allegorical Commentary: Philo's Interpretation of the Burning Bush." In *"Rewritten Bible" after Fifty Years: Texts, Terms, or Techniques? A Last Dialogue with Géza Vermes*, edited by József Zsengellér, 221–32. SJSJ 166. Leiden: Brill, 2014.

Frei, Hans W. *The Eclipse of Biblical Narrative: A Study in Eighteenth and Nineteenth Century Hermeneutics*. New Haven: Yale University Press, 1975.

Fung, Ronald Y. K. *The Epistle to the Galatians*. NICNT. Grand Rapids: Eerdmans, 1988.

Funk, Robert W. *A Beginning-Intermediate Grammar of Hellenistic Greek*. Missoula, MT: Scholars, 1977.

Gabbay, Uri. "Akkadian Commentaries from Ancient Mesopotamia and Their Relation to Early Hebrew Exegesis." *DSD* 19 (202) 267–312.

Gale, Monica R. *Myth and Poetry in Lucretius*. Cambridge Classical Studies. Cambridge: Cambridge University Press, 2007.

Galloway, Lincoln E. *Freedom in the Gospel: Paul's Exemplum in 1 Cor 9 in Conversation with the Discourses of Epictetus and Philo*. CBET. Dudley, UK: Peeters, 2004.

Gaventa, Beverly Roberts, ed. *Apocalyptic Paul: Cosmos and Anthropos in Romans 5–8*. Waco: Baylor University Press, 2013.

George, Timothy. *Galatians*. NAC 30. Nashville: Broadman & Holman, 1994.

Gerber, Daniel. "Ga 4,21–31 ou l'indéfinissable méthode?" In *Typologie biblique: De quelques figures vives*, edited by Raymond Kuntzmann, 165–76. Paris: Cerf, 2002.

Gese, Hartmut. "Hagar Is a Mountain in Arabia." [In Greek.] In *Vom Sinai zum Zion. Alttestamentliche Beiträge zur biblischen Theologie*, 49–62. BEvT 64. Munich: Kaiser, 1974.

Gignilliat, Mark. "Paul, Allegory, and the Plain Sense of Scripture: Galatians 4:21–31." *JTI* 2 (2008) 135–46.

Gil-Tamayo, Juan A. "'Todo esto tiene un sentido alegórico' (Ga 4,24). La Exégesis antioquena de Gálatas 4,21–31." *ScrTh* 40 (2008) 35–63.

Goldingay, John, and David Payne. *A Critical and Exegetical Commentary on Isaiah 40–55*. 2 vols. ICC. New York: T&T Clark, 2006.

Goldman, Liora. "Biblical Exegesis and Pesher Interpretation in the Damascus Document." PhD diss., University of Haifa, 2008.

———. "The Exegesis and Structure of Pesharim in the Damascus Document." In *The Dynamics of Exegesis and Language at Qumran*, edited by Devorah Dimant and Reinhard G. Kratz, 193–202. FAT 2/35. Tübingen: Mohr Siebeck, 2009.

Goodspeed, Edgar. *New Solutions of New Testament Problems*. Chicago: University of Chicago Press, 1927.

Goppelt, Leonhard. *Typos: The Typological Interpretation of the Old Testament in the New*. Grand Rapids: Eerdmans, 1982.

Gräßer, Erich. *Der Alte Bund im Neuen. Exegetische Studien zur Israelfrage im Neuen Testament*. WUNT 1/35. Tübingen: Mohr Siebeck, 1985.

Greene, J. T. "Paul's Hermeneutic Versus Its Competitors." *JRT* 42 (1985) 7–21.
Griffiths, Janice. "Allegory in Greece and Egypt." *JEA* 53 (1967) 79–102.
Grossouw, W. "Over de echtheid van 2 Cor 6:14–7:1." In *Liturgica. Second Century. Alexandria before Nicaea. Athanasius and the Arian Controversy*, edited by E. A. Livingstone, 203–6. StC 26. Leuven: Peeters, 1951.
Grundmann, Walter. "The Teacher of Righteousness of Qumran and the Question of Justification by Faith in the Theology of the Apostle Paul." In *Paul and Qumran: Studies in New Testament Exegesis*, edited by Jerome Murphy-O'Connor, OP, 85–114. Chicago: Priority, 1968.
Gunther, John. "The Epistle of Barnabas and the Final Rebuilding of the Temple." *JSJ* 7 (1976) 143–51.
Hamerton-Kelly, Robert G. "Some Techniques of Composition in Philo's Allegorical Commentary, with Special Reference to 'De Agricultura': A Study in the Hellenistic Midrash." In *Jews, Greeks, and Christians: Religious Cultures in Late Antiquity: Essays in Honor of William David Davies*, edited by Shimon Applebaum et al., 45–56. SJLA 21. Leiden: Brill, 1976.
Hansen, Walter. *Abraham in Galatians: Epistolary and Rhetorical Contexts*. JSNTSup 29. Sheffield: JSOT, 1989.
Hanson, Anthony Tyrrell. *Studies in Paul's Technique and Theology*. Grand Rapids: Eerdmans, 1974.
Hanson, R. P. C. *Allegory and Event: A Study of the Sources and Significance of Origen's Interpretation of Scripture*. Richmond, VA: John Knox, 1959.
Harmon, Matthew S. *She Must and Shall Go Free: Paul's Isaianic Gospel in Galatians*. BZNW. Berlin: de Gruyter, 2010.
Harrisville, Roy. *The Figure of Abraham in the Epistles of St. Paul: In the Footsteps of Abraham*. San Francisco: Mellen Research University Press, 1992.
Hay, David M. "Philo's References to Other Allegorists." In *The Studia Philonica Annual Studies in Hellenistic Judaism 6*, edited by Alan Mendelson et al., 41–75. SPhiloA. Atlanta: Scholars, 1994.
———. "References to Other Exegetes." In *Both Literal and Allegorical: Studies in Philo of Alexandria's Questions and Answers on Genesis and Exodus*, edited by David M. Hay, 81–97. BJS 232. Atlanta: Scholars, 2009.
Hays, Richard B. *Echoes of Scripture in the Letters of Paul*. New Haven, CT: Yale University Press, 1989.
———. *The Faith of Jesus Christ: An Investigation into the Narrative Substructure of Galatians 3:1—4:11*. SBLDS 56. Atlanta: Scholars, 1983.
Hegedus, Tim. "Midrash and the Letter of Barnabas." *BTB* (2007) 20–26.
Heldt, Petra. "Delineating Identity in the Second and Third Century CE: The Case of the Epistle of Paul to the Galatians 4:21–31 in the Writings of Hippolytus." In *Other Greek Writers. John of Damascus and Beyond. The West to Hilary*, edited by F. Young et al., 163–68. StPatr 42. Leuven: Peeters, 2006.
———. "The Epistle of Paul to the Galatians 4:21–31 in the Reading of the Early Church." PhD diss., Jerusalem University, 2002.
Helleman, Wendy. "'Abraham Had Two Sons': Augustine and the Allegory of Sarah and Hagar (Galatians 4:21–31)." *CTJ* 48 (2013) 35–64.
Hendriksen, William. *Galatians*. New Testament Commentary. Grand Rapids: Baker, 1968.
Hersman, Anne. *Studies in Greek Allegorical Interpretation*. Chicago: Blue Sky, 1906.

Hilgenfeld, Adolphus. "Die Abfassungszeit und die Zeitrichtung des Barnabasbriefes." *ZWT* 13 (1870) 115–23.

Himmelfarb, Martha. *A Kingdom of Priests: Ancestry and Merit in Ancient Judaism*. Jewish Culture and Contexts. Philadelphia: University of Pennsylvania Press, 2006.

Hogeterp, Albert. "Hagar and Paul's Covenant Thought." In *Abraham, the Nations, and the Hagarites: Jewish, Christian, and Islamic Perspectives on Kinship with Abraham*, edited by Martin Goodman et al., 345–59. TBN 13. Leiden: Brill, 2010.

Hong, In-Gyu. *The Law in Galatians*. JSNTSup 81. Sheffield: JSOT, 1993.

Horbury, William. *Jews and Christians: In Contact and Controversy*. New York: T&T Clark, 1998.

Horgan, Maurya P. *Pesharim: Qumran Interpretations of Biblical Books*. CBQMS 8. Washington, DC: Catholic Biblical Association of America, 1979.

Horsley, Richard A. "Pneumatikos vs. Psychikos: Distinctions of Spiritual Status among the Corinthians." *HTR* 69 (1976) 269–88.

Hübner, Hans. *Law in Paul's Thought: A Contribution to the Development of Pauline Theology*. Translated by James C. G. Greig. Edinburgh: T. & T. Clark, 1984.

Hugenberger, G. P. "Introductory Notes on Typology." In *The Right Doctrine from the Wrong Texts? Essays on the Use of the Old Testament in the New*, edited by G. K. Beale, 331–41. Grand Rapids: Baker Academic, 1994.

Hurtado, Larry W. "Does Philo Help Explain Early Christianity?" In *Philo und das Neue Testament: Wechselseitige Wahrnehmungen; I. Internationales Symposium zum Corpus Judaeo-Hellenisticum. 1.-4. Mai 2003, Eisenach/Jena*, edited by Roland Deines and Karl-Wilhelm Niebuhr, 73–92. WUNT 1/172. Tübingen: Mohr Siebeck, 2004.

Hvalvik, Reidar. *The Struggle for Scripture and Covenant: The Purpose of the Epistle of Barnabas and Jewish-Christian Competition in the Second Century*. WUNT 2/82. Tübingen: Mohr Siebeck, 1996.

Hyun, Young Min. "The Bible, Allegory, and Poetry." *Modern Studies in English Language & Literature* 52 (2008) 295–322.

Instone-Brewer, David. *Techniques and Assumptions in Jewish Exegesis before 70 CE*. TSAJ 30. Tübingen: Mohr Siebeck, 1992.

Jeffrey, David Lyle. "(Pre) Figuration: Masterplot and Meaning in Biblical History." In *"Behind" the Text: History and Biblical Interpretation*, edited by Craig Bartholomew et al., 363–93. Scripture and Hermeneutic. Grand Rapids: Zondervan, 2003.

Jewett, Paul K. "Concerning the Allegorical Interpretation of Scripture." *WTJ* 17 (1954) 1–20.

Jewett, Robert. "Agitators and the Galatian Congregation." *NTS* 17 (1971) 198–212.

———. *Paul's Anthropological Terms*. AGJU 10. Leiden: Brill, 1971.

Jobes, Karen H. "Jerusalem, Our Mother: Metalepsis and Intertextuality in Galatians 4.21–31." *WTJ* 55 (1993) 299–320.

Johnson, Sherman E. "The Dead Sea Manual of Discipline and the Jerusalem Church of Acts." *ZAW* 66 (1954) 106–20.

———. "Paul and the Manual of Discipline." *HTR* 48 (1955) 157–66.

Jokiranta, Jutta. "Pesharim: A Mirror of Self-Understanding." In *Reading the Present in the Qumran Library: The Perception of the Contemporary by Means of Scriptural Interpretations*, edited by Kristin De Troyer and Armin Lange, 23–34. SymS 30. Atlanta: SBL, 2005.

Kahl, Brigitte. "Hagar between Genesis and Galatians: The Stony Road to Freedom." In *From Prophecy to Testament: The Function of the Old Testament in the New*, edited by Craig A. Evans, 219–32. Peabody, MA: Hendrickson, 2004.

———. "Hagar's Babylonian Captivity: A Roman Re-imagination of Galatians 4:21–31." *Int* 68 (2014) 257–69.

Kamesar, Adam. "Biblical Interpretation in Philo." In *The Cambridge Companion to Philo*, edited by Adam Kamesar, 65–91. Cambridge Companions to Philosophy. New York: Cambridge University Press, 2009.

Kaplan, Jonathan. *My Perfect One: Typology and Early Rabbinic Interpretation of Song of Songs*. New York: Oxford University Press, 2015.

———. "The Song of Songs from the Bible to the Mishnah." *HUCA* 81 (2010) 43–66.

Kaufman, Stephen A. "The Temple Scroll and Higher Criticism." *HUCA* 53 (1982) 34–43.

Keener, Craig S. *Galatians*. NCBC. Cambridge: Cambridge University Press, 2018.

Kennedy, Harry. *Philo's Contribution to Religion*. London: Hodder & Stoughton, 1919.

Kepple, Robert. "Analysis of Antiochene Exegesis of Galatians 4:24–6." *WTJ* 39 (1977) 239–49.

King, Daniel. "Paul and the Tannaim." *WTJ* 45 (1983) 340–70.

Kister, Menahem. "Biblical Phrases and Hidden Biblical Interpretations and *Pesharim*." In *The Dead Sea Scrolls: Forty Years of Research*, edited by Devorah Dimant and Uriel Rappaport, 37–39. STDJ 10. Leiden: Brill, 1992.

———. "A Common Heritage: Biblical Interpretation at Qumran and Its Implications." In *Biblical Perspectives: Early Use and Interpretation of the Bible in Light of the Dead Sea Scrolls: Proceedings of the First International Symposium of the Orion Center for the Study of the Dead Sea Scrolls and Associated Literature, 12–14 May, 1996*, edited by Michael Stone and Esther G. Chazon, 101–11. STDJ 28. Leiden: Brill, 1998.

Knox, Wilfred L. *St Paul and the Church of Jerusalem*. Cambridge: Cambridge University Press, 1925.

Kosmala, Hans. "At the End of the Days." *ASTI* 2 (1963) 27–37.

Kovelman, Arkady. "Jeremiah 9:22–23 in Philo and Paul." *RRJ* 10 (2007) 162–75.

Kraft, Robert Alan. "The Epistle of Barnabas: Its Quotations and Their Sources." PhD diss., Harvard University, 1961.

———. Review of *Les Testimonia dans le Christianisme Primitif*, by Pierre Prigent. *JTS* 13 (1962) 401–8.

Kronenberg, Leah. *Allegories of Farming from Greece and Rome: Philosophical Satire in Xenophon, Varro, and Virgil*. Cambridge: Cambridge University Press, 2009.

Kuhn, Heinz-Wolfgang. "Die Bedeutung der Qumrantexte für das Verständnis des Galaterbriefes." In *New Qumran Texts and Studies: Proceedings of the First Meeting of the International Organization of Qumran Studies, Paris 1992*, edited by George Brooke and Florentino García Martínez, 169–221. STDJ 15. Leiden: Brill, 1992.

———. "The Impact of Selected Qumran Texts on the Understanding of Pauline Theology." In *The Bible and the Dead Sea Scrolls: The Princeton Symposium on the Dead Sea Scrolls*, edited by James H. Charlesworth, 3:153–85. Waco: Baylor University Press, 2006.

———. "The Impact of the Qumran Scrolls on the Understanding of Paul." In *The Dead Sea Scrolls: Forty Years of Research*, edited by Devorah Dimant and Uriel Rappaport, 327–39. STDJ 10. Leiden: Brill, 1992.

Kwon, Yon-Gyong. *Eschatology in Galatians: Rethinking Paul's Response to the Crisis in Galatia*. WUNT 2/183. Tübingen: Mohr Siebeck, 2004.

Lagrange, Marie-Joseph. *Saint Paul: Épitre aux Galates*. Paris: Gabalda, 1942.

Lambrecht, Jan, SJ. "Abraham and His Offspring. A Comparison of Galatians 5,1 with 3,13." *Bib* 80 (1999) 525–36.

LaSor, William. *The Dead Sea Scrolls and the New Testament*. Grand Rapids: Eerdmans, 1972.

Lauterbach, Jacob Z. "The Ancient Jewish Allegorists in the Talmud and Midrash." *JQR* 1 (1911) 291–333.

———. "The Ancient Jewish Allegorists in the Talmud and Midrash (Continued)." *JQR* 1 (1911) 503–31.

Leipold, Johannes. *Geschichte des neutestamentlichen Kanons*. 2 vols. Leipzig: Hinrichs, 1907.

Lémonon, Jean-Pierre. *L'Épitre aux Galates*. Paris: Cerf, 2008.

Leverett, Frederick. *A New and Copious Lexicon of the Latin Language*. Philadelphia: Lippincott, 1855.

Liao, Paul S. H. "The Meaning of Galatians 4:21–31: A New Perspective." *Northeast Asia Journal of Theology* 22–23 (1979) 115–32.

Lietzmann, Hans. *An die Galater*. HNT 10. Tübingen: Mohr Siebeck, 1923.

———. *Geschichte der alten Kirche*. Berlin: de Gruyter, 1975.

Lightfoot, J. B. *Saint Paul's Epistle to the Galatians*. London: MacMillan and Co., 1865.

Lim, Timothy H. *Holy Scripture in the Qumran Commentaries and Pauline Letters*. Oxford: Clarendon, 1997.

———. *Pesharim*. Companion to the Qumran Scrolls. Sheffield: Academic, 2002.

———. "Studying the Qumran Scrolls and Paul in their Historical Context." In *The Dead Sea Scrolls as Background to Postbiblical Judaism and Early Christianity: Papers from an International Conference at St. Andrews in 2001*, edited by James Davila, 135–56. STDJ 46. Leiden: Brill, 2003.

Lincicum, David. "Paul and the Temple Scroll: Reflections on a Shared Engagement with Deuteronomy." *Neot* 43 (2009) 69–92.

Lincoln, Andrew T. *Paradise Now and Not Yet: Studies in the Role of the Heavenly Dimension in Paul's Thought with Special Reference to His Eschatology*. SNTSMS. Cambridge: Cambridge University Press, 1981.

Lindemann, Andreas. *Paulus im ältesten Christentum: Das Bild des Apostels und die Rezeption der paulinischen Theologie in der frühchristlichen Literatur bis Marcion*. BHT 58. Tübingen: Mohr Siebeck, 1979.

Loewe, Ralph. "The 'Plain' Meaning of Scripture in Early Jewish Exegesis." In *Papers for the Institute of Jewish Studies London*, edited by J. G. Weiss, 1:140–85. Jerusalem: Magnes, 1964.

Löfstedt, Torsten. "The Allegory of Hagar and Sarah: Gal 4.21–31." *EstBib* 58 (2000) 475–94.

Loisy, Alfred. "The Christian Mystery." *Hibbert Journal* 10 (1911–12) 51.

Longenecker, Richard N. *Biblical Exegesis in the Apostolic Period*. Grand Rapids: Eerdmans, 1999.

———. *Galatians*. WBC 41. Dallas: Word, 1990.

López, Renè A. "Vice Lists in Non-Pauline Sources." *BSac* 168 (2011) 178–95.

Loubster, J. A. "The Contrast Slavery/Freedom as Persuasive Device in Galatians." *Neot* 28 (1994) 163–76.

Lowe, Dunstan M. "Personification Allegory in the 'Aeneid' and Ovid's 'Metamorphoses.'" *Mnemosyne* 61 (2008) 414–35.
Lowy, Simeon. "The Confutation of Judaism in the Epistle of Barnabas." In *Early Christianity and Judaism*, edited by Everett Ferguson, 303–35. Studies in Early Christianity 6. New York: Garland, 1993.
Lucchesi, Enzi. "Nouveau parallèle entre Saint Paul (Gal. III 16) et Philon d'Alexandrie (*Quaestiones in Genesim*)?" *NovT* 21 (1979) 150–55.
Lührmann, Dieter. *Galatians: A Continental Commentary*. Translated by O. C. Dean. Continental Commentaries. Minneapolis: Fortress, 1992.
Lütgert, Wilhelm. *Gesetz und Geist: Eine Untersuchung zur Vorgeschichte des Galaterbriefes*. Gütersloh: Bertelsmann, 1919.
Machiela, Daniel. "The Qumran Pesharim as Biblical Commentaries: Historical Context and Lines of Development." *DSD* 19 (2012) 313–62.
Mack, Burton. "Philo Judaeus and Exegetical Traditions in Alexandria." *ANRW*, edited by Hildegard Temporini and Wolfgang Haase, II.212.2:236–41. New York: de Gruyter, 1989.
MacQueen, John. *Allegory*. London: Methuen, 1970.
Malan, F. S. "The Strategy of Two Opposing Covenants." *Neot* 26 (1992) 425–40.
Manns, Frédéric. "Jewish Interpretations of the Song of Songs." *LASBF* 58 (2008) 277–95.
Martín, José Pablo. "L'interpretazione allegorica nella Lettera di Barnaba e nel Giudaismo alessandrino." *Studi Storico Religiosi* 6 (1982) 173–83.
Martyn, J. Louis. "Apocalyptic Antinomies in Paul's Letter to the Galatians." *NTS* 31 (1985) 410–24.
———. "The Covenants of Hagar and Sarah." In *Faith and History: Essays in Honor of Paul Meyer*, edited by John T. Carroll et al., 160–92. Atlanta: Scholars, 1990.
———. *Galatians*. AB 33a. New York: Doubleday, 1997.
———. "A Law-Observant Mission to the Gentiles: The Background of Galatians." *SJT* 38 (1985) 307–24.
Maschke, Timothy. "The Authority of Scripture: Luther's Approach to Allegory in Galatians." *Logia* 4 (1995) 25–31.
Massaux, Édouard. *Influence de l'Évangile de Saint Matthieu sur la littérature chrétienne avant Saint Irénée*. Leuven: Leuven University Press, 1986.
Matera, Frank J. *Galatians*. Edited by Daniel J. Harrington, SJ. SP. Collegeville: Liturgical, 1992.
Matusova, Ekaterina. "Allegorical Interpretation of the Pentateuch in Alexandria: Inscribing Aristobulus and Philo in a Wider Literary Context." In *The Studia Philonica Annual 22, 2010: Studies in Hellenistic Judaism*, edited by David T. Runia and Gregory E. Sterling, 1–51. SPhiloA. Atlanta: SBL, 2010.
McClane, Curtis D. "The Hellenistic Background to the Pauline Allegorical Method in Galatians 4:21–31." *RQ* 40 (1998) 125–35.
McFarland, Orrey. "Whose Abraham, Which Promise? Genesis 15.6 in Philo's *De Virtutibus* and Romans 4." *JSNT* 35 (2012) 107–29.
McNamara, Martin. "'To de (Hagar) Sina oros estin en tê Arabia' (Gal. 4:25a)." *MilS* 2 (1978) 24–41.
McNutt, Walter Buswell. "Philo of Alexandria: An Exegete of Scripture." PhD diss., University of Missouri Kansas City, 2001.
Meinhold, Peter. "Geschichte und Exegese im Barnabasbrief." *ZKG* 59 (1940) 255–303.

Ménard, Dom. *Sancti Barnabae Apostoli (ut fertur) Epistola Catholica*. Paris: Bibliothèque Nationale, 1645.
Menken, Maarten J. J. "Old Testament Quotations in the *Epistle of Barnabas* with Parallels in the New Testament." In *Textual History and the Reception of Scripture in Early Christianity*, edited by Johannes de Vries and Martin Karrer, 295–321. SCS 60. Atlanta: SBL, 2013.
Miller, Troy. "Surrogate, Slave and Deviant? The Figure of Hagar in Jewish Tradition and Paul (Galatians 4.21–31)." In *Early Christian Literature and Intertextuality*, edited by Craig A. Evans and H. Daniel Zacharias, 2:138–54. LNTS 392. London: T. & T. Clark, 2009.
Mitchell, Margaret M. *Paul, the Corinthians and the Birth of Christian Hermeneutics*. Cambridge: Cambridge University Press, 2010.
Montagnini, Felice. "Il Monte Sinai Si Trova in Arabia (Gal 4,25)." *BeO* 11 (1969) 33–37.
Moo, Douglas J. *Galatians*. BECNT. Grand Rapids: Baker Academic, 2013.
Mußner, Franz. *Der Galaterbrief: Auslegung*. Vienna: Herder, 1974.
———. "Hagar, Sinai, Jerusalem: Zum Text von Gal 4:25a." *TQ* 135 (1955) 56–60.
Murphy-O'Connor, Jerome, OP. "Truth: Paul and Qumran." In *Paul and Qumran: Studies in New Testament Exegesis*, edited by Jermoe Murphy-O'Connor, OP, 179–230. Chicago: Priority, 1968.
Ngewa, Samual. *Galatians*. African Bible Commentary. Grand Rapids: Hippo, 2010.
Nickelsberg, George W. E. "Philo among Greeks, Jews, and Christians." In *Philo und das Neue Testament: Wechselseitige Wahrnehmungen; I. Internationales Symposium zum Corpus Judaeo-Hellenisticum. 1.–4. Mai 2003, Eisenach/Jena*, edited by Roland Deines and Karl-Wilhelm Niebuhr, 53–72. WUNT 1/172. Tübingen: Mohr Siebeck, 2004.
Nikiprowezky, Valentin. *Le commentaire de l'Écriture chez Philon d'Alexandrie: Son caractère et sa portée, observations philologiques*. ALGHJ 11. Leiden: Brill, 1977.
Nitzan, Bilha. *Pesher Habakkuk: A Scroll from the Wilderness of Judea (1QpHab)*. Jerusalem: Bialik Institute, 1986.
Oepke, D. Albrecht. *Der Brief des Paulus an die Galater*. Berlin: Evangelisch, 1960.
O'Hagan, Angelo. "Early Christian Exegesis Exemplified from the Epistle of Barnabas." *ABR* 11 (1963) 33–41.
Olsen, Glenn. "Allegory, Typology, and Symbol: The Sensus Spiritalis, Pt 1: Definitions and Earliest History." *Comm* 4 (1977) 161–79.
O'Neill, J. C. "'For This Is Mount Sinai in Arabia' (Galatians 4:25)." In *The Old Testament in the New Testament: Essays in Honour of J. L. North*, edited by Steve Moyise, 210–19. JSNTSup 189. Sheffield: Sheffield Academic, 2000.
Paget, James. "Barnabas 9:4: A Peculiar Verse on Circumcision." *VC* 45 (1991) 242–54.
———. "Barnabas and the Outsiders: Jews and Their World in the *Epistle of Barnabas*." In *Early Christian Communities between Ideal and Reality*, edited by Mark Grundeken and Joseph Verheyden, 175–202. WUNT 1/342. Tübingen: Mohr Siebeck, 2015.
———. "The Epistle of Barnabas." *ExpTim* 117 (2006) 441–46.
———. *The Epistle of Barnabas: Outlook and Background*. WUNT 2/64. Tübingen: Mohr Siebeck, 1994.
———. "Paul and the Epistle of Barnabas." *NovT* 4 (1996) 359–81.
Parsons, Mikael. "'Allegorizing Allegory': Narrative Analysis and Parable Interpretation." *PRSt* 15 (1988) 147–64.

Pastor, Federico. "Alegoría o Tipología en Gal 4,21–31." *EstBib* 34 (1975) 113–19.
———. "A Propósito de Gal 4,25." *EstBib* 31 (1972) 205–10.
Pearson, Birger Albert. *The Pneumatikos-Psychikos Terminology in 1 Corinthians: A Study in the Theology of the Corinthian Opponents of Paul and its Relation to Gnosticism*. SBLDS 12. Missoula, MT: Scholars, 1973.
Peisker, C. H. "Parable, Allegory, Proverb." *NIDNTT* 5 (1976) 743–49.
Pépin, Jean. *Mythe et Allégorie: Les origines grecques et les contestations judéo-chrétiennes*. Paris: Montaigne, 1958.
Perriman, Andrew C. "The Rhetorical Strategy of Galatians 4:21–5:1." *EvQ* 65 (1993) 27–42.
———. "Typology in Paul." *Th* 90 (1987) 200–206.
Pfleiderer, Otto. *Der Paulinismus. Ein Beitrag zur Geschichte der urchristlichen Theologie*. Leipzig: Reisland, 1890.
———. *Das Urchristentum, seine Schriften und Lehren in geschichtlichem Zusammenhang*. Berlin: Reimer, 1902.
Prigent, Pierre. *Les Testimonia dans le christianisme primitif. L'Épitre de Barnabe I–XVI et ses sources*. Paris: Lecoffre, 1961.
Prostmeier, Ferdinand R. *Der Barnabasbrief*. KAV 8. Göttingen: Vandenhoeck & Ruprecht, 1999.
Punt, Jeremy. "Hermeneutics in Identity Formation: Paul's Use of Genesis in Galatians 4." *HTS* 67 (2011) 1–8.
———. "Revealing Rereading. Part 1: Pauline Allegory in Galatians 4:21–5:1." *Neot* 40 (2006) 87–100.
———. "Revealing Rereading. Part 2: Paul and the Wives of the Father of Faith in Galatians 4:21—5:1." *Neot* 40 (2006) 101–18.
———. "Subverting Sarah in the New Testament: Galatians 4 and 1 Peter 3." In *Exegetical Studies*, edited by Craig A. Evans, 155–74. Vol. 2 of *Early Christian Literature and Intertextuality*. SSEJC 392. New York: T&T Clark, 2009.
Ramsay, William. *A Historical Commentary on St. Paul's Epistle to the Galatians*. London: Hodder & Stoughton, 1900.
Renouf, P., and E. Naville. *The Egyptian Book of the Dead*. London: Society of Biblical Archaeology, 1904.
Rhode, Joachim. *Der Brief des Paulus an die Galater*. Berlin: Evangelisch, 1989.
Rhodes, James N. *The Epistle of Barnabas and the Deuteronomic Tradition: Polemics, Paraenesis, and the Legacy of the Golden-Calf Incident*. WUNT 2/188. Tübingen: Mohr Siebeck, 2004.
———. "The Two Ways Tradition in the Epistle of Barnabas: Revisiting an Old Question." *CBQ* 73 (2011) 797–816.
Rhoers, Walter R. "The Typological Use of the Old Testament in the New Testament." *Concordia Journal* 10 (1984) 204–16.
Ridderbos, Herman N. *The Epistle of Paul to the Churches of Galatia*. Grand Rapids: Eerdmans, 1984.
Rogers, Justin M. "The Philonic and the Pauline: Hagar and Sarah in the Exegesis of Didymus the Blind." In *Studia Philonica Annual 26, 2014: Studies in Hellenistic Judaism*, edited by David T. Runia and Gregory E. Sterling, 57–77. SPhiloA. Atlanta: SBL, 2014.
Ropes, J. H. *The Singular Problem of the Epistle to the Galatians*. Cambridge: Harvard University Press, 1929.

Runia, David T. *Exegesis and Philosophy: Studies on Philo of Alexandria.* VCS 332. Brookfield: Variorum, 1991.

———. "Further Observations on the Structure of Philo's Allegorical Treatises." *VC* 41 (1987) 105–38.

———. *Philo in Early Christian Literature.* CRINT III/3. Minneapolis: Fortress, 1993.

———. "The Structure of Philo's Allegorical Treatises: A Review of Two Recent Studies and Some Additional Comments." *VC* 39 (1984) 209–56.

Russell, Letty M. "Twists and Turns in Paul's Allegory." In *Hagar, Sarah, and Their Children: Jewish, Christian, and Muslim Perspectives*, edited by Phyllis Trible and Letty M. Russell, 71–97. Louisville: Westminster John Knox, 2006.

Ruzer, Serge. "Exegetical Patterns Common to the Dead Sea Scrolls and the New Testament, and Their Implications." In *Text, Thought, and Practice in Qumran and Early Christianity*, edited by Ruth Clements and Daniel R. Schwartz, 231–51. STDJ 84. Leiden: Brill, 2009.

Sanders, James A. "Habakkuk in Qumran, Paul, and the Old Testament." *JR* 39 (1959) 323–44.

Sandmel, Samuel. "Philo Judaeus: An Introduction to the Man, His Writings, and His Significance." *ANRW* II.21.2:3–46, edited by Hildegard Temporini and Wolfgang Haase. Berlin: de Gruyter, 1989.

———. *Philo of Alexandria: An Introduction.* New York: Oxford University Press, 1979.

Sänger, Dieter. "Sara, die Freie—unsere Mutter. Namenallegorese als Interpretament christlicher Identitätsbildung in Gal 4,21–31." In *Neues Testament und hellenistisch-jüdische Alltagskultur. Wechselseitige Wahrnehmungen. III. Internationales Symposium zum Corpus Judaeo-Hellenisticum Novi Testamenti 21.–24. Mai 2009, Leipzig*, edited by Roland Deines et al., 213–39. WUNT 1/274. Tübingen: Mohr Siebeck, 2011.

Schenck, Kenneth. *A Brief Guide to Philo.* Louisville: Westminster John Knox, 2005.

Schlier, Heinrich. *Der Brief an die Galater.* Meyers kritisch-exegetischer Kommentar über das Neue Testament. Göttingen: Vandenhoeck & Ruprecht, 1989.

Schmithals, W. "Die Häretiker in Galatien." *ZNW* 47 (1956) 25–67.

Schoeps, H. J. *Paul: The Theology of the Apostle in the Light of Jewish Religious History.* Translated by Harold Knight. Philadelphia: Westminster, 1961.

Schreiner, Thomas R. *Galatians.* Edited by Clinton E. Arnold. Zondervan Exegetical Commentary on the New Testament 9. Grand Rapids: Zondervan, 2010.

Schwemer, Anna Maria. "Himmlische Stadt und himmlische Bürgerrecht bei Paulus (Gal 4,26 und Phil 3,20)." In *La Cité de Dieu/Die Stadt Gottes*, edited by Martin Hengel et al., 195–243. WUNT 1/129. Tübingen: Mohr Siebeck, 2000.

Scott, James M. *The Apocalyptic Letter to the Galatians: Paul and the Enochic Heritage.* Lanham, MD: Fortress Academic, 2021.

Segal, Michael. "Between Bible and Rewritten Bible." In *Biblical Interpretation at Qumran*, edited by Matthias Henze, 10–28. SDSS. Grand Rapids: Eerdmans, 2005.

Seland, Torrey. *Establishment Violence in Philo and Luke: A Study of Non-Conformity to the Torah and Jewish Vigilante Reactions.* BibInt 15. Leiden: Brill, 1995.

Sellin, Gerhard. "Hagar und Sara. Religionsgeschichtliche Hintergründe der Schriftallegorese Gal 4,21–31." In *Das Urchristentum in seiner literarischen Geschichte: Festschrift für Jürgen Becker zum 65*, edited by Ulrich Meil et al., 59–84. BZAW 100. Berlin: de Gruyter, 1999.

———. *Der Streit um die Auferstehung der Toten: Eine religionsgeschichtliche und exegetische Untersuchung von 1 Korinther 15*. FRLANT 138. Göttingen: Vandenhoeck & Ruprecht, 1986.
Siegert, Folker. "Philo and the New Testament." In *The Cambridge Companion to Philo*, edited by Adam Kamesar, 175–209. Cambridge Companions to Philosophy. New York: Cambridge University Press, 2009.
Siegfried, Carl. *Philo von Alexandria als Ausleger des Alten Testament. An sich selbst und nach seinem geschichtlichen Einfluss betrachtet. Nebst Untersuchungen über Graecotaet Philo's*. Jena: Dufft, 1875.
Silva, Moisés. *Explorations in Exegetical Methods: Galatians as a Test Case*. Grand Rapids: Baker, 1996.
Smit, Joop. "The Letter of Paul to the Galatians: A Deliberative Speech." *NTS* 35 (1989) 1–26.
Smith, Gary V. *Isaiah 40–66*. NAC 15b. Nashville: B&H, 2009.
Smith, Jonathan Z. *Drudgery Divine: On the Comparison of Early Christianities and the Religions of Late Antiquity*. Chicago: University of Chicago Press, 1990.
———. "The 'End' of Comparison: Redescription and Rectification." In *A Magic Still Dwells: Comparative Religion in the Postmodern Age*, edited by Kimberly C. Patton and Benjamin C. Ray, 237–41. Berkeley: University of California Press, 2000.
———. "In Comparison a Magic Dwells." In *A Magic Still Dwells: Comparative Religion in the Postmodern Age*, edited by Kimberly C. Patton and Benjamin C. Ray, 23–44. Berkeley: University of California Press, 2000.
Smith, Julien. "The Epistle of Barnabas and the Two Ways of Teaching Authority." *VC* 68 (2014) 465–97.
Smyth, Herbert Weir. *Greek Grammar for Colleges*. Cambridge: Harvard University Press, 2002.
Snodgrass, Klyne. "The Use of the Old Testament in the New." In *New Testament Criticism and Interpretation*, edited by David Alan Black and David S. Dockery, 29–51. Grand Rapids: Zondervan, 1991.
Söding, Thomas. "'Sie ist unsere Mutter': Die Allegorie über Sara und Hagar (Gal 4,21–31) in der Einheitsübersetzung und bei Paulus." In *Für immer verbündet: Studien zur Bundestheologie der Bibel; Festgabe für Frank-Lothar Hossfeld zum 65. Geburtstag*, edited by Christoph Dohmen and Christian Frevel, 231–37. SBS 211. Stuttgart: Katholisches Bibelwerk, 2017.
Sowers, Sidney G. "The Hermeneutics of Philo and Hebrews." PhD diss., Basel University, 1965.
Stegmann, Basil Augustine. "Christ, the 'Man from Heaven'; A Study of 1 Cor. 15, 45–7 in the Light of the Anthropology of Philo Judaeus." PhD diss., Catholic University of America, 1927.
Steinhauser, Michael. "Gal 4,25a: Evidence of Targumic Tradition in Gal 4,21–31?" *Bib* 70 (1989) 234–40.
Sterling, Gregory E. "The Place of Philo in the Study of Christian Origins." In *Philo und das Neue Testament: Wechselseitige Wahrnehmungen; I. Internationales Symposium zum Corpus Judaeo-Hellenisticum. 1.–4. Mai 2003, Eisenach/Jena*, edited by Roland Deines and Karl-Wilhelm Niebuhr, 21–52. WUNT 1/172. Tübingen: Mohr Siebeck, 2004.
———. "'The School of Sacred Laws': The Social Setting of Philo's Treatises." *VC* 53 (1999) 148–64.

———. "'Wisdom among the Perfect': Creation Traditions in Alexandrian Judaism and Corinthian Christianity." *NovT* 37 (1995) 355–84.
Steudel, Annette. "אחרית הימים in the Texts from Qumran." *RevQ* 62 (1993) 225–43.
Stevens, John A. "Seneca and Horace: Allegorical Technique in Two Odes to Bacchus (Hor. 'Carm.' 2.19 and Sen. 'Oed.' 403–508)." *Phoenix* 53 (1999) 281–307.
Still, Todd D. "'Once upon a Time': Galatians as an Apocalyptic Story." *JSPL* 2 (2012) 133–41.
Strawbridge, Jennifer. "A School of Paul? The Use of Pauline Texts in Early Christian Schooltext Papyri." In *Ancient Education and Early Christianity*, edited by Matthew Ryan Hauge and Andrew W. Pitts, 165–78. LNTS. New York: T&T Clark, 2016.
Svendsen, Stefan. *Allegory Transformed: The Appropriation of Philonic Hermeneutics in the Letter to the Hebrews*. WUNT 2/269. Tübingen: Mohr Siebeck, 2009.
Tamez, Elsa. "Hagar and Sarah in Galatians: A Case Study in Freedom." *WW* 20 (2000) 265–71.
Tate, Jonathan. "The Beginnings of Greek Allegory." *CR* 41 (1927) 214–15.
———. "On the History of Allegorism." *CQ* 28 (1934) 105–14.
———. "Plato and Allegorical Interpretation." *CQ* 23(1929) 142–54.
———. "Plato and Allegorical Interpretation (Continued)." *CQ* 24 (1930) 1–10.
Tedder, Samuel John. "Children of Laughter and the Re-Creation of Humanity: The Theological Vision and Logic of Paul's Letter to the Galatians from the Vantage Point of 4:21–5:1." PhD diss., Durham University, 2017.
Thackeray, Henry. *The Relation of St. Paul and Jewish Thought*. New York: Macmillan, 1900.
Theilman, Frank. *From Plight to Solution: A Jewish Framework for Understanding Paul's View of the Law in Galatians and Romans*. NovTSup 61. Leiden: Brill, 1989.
Todd, James. *The Apostle Paul and the Christian Church at Philippi*. Cambridge: Bell, 1864.
Tolmie, D. F. "Allegorie as Argument: Galasiërs 4:21—5:1 in Retoriese Perspektief." *AcT* 2 (2002) 163–78.
———. *Persuading the Galatians: A Text-Centered Rhetorical Analysis of a Pauline Letter*. WUNT 2/190. Tübingen: Mohr Siebeck, 2005.
Trible, Phyllis. *Texts of Terror: Literary-Feminist Readings of Biblical Narratives*. OBT. Minneapolis: Fortress, 1984.
Trigg, J. W. *Origen: The Bible and Philosophy in the Third-Century Church*. Atlanta: John Knox, 1983.
Vanderkam, James C. *The Dead Sea Scrolls Today*. Grand Rapids: Eerdmans, 1994.
Van Kooten, George. "Philosophical Criticism of Genealogical Claims and Stoic Depoliticization of Politics: Greco-Roman Strategies in Paul's Allegorical Interpretation of Hagar and Sarah (Gal 4:21–31)." In *Abraham, the Nations, and the Hagarites: Jewish, Christian, and Islamic Perspectives on Kinship with Abraham*, edited by Martin Goodman et al., 361–85. TBN 13. Leiden: Brill, 2010.
Van Os, Bas. "Children of the Slave Woman: The Gnostic Christian Reinterpretation of Paul's Allegory of Hagar and Sarah." In *Abraham, the Nations, and the Hagarites: Jewish, Christian, and Islamic Perspectives on Kinship with Abraham*, edited by Martin Goodman et al., 387–400. TBN 13. Leiden: Brill, 2010.
Vermes, Géza. *Scripture and Tradition in Judaism: Haggadic Studies*. StPB. Leiden: Brill, 1961.
Vouga, François. *An die Galater*. HNT 10. Tübingen: Mohr Siebeck, 1998.

Wagner, Guy. "Les enfants d'Abraham ou les chemins de la promesse et de la liberté: Exégèse de Galates 4,21 à 31." *RHPR* 71 (1991) 285–95.
Wan, Sze-Kar. "Allegorical Interpretation East and West: A Methodological Enquiry into Comparative Hermeneutics." In *Text & Experience: Towards a Cultural Exegesis of the Bible*, edited by Daniel Smith-Christopher, 154–79. Biblical Seminar 35. Sheffield: Sheffield Academic, 1995.
———. "Charismatic Exegesis." In *The Studia Philonica Annual 6, 1994: Studies in Hellenistic Judaism*, edited by Alan Mendelson et al., 71–78. SPhiloA 6. Atlanta: Scholars, 1994.
Warren, William. "Paul's Hermeneutical Method and Ours." *TTE* 50 (1994) 115–26.
Watson, Francis. *Paul and the Hermeneutics of Faith*. T & T Clark Cornerstones. London: T. & T. Clark International, 2004.
Wengst, Klaus. *Didache (Apostellehre). Barnabasbrief. Zweiter Klemensbrief. Schrift an Diognet*. Schriften des Urchristentums 2. Darmstadt: Wissenschaft, 1984.
———. *Tradition und Theologie des Barnabasbriefes*. AzK 42. Berlin: de Gruyter, 1971.
Whitman, Jon. *Allegory: The Dynamics of an Ancient and Medieval Technique*. Cambridge: Harvard University Press, 1987.
———, ed. *Interpretation and Allegory: Antiquity to the Modern Period*. Leiden: Brill, 2000.
Williams, Arthur. "The Date of the Epistle of Barnabas." *JTS* 34 (1933) 339–46.
Williams, Sam K. *Galatians*. ANTC. Nashville: Abingdon, 2007.
Williamson, Ronald. *Philo and the Epistle to the Hebrews*. ALGHJ 4. Leiden: Brill, 1970.
Willitts, Joel. "Isa 54,1 in Gal 4,24b: Reading Genesis in Light of Isaiah." *ZNW* 96 (2005) 188–210.
Wilson, Todd A. *The Curse of the Law and the Crisis in Galatians: Reassessing the Purpose of Galatians*. WUNT 2/225. Tübingen: Mohr Siebeck, 2007.
Windisch, Hans. *Der Barnabasbrief*. HNT 3. Tübingen: Mohr Siebeck, 1920.
Witherington, Ben, III. *Grace in Galatia: A Commentary on St. Paul's Letter to the Galatians*. Grand Rapids: Eerdmans, 1998.
Wolfson, Harry. *Philo: Foundations of Religious Philosophy in Judaism, Christianity, and Islam*. Cambridge: Harvard University Press, 1947.
Wolter, Michael. "Das Israelproblem nach Gal 4,21–31 und Rom 9–11." *ZTK* 107 (2010) 1–30.
Wood, James. "Pauline Studies and the Dead Sea Scrolls." *ExpTim* 78 (1967) 308–11.
Woollcombe, K. J. "The Biblical Origins and Patristic Development of Typology." In *Essays on Typology*, 39–75. London: SCM, 1957.
Wright, N. T. *Galatians*. CCF. Grand Rapids. Eerdmans, 2021.
———. *Paul and the Faithfulness of God*. Christian Origins and the Question of God 4. Minneapolis: Fortress, 2013.
Young, Francis. "Alexandrian and Antiochene Exegesis." In *A History of Biblical Interpretation*, edited by Alan J. Hauser and Duane F. Watson, 1:334–54. History of Biblical Interpre-tation. Grand Rapids: Eerdmans, 2003.
———. "Typology." In *Crossing the Boundaries: Essays in Biblical Interpretation in Honour of Michael D. Goulder*, edited by Stanley E. Porter et al., 28–48. BibInt 8. Leiden: Brill, 1994.
Zsengellér, József, ed. *"Rewritten Bible" after Fifty Years: Texts, Terms, or Techniques? A Last Dialogue with Géza Vermes*. SJSJ 166. Leiden: Brill, 2014.

Zucker, David, and Rebecca Brinton. "'The Other Woman': A Collaborative Jewish-Christian Study of Hagar." In *Perspectives on Our Father Abraham: Essays in Honor of Marvin R. Wilson*, edited by Stephen A. Hunt, 339–83. Grand Rapids: Eerdmans, 2010.

Zurawski, Jason. "Mosaic Torah as Encyclical Paideia: Reading Paul's Allegory of Hagar and Sarah in Light of Philo of Alexandria's." In *Pedagogy in Ancient Judaism and Early Christianity*, edited by Karina Martin Hogan et al., 283–308. EJL 41. Atlanta: SBL, 2017.

Ancient Documents Index

OLD TESTAMENT/ HEBREW BIBLE

Genesis

11:7 (LXX)	8n35
14:14	138
15:6	87–88, 111–12, 139–40
16–21	xxv–xxvi, xxx, 2, 6–9, 12–14, 23, 23n110, 26–28, 32–33, 77, 92, 103, 130, 158, 161, 164
16:10–11	9
17	11n54, 33n145
17:11–14	10n48
17:24–25	10n48
17:25	10n49
21:9	27–28, 28n125, 28n126
21:9 (LXX)	28n126
21:10	29, 29n129, 102, 153n87, 164–65
21:12	29
21:17–18	9n41
25:21–23	150
48	150

Exodus

15:17–18	103
15:25	66
17:8	66
34:33–35	xxix

Leviticus

11:7–15	150

Numbers

12:12	125–26
19:1–22	150
19:16	165
21:18	59–61, 103, 103n37
24:7–8 (LXX)	166

Deuteronomy

10:16	137n44
12:3	66
14:8–14	150
18:3	66
28:49 (LXX)	8n35

2 Samuel

11:26–12:15	50, 53, 58
12:7	58

Psalm

1:1	153, 153n87, 166
80:7–14	58

Proverbs

3:18	66

Ancient Documents Index

Song of Songs

    67, 67n70

Isaiah
50:1	21n100
51:2	23
51:18	21n100
54:1	21–26, 23n110, 24n112, 24n115, 26n121, 41, 85n13, 103n37, 127, 129, 153, 163
54:16	59, 103n37
66:7–11	21n100

Jeremiah
50:12	21n100

Ezekiel
37:1–14	58

Daniel
7	145n68

Hosea
2:4	21n100

APOCRYPHA

1 Maccabees
2:52	88n22

2 Esdras
10:7	21n100
14:4	21n100

PSEUDEPIGRAPHA

2 Baruch
3:1	21n100

2 Clement
2:1–3	23n110

Letter of Aristeas
	43n22
150–52	43–44

NEW TESTAMENT

Matthew
13:13	8n35
24:42–44	62, 62n60
25:14–30	62n60

Luke
	104, 104n1
10:30–35	62n60
15:11–31	62n60
16:29	8n35

John
	104, 104n2

Romans
	31n142, 105, 105n7, 132–33
1–2	108n29
1:18	116–17
1:22–23	116–17
2	137n42
2:25–29	107n18
2:28–29	110
2:29	136n35, 137
3	137n37
3:1–2	138
3:31	135n28
4	9n42, 134, 135n28, 167
4:3	111n42
4:9	111n42
4:11	135n28
5:13	107n19, 108n32
7:5	108n33
7:8	107n21

7:24	108n30
8:5	108n33
8:34	108n28
9	135n28
9:11	9, 9n46
9:12	137n41
10:6–7	101n35
11	136n36
11:11–24	107n23
11:12	132

1 Corinthians

	105, 105n8, 156
1:26–31	107n24
2:13	136n34
2:15	136n34
3–4	135n28
3:1–3	12, 53, 64, 68–69
3:16–17	136n32
4:13	133
4:14–15	9
5:6–7	63, 69
5:11	107n20
6:16	108n37
6:19	136n32
7:31	108n35
9:9–10	63, 68
9:21	135n28
9:24–27	113
9:27	137n40
10:1–11	28n128, 63–64, 68, 76
10:3	107n22
10:4	28n128, 64, 76
10:6	28n128, 64. 76
10:11	64, 76
10:12	108n34
11:25	136n36
12:2	130
12:12–25	12, 65, 68
12	43n21
13	107n16
13:12	107n26
14:2	8n35
14:37	136n34
15:8	135n28
15:32	113n46
15:45–49	107n15, 109
15:46	108n31

2 Corinthians

	105, 105n8
3:5–6	117
3:6	136n36
3:7	135n28
3:12–18	12, 64
3:12–16	xxix
3:18	107n26
4:4	107n17
4:6	137n42
5:10	137n38
6:4	108n36
6:16–17	107n25

Galatians

	xxv–xxvi, 5–6, 7n34, 31n143, 85–86, 105, 105n9, 161–62, 164–67
1:4	137n39
1:6–9	119
1:6	90
1:8–9	31
1:15–17	117
2:2	113
2:6	135n28
2:12	10
2:16	86
3	8n39, 139
3:6–9	166
3:6–7	8, 87, 111, 139
3:19	135n28
3:23–26	7–8, 130
3:28	31n143
3:29	136n33
4:3	89
4:7	31n143
4:8–9	130
4:9	89
4:17	31
4:21–31	xxv–xxvi, xxx, 1–34, 36–41, 76–77, 92, 157–64
4:21–23	7–11

Galatians (continued)

4:21	7n33, 8, 151
4:22–27	123–28, 149–54
4:22–25	99–101
4:23	9, 9n40
4:24–27	9, 11–26, 28
4:24–25	18–19
4:24	xxv, 12, 14n68, 15n75, 64, 69–70, 87, 100, 126–27, 136n36, 151–53, 158–60
4:25–27	4n13
4:25–26	19–21
4:25	xxv, 7n31, 16, 18, 153
4:26–27	85n13
4:26	19n93, 21–22
4:27	8n38, 22–24, 24n112, 103n37, 153, 163
4:28–31	10, 17, 27–43
4:28	10, 27, 129
4:29	8n38, 9, 27–29, 91
4:30	8, 29, 153n87, 164–65
4:31	3, 3n9, 31
5:1	3–4, 3n9, 137n37
5:2–10	90n24
5:10	31
5:19–21	88, 112, 140
6:1–10	90n24
6:1	136n34

Ephesians

	133–34
1:22	43n21
2:15	135n28
3:8	135n28

Philippians

	106, 106n10
3:14	113n46

Colossians

	106, 106n11, 134
1:15–20	107n17
1:18	43n21

1 Thessalonians

5:5	137n42

1 Timothy

1:15	135n28

Philemon

10	9

Hebrews

	104, 104n3

James

2:23	88n22

DEAD SEA SCROLLS

xxxii, 59–61, 83–103, 109, 111, 131, 131n1, 160

1QpHab (Pesher Habakkuk)

	60, 69, 90–92
I, 16—II, 4a	60
II, 1b–4	87
II, 3b–4	90
II, 5–10a	95
II, 10b–15	94
II, 10b–13a	99–100
III, 2–6a	95
III, 6b–13a	95
IV, 1–3a	95
IV, 3b–9a	95
IV, 9b–12a	95
V, 1–6a	97
V, 6b–8a	95
V, 8b–12a	95
VI, 2b–5a	95
VI, 5b–8a	95
VI, 8b–12a	95
VII, 3–5a	95
VII, 5b–14a	92
VII, 5b–8	95
VII, 9–14a	95
VII, 14b–16	95
VII, 17—VIII, 3a	95

VIII, 3b–13a	95
VIII, 13b—IX, 2a	96
IX, 3b–7a	95
IX, 8–12a	95
IX, 12b—X, 1a	96
X, 1b–5a	98
X, 5b–13	96
X, 14—XI, 2a	97
XI, 2b–8a	95
XI, 8b–15	95
XI, 17—XII, 6a	96
XII, 6b–10a	98
XII, 10b–14a	96
XII, 14b—XIII, 4	95

1QM (War Scroll)

X, 5b–9a	93n29

1QS (Rule of the Community)

III, 13—IV, 26	140n48
IV, 9–14a	88
VIII, 14–16a	98

4QCat^a (Catena A)

1–4, 14, 24, 31 I, 6	96
1–4, 14, 24, 31 I, 13	98
7, 9–11, 20, 26 I, 9	96
7, 9–11, 20, 26 I, 12	98

4QFlor (Florilegium)

1–2, 21 I, 3b–7a	98, 103
1–2, 21 I, 7b–9	98
1–2, 21 I, 10–12a	98
1–2, 21 I, 12b–12	98
1–2, 21 I, 14–15a	97
1–2, 21 I, 15b–16a	98
1–2, 21 I, 16b–17	98
1–2, 21 I, 18–19	97

4QMMT, 4Q397
(Miqṣat Ma‘ aśê ha-Torah)

14–21 I, 12b–13a	89
14–17 I	93n29

4QMMT, 4Q398
(Miqṣat Ma‘ aśê ha-Torah)

14–17 II, 2b–4a	86
14–17 II, 4b–8	89
14–17 II, 7–8	88

4QpIsa^a (Isaiah Pesher 4)

8–10 III, 6–8	98
8–10 III, 9	98
8–10 III, 10–11a	98
8–10 III, 11b–13	98
8–10 III, 26b–29	96

4QpIsa^b (Isaiah Pesher 2)

I, 1–3a	97
II, 1–2a	96
II, 6b–7a	98
II, 9b–10	98

4QpIsa^c (Isaiah Pesher 3)

6–7 II, 1–8a	96
6–7 II, 14–16	97
6–7 II, 17–18	98
23 II, 3–13	97

4QpIsa^d (Isaiah Pesher 6)

I, 3b–8	95

4QpNah (Nahum Pesher)

3–4 I, 6–8a	95
3–4 II, 1b–2	98, 100n34
3–4 II, 3–6	95
3–4 II, 7–10a	95
3–4 III, 1b–5a	95
3–4 III, 5b–8a	95
3–4 III, 8b–9	98, 100n34
3–4 III, 10–11a	98, 100n34
3–4 III, 11b—IV, 1a	98, 100n34
3–4 IV, 1b–4a	95
3–4 IV, 4b–6a	95

4QpPs^a (Psalm Pesher 1)

1–10 I, 25—II, 1a	95
1–10 II, 1b–4a	95
1–10 II, 4b–5a	98, 100n34
1–10 II, 7–9a	95
1–10 II, 9b–12	95
1–10 II, 13–16a	95
1–10 II, 16b–20	95
1–10 III, 2b–5a	96
1–10 III, 7–8a	95
1–10 III, 14–17a	95
1–10 III, 17b–19	96
1–10 IV, 7–10a	95
1–10 IV, 13–15	95
1–10 IV, 16–17a	95

11QMelch, 11Q13 (Melchizedek)

II, 11b–15a	95
II, 15b–18a	98

11QTemple, 11Q19 (Temple Scroll)

L, 4b–6	165

CD (Damascus Document)

	69, 84, 90, 92, 98n33
II, 14–6	90
III, 13—VI, 26	140n48
III, 20b—IV, 4a	99
IV, 12b–17a	98
VI, 2b–11a	59, 61, 99, 103, 103n37
VI, 14	87
VI, 18b–19	87
VII, 14b–21a	92
VIII, 8b–12a	99, 103
VIII, 21	87n19
XIX, 7b–9	99, 103
XIX, 20–24a	99
XIX, 33b–35a	90
XIX, 33b–34	87n19
XX, 10–12	87n19

OTHER JEWISH WRITINGS

Aristobulus (apud Eusebius)

Praeparatio evangelica

8.10.6	44n24
8.10.7–9	xxviiin9, 44

Josephus

	61–62

Antiquitates judaicae

1.24	62n58
1.215	28n125
3.179–183	61

Vita

1–3	61n57

Philo

	xxvii, xxxii, 12–13, 12n56, 13n60, 38, 38n8, 45–47, 45n26–27, 47n35, 61–63, 62n58, 62n60, 65, 67, 69–70, 73, 76, 88n22, 88n23, 93, 104–31, 140, 146, 146n74, 149n85, 156, 160, 163, 166

De Abrahamo

68	45n27
262–274	111n42

De agricultura

9	65, 107n22, 140

De cherubim

55	130
81–82	113
119	108n35

Ancient Documents Index

De confusione linguarum

146–147	107n17

De congressu eruditionis gratia

5–6	12n56
19	65, 107n22, 140
23	69, 129

De decalogo

53–54	116
66	116n56
80	116n56
105	107n26
142	107n21

De fuga et invention

46	107n24
97	113n46

De gigantibus

	124n70
7	108n33
29	108n33
52	108n28

De Iosepho

28	45n26
144	107n20

De migratione Abrahami

29	65, 107n22, 140
34–35	117–18
44	111n42
86–93	114
89–93	107n18
89	45, 118
92	110
102	108n28
190	107n26

De mutatione nominum

81	113n46
177	111n42

186	111n42
218	111n42

De opificio mundi

134	107n15, 110n41
157	130

De posteritate Caini

7	45n27
14	67

De praemiis et poenis

27–30	111n42
27	113n46
49–51	111n42
91–97	119
95	120
165–172	119
168	119

De sacrificiis Abelis et Caini

32	88n23, 112–13

De somniis

1.73	45n27
1.102	45n27
1.203	108n29
1.239	107n17
2.248	107n25
2.252	118

De specialibus legibus

1.84–97	114n51
1.287	45n27
1.295	108n35
4.122–124	108n31

De virtutibus

102	114–15
215–216	111n42

De vita Mosis

1.290	166

De vita Mosis (continued)

2.171	108n27
2.190	45n26
2.43–44	107n23, 119
2.44	120

Legatio ad Gaium

166–183	115n52
349–373	115n52

Legum allegoriae

	120–21
1–3	121, 121n62
1.24	123
1.31	107n15, 109, 110n41
1.61–62	121n62
1.63–76	123–28
1.63	123
1.65	122–23, 128
1.68	123
1.72	122, 123n65
1.79	121n62
1.100	121n62
2.21	67
2.38	123n66
2.41	123n66
2.44	121
2.49	108n37
2.77	123n66
2.89	122n63
2.92	123n66
2.108	113n46
3.4	45n26
3.10	107n24
3.15	123n66
3.16	121n62
3.19	122
3.48	113n46
3.83	121n62
3.97	108n29
3.153–154	123n66
3.157	123n66
3.164	108n34
3.183	121n62
3.209	123
3.211	108n30
3.225	122n63
3.228	88n22, 111
3.236	45n26
3.246	122
3.253	122n64

Quaestiones et solutiones in Genesin

	120
3.13–37	12n56

Quaestiones et solutiones in Exodum

	120
2.2	110

Quis rerum divinarum heres sit

12	108n33
55	108n31
90–95	111n42
188	107n17
270	108n30

Quod deterius potiori insidari soleat

20–21	107n16
34	108n36
78	130

Quod Deus sit immutabilis

4	111n42
134–135	107n19
134	108n32

RABBINIC WRITINGS

Genesis Rabbah

53.11	28n125

Mekilta De-Rabbi Ishmael

52b	67

Ancient Documents Index

Mekilta De Rabbi Shimon
53a	67
73	66
82	66

Pesiqta Rabbati
48.2	28n125

Pirqe Rabbi Eliezer
30	28n125

Semahot
8	66–67

Sifre Devarim
165	66

Sotah
6.6	28n125

Targum Neofiti
Gen 21:9	28n125

Targum Onqelos
Gen 21:9	28n125

Targum Pseudo-Jonathan
Gen 21:9–11	28n125

GRECO-ROMAN WRITINGS

Artemidorus

Oneirocritica
1.2	49
1.11	49

Athenaeus

Deipnosophistae
2.80	48

Aristotle

Analytica priora
66b	16n80

Metaphysica
$986^{a}23$	17n82
$1004^{b}27$	16n80
$1066^{a}15$	16n80
$1072^{a}31$	16n80

Rhetorica
3.1412a–b	48n41

Cicero

De oratore
2.261–262	56
3.166	56

Orator
94	52

Demetrius

De elocutione
99–102	52
243	52
282–283	48

Heraclitus

Quaestiones Homericae
5	51, 53, 55

Hermogenes

Peri ideon
246	52

Homer

Odyssea
22.195–196	51

Horace

Carmina

1.5	55n50
1.14	55n50
3.1	55n50
3.1.7	55n50
3.3	55n50
3.4.42–68	55n50

Epistulae

1:2.36	55, 70

Livy

Ab urbe condita

2.32	43, 65

Lucretius

55n51

De rerum natura

601–603	55–56, 70

Ovid

Metamorphoses

2:768–795	54–55

Plato

Republic

7.514a–541b	xxix, 46, 70
7.517b	46–47

Plutarch

Caius Marcius Coriolanus

6	43, 65

De communibus notitiis contra stoicos

1078e	49

De Iside et Osiride

363d–64a	49

De liberis educandis

7d	106n13

De vita et poesi Homeri

70	51

Moralia

19e–f	47n39

Polybius

Historiae

10.23.7	16n81

Porphyry

Quaestionum homericarum ad Odysseam pertinentium reliquiae

20.67.1–75.7	46n30

Vita Pythagorae

12	50

Quintilian

Institutio oratoria

8.6.44	56–57, 56n52
8.6.47–49	57n53
8.6.50–51	57n53
9.2.92	52

Rhetorica ad Herennium

4.34.46	57

Strabo

Geographica

1.2.7	49
1.2.17	49

Tryphon

Peri tropon

γ 50–51

Tryphon II

De tropis

216.1 51

Virgil

Aeneid

4.173–188	54
4.189–197	54
5.834–871	55

Georgics

55

EARLY CHRISTIAN WRITINGS

Ambrosiaster

Commentaries on Galatians

25	20n94
26	30n132

Augustine

Expositio in epistulam ad Galatas

193–99 30n132

Clement of Alexandria

Stromateis

2.6:31	141n50
2.7:35	141n50
2.20:116	141n50
5.10:63	141n50

Didache

3.1–6 140n48

Epistle of Barnabas

xxxii, xxxiin14, 76, 88n22–23, 112n44–45, 130–56, 160, 166

1.3–4	143–44, 147
1.8	143–44, 147
2.6	135n28, 137n37
2.9	143n59, 148n82
3.1	148n82
4	135n28
4.2	143n59
4.3–5	144n64
4.6–8	143n59
4.6–7	146
4.6	135n28, 144, 147
4.8	136n36, 139, 142n56
4.9	133, 137n39–40
4.11	136n34
4.12	137n38
5.2	148n82
5.9	135n28
6.10	148n82
6.11	156
6.13	148n82
6.17	140
7.3	156
7.7	156
7.10–11	156
8.1–3	149–54
8.1	156
8.2	148
8.7	143n59
9	135n28
9.1–3	138
9.1	136n35, 137
9.4	138, 143n59, 147, 154
9.6	138
9.8	138n47
9.9	144, 147
10.1–11	149–54
10.2	148
10.3	149
10.9	143n59, 147, 154
10.10	153, 166
10.11	143
11.8	148

Epistle of Barnabas (continued)

11.10–11	148–49, 154–55
12.2–10	156
12.2	156
12.5–6	156
12.10	156
13.1–6	149–55
13.1–3	136n33
13.3	149
13.5	156
13.6–7	143n59
13.7	88n22, 112n44, 134, 135n28, 139
15.4	147, 149
16	144n63
16.1–2	143n59, 147
16.3–4	145n69
17–20	137n42
18.2	137n39
19.7	156
20.1	88n23, 112n45, 140

Eusebius

Praeparatio evangelica

8.10.6	44n24
8.10.7–9	xxvin9, 44

Jerome

Commentarius in epistolam ad Galatas

4:22–23	9n42, 10
4:24	12n58
4:28	7n33
4:29–31	30n132

John Chrysostom

Homiliae in epistulam ad Galatas commentaries

4.24	12n58, 14n64, 76n17
4.25	19n89

Marius Victorinus

In epistolam Pauli ad Galatas libri duo

322	12, 30n132

Origen

	12–13, 13n60

Contra Celsum

6.42	46n31

Severian of Gabala

Commentary on Galatians

302–303	12n58

Tertullian

Adversus Marcionem

5.4	29n130

De jejunio adversus psychicos

14	147n80

Theodore of Mopsuestia

The Commentaries on the Minor Epistles of Paul

73–79	12n58
115	13, 19n91

www.ingramcontent.com/pod-product-compliance
Lightning Source LLC
Chambersburg PA
CBHW020408230426
43664CB00009B/1236